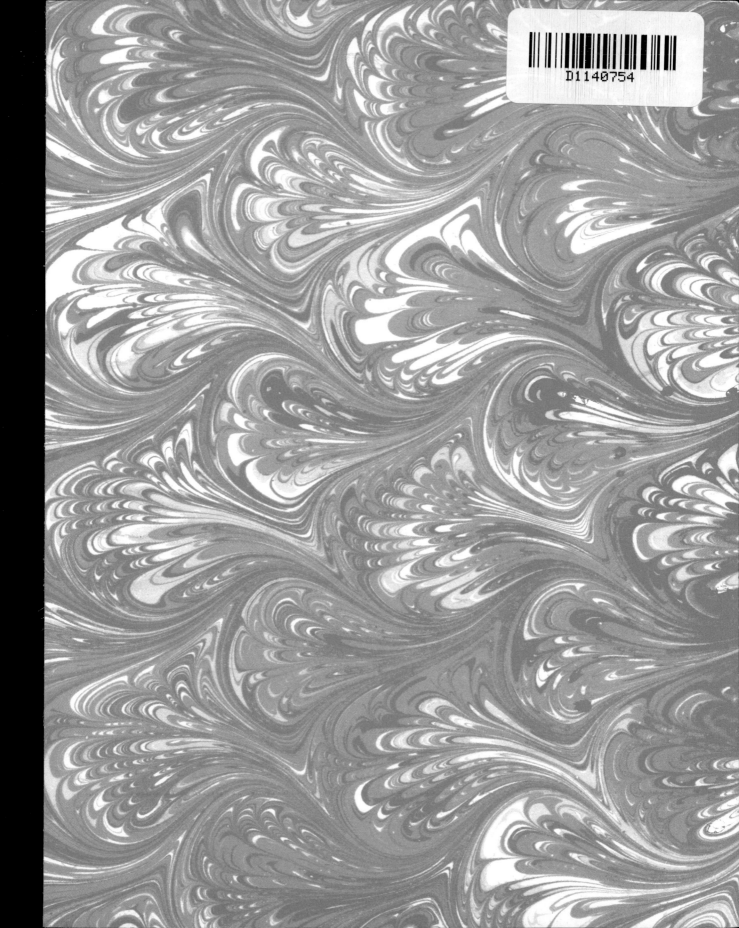

The DARING Book for Girls

Andrea Buchanan and Miriam Peskowitz

HarperCollins*Publishers*

HarperCollins*Publishers*
77–85 Fulham Palace Road,
Hammersmith, London W6 8JB

www.harpercollins.co.uk

Published by HarperCollins*Publishers* 2008

1

First published in the US, in a slightly different edition
by HarperCollins*Publishers* 2007

Copyright © Andrea Buchanan and Miriam Peskowitz 2007
Except the following chapters which are written by Clare Hey. Copyright © HarperCollins*Publishers* 2008:
Women Who Changed the World: Indira Gandhi; Women Who Changed the World: Jane Goodall;
Message in a Bottle; Poems Every Girl Should Read; Seven Daring Wonders of the World;
Women Who Changed the World: Marie Stopes; Exploring: Top Five Islands; Hula Hooping; Origami;
Secret Garden Fun at the Seaside; Making Your Own Jewellery; Great Films for Girls;
Bird Watching; Rules of the Game: Lacrosse; Women Who Changed the World: the Suffrage Movement;
Cat's Cradle; Women Who Changed the World: Florence Nightingale, Clara Barton and Mary Seacole;
Gardens, Allotments and Window Boxes; Women Who Changed the World: Anne Frank;
Women Who Changed the World: Mary Wollstonecraft; Rules of the Game: Hockey; Hiking;
Fables and Stories; Cycling; Games for a Rainy Day; Letters Home from a Great Adventurer;
Making and Flying a Kite
Italian Terms of Endearment written by Catherine Castledine. Copyright © HarperCollins*Publishers* 2008.

Andrea Buchanan and Miriam Peskowitz assert the moral right to
be identified as the authors of this work

A catalogue record for this book is available from the British Library

ISBN: 978 0 00 726855 9

Printed and bound in Italy by
L.E.G.O. SpA - Vicenza

NOTE TO PARENTS: This book contains a number of activities which may be dangerous
if not done exactly as directed or which may be inappropriate for young children.
All of these activities should be carried out under adult supervision only. The authors
and publishers expressly disclaim liability for any injury or damages that result from
engaging in the activities contained in this book.

To the most daring girl I know:
my grandmother Margaret Mullinix – A.B.

To my daughters, Samira and Amelia Jane – M.P.

This book wouldn't be complete without some Daring Girl badges,
which you can print out at our website: www.daringbookforgirls.com

CONTENTS

CONTENTS

The publisher and authors acknowledge the inspiration of
The Dangerous Book for Boys for the concept and design for this book
and are grateful to Conn and Hal Iggulden for their permission.

INTRODUCTION

WE WERE GIRLS in the days before the Internet, mobile phones or even voicemail. Telephones had cords and were dialled by, well, actually dialling. We listened to records and cassette tapes – we were practically grown-ups before CDs came to pass – and more often than not, we did daring things like walk to school by ourselves. Ride our bikes to the local shop. Babysit when we were still young enough to be babysat ourselves. Spent hours on our own, playing hopscotch or swingball, building a den in our rooms, or turning our suburban neighbourhood into the perfect setting for covert ops, impromptu games and imaginary medieval kingdoms.

Girls today are girls of the twenty-first century, with email accounts, digital cable, MP3 players and complex video games. Their childhood is in many ways much cooler than ours – what we would have given for a remote control, a rock-climbing wall or video phones! In other ways, though, girlhood today has become high-pressured and competitive, and girls are inducted into grownup-hood sooner, becoming teenagers and adult women before their time.

In the face of all this pressure, we present stories and projects galore, drawn from the vastness of history, the wealth of girl knowledge, the breadth of sport and the great outdoors. Consider *The Daring Book for Girls* a book of possibilities and ideas for filling a day with adventure, imagination – and fun. The world is bigger than you can imagine, and it's yours for the exploring – if you dare.

Bon voyage.

Andrea Buchanan
Miriam Peskowitz

ESSENTIAL GEAR

1 **Swiss Army Knife.** A key tool for survival, exploring and camping, it's a knife, screwdriver and saw with loads of extras like a magnifying glass, nail file, bottle opener, scissors and tweezers. Best of all it fits in your pocket. Clean with hot soapy water and add a tiny drop of mechanical oil once every three blue moons.

2 **Bandana.** Can be used to keep your head cool, protect your belongings, wrap a present. Tied to a stick, it can carry your treasured possessions on your adventures.

3 **Rope and String.** A stretch of rope and a knowledge of knots will take you many places – and may also help get you out of them.

4 **Notepad and Pencil, with a Back-up Pen.** Life is about memories: a quick sketch of a bird or plant, a wish list, a jot of the most important thought ever. A pad and pencil is also perfect for spying or for writing.

5 **Hair Band.** For when hair gets in the way. At a pinch, you can also use your bandana or a pencil.

6 **Bungee Strap.** For strapping things down on the go.

7 **Torch.** Basic tool for camping and reading under the covers late at night. A small piece of red Cellophane over the lens makes ghost stories even creepier. Eventually you can graduate to a headlamp, so your hands are free.

8 **Compass.** You need to know where you are and a compass can help. Hang it around your neck along with a whistle.

9 **Safety Pins.** Because they're good to have on hand when things need to be put back together, or when you want to express eternal friendship to a new friend by decorating with a few beads as a gift.

10 **Gaffer tape.** Two inches wide and hard as nails. It can fix almost everything. Good for treehouse construction.

11 **Deck of cards and a good book.** Old standbys.

12 **Patience.** It's a quality and not a thing, but it's essential so we'll include it here. Forget perfect on the first try. In the face of frustration, your best tool is a few deep breaths, and remembering that you can do anything once you've practised two hundred times. Seriously.

THE DARING GIRL'S GUIDE TO DANGER

◆

FACING YOUR FEARS can be a rewarding experience and pushing yourself to new heights will inspire you to face challenges throughout life. Here in no particular order is a checklist of danger and daring. Some you should be able to do right away, but a few you might need to work up to:

1 **Ride a roller coaster.** The tallest roller coaster in the UK is Oblivion at Alton Towers in Staffordshire with a terrifying near vertical drop of over 50 metres. The Colossus at Thorpe Park, Chertsey, has the greatest number of rolls in the country, looping the loop ten times during the ride. And the longest roller coaster in the UK is the Ultimate at Lightwater Valley near Ripon – it's nearly one and a half miles long and takes five minutes to complete.

2 **Ride a zip line across the canopy of a rainforest.** A trip to Costa Rica offers incredible adventures, including 'flying' across the roof of the world 60 metres off the ground with distances between trees of up to 360 metres. Many outdoor centres around the UK also offer zip line courses.

3 **Go white-water rafting.** Most people think looking at the Grand Canyon from the rim down is scary, but a true act of daring is to take a white-water rafting trip down the stretch of Colorado River that cuts through it. Some trips even include a helicopter ride for an extra dose of danger!

4 **Have a scary movie festival in your living room.** Some good ones are *The Exorcist, Jaws, Alien, The Shining* and Alfred Hitchcock's classic but still frightening *Psycho*. But don't blame us if you can't go to sleep without wondering what's under the bed.

5 **Wear high heels.** This may not sound so dangerous, but without practice you can fall or twist an ankle. For your first time in heels, borrow someone else's and make sure to start on a hard surface like wood. Once you're feeling steady on your feet, give carpeting a try. If you can wear heels on a thick carpet, you can do anything. Eventually, if it's a skill you want to learn, you'll be able to run, jump and do karate in three-inch heels.

6 **Stand up for yourself – or someone else.** It's scary to feel like you're the only one who doesn't agree, but when something's wrong, a daring girl speaks up, for herself or someone who needs an ally. Summon your courage and raise your voice – real bravery is feeling the fear and doing it anyway.

7 **Try sushi or another exotic food.** Rice in seaweed does not count. For the true daring girl try some *natto* (fermented soya beans) or *escargots* (snails).

8 **Dye your hair purple.** Sometimes the scariest thing is just being a little bit different, even for a day. There are many hair dyes that wash out after a few weeks – so you can experience what it would be like to have a lime-green ponytail without having to wait for all your hair to grow out to change it again.

RULES OF THE GAME:
NETBALL

❖

THE FIRST GAMES of netball in the UK can be traced back to 1895 where it was played with a loose set of rules by ladies at Madame Ostenburg's College. Broadly based on the American game of basketball, it wasn't until Clara Baer, a US gymnastics teacher, formalized the rules that the more modern game of netball was born. Its popularity in Britain in the early twentieth century was huge and it soon spread like wildfire through the British Commonwealth. That's why netball now has a storied history in Australia, New Zealand, Jamaica, Barbados, Trinidad and Tobago, and India. Poly Netball Club, based in Chiswick, West London, holds claim to being the oldest netball club in the UK, harking back to their first recorded competitive game played in 1907. In 1995, netball was recognized as an Olympic sport, but it has not yet been added to the roster of competition.

Played with a ball slightly smaller than a football, netball is primarily played by girls. The uniform is usually gym skirts with bibs to show what position each girl is playing in.

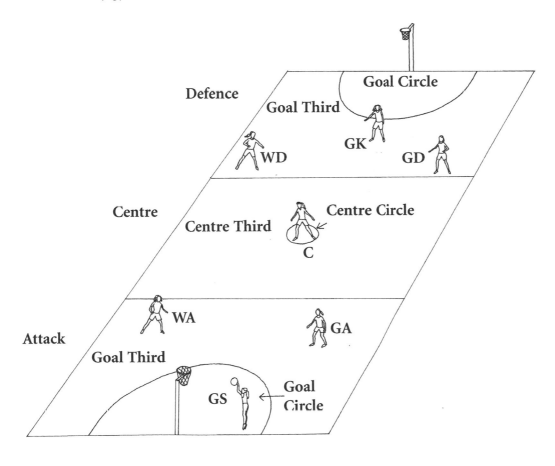

SOME THINGS TO KNOW

1 Netball is a game of passing; there is no dribbling. You don't bounce the ball and run the full length of the court. The netball court is divided into three zones. Players are limited to specific thirds of the court and they pass the ball quickly, from one zone to another. A player with the ball must pass to the next player within three seconds. She can pass the ball within a zone or into the next zone, but can neither skip a zone, nor throw the ball way down the court.

2 A netball team has seven active positions. Each player has a particular position, one opposing player she defends against and a specific part of the court she plays in.

Netball Positions			
Abbreviation	**Position**	**Defends against the:**	**Playing Area**
GS	Goal Shooter	GK: Goal Keeper	A, goal circle
GA	Goal Attack	GD: Goal Defence	A and C, goal circle
WA	Wing Attack	WD: Wing Defence	A and C, not goal circle
C	Centre	C: Centre	All thirds, not goal circles
WD	Wing Defence	WA: Wing Attack	C and D, not goal circle
GD	Goal Defence	GA: Goal Attack	C and D, goal circle
GK	Goal Keeper	GS: Goal Shooter	D, goal circle

3 A player with the ball cannot run. Instead, netball players perfect the pivot and move their bodies while keeping one foot planted on the court. Fouls committed against these rules, breaking the three-second rule, or the ball going offside result in a free pass by the opposing team.

4 The basket is suspended on a three-metre-high pole. There is no backboard. To make a goal, one stands within the goal circle, aims for the front or back of the rim, and shoots high, with some backspin. Oh, and no jumpshots, as at least one foot must stay on the floor. Each goal is worth one point, though a goal shot from outside the goal circle yields two points.

5 Defence players can intercept passes any way they like, but they cannot charge, intimidate or move closer than ninety centimetres towards the player with the ball. Moving in too close is called obstruction and results in a penalty pass.

6 A game has four fifteen-minute quarters, with three minutes between the first two and the last two, and a luxurious five-minute break at halftime.

7 Netball is a no-contact sport, which means players cannot push, trip, knock, bump, elbow, hold or charge each other. Although a player should attempt to intercept the ball while it is being passed, grabbing the ball while another player holds it is considered a foul. Breaking the personal contact rule results in a penalty pass for the opposing team and a penalty shot should any of this – or any untoward attempt to move the goalpost – happen within the goal circle.

WOMEN WHO CHANGED THE WORLD

Indira Gandhi (1917–84)

THE INDIA IN WHICH Indira Gandhi (then Nehru, before her marriage to Feroze Gandhi) was born was one of turmoil and unrest. Growing up in the 1920s and 1930s, she was surrounded by politics – her father was an important member of the pro-independence party, the Indian National Congress, which was led by Mahatma Gandhi. Even as a young girl she wanted her country to be independent of Britain and so, determined to help in any way she could, she formed Vanara Sena. Meaning 'Army of Monkeys', Vanara Sena was a group of Indian boys and girls, all committed to independence, who joined together under Indira's leadership to make flags and sing patriotic songs. Indira is said to have used her schoolbag to smuggle out of her father's house a document important to the revolutionaries, right under the noses of the police who kept them under constant surveillance.

When India achieved autonomy from Britain in 1947 and India and Pakistan were formed as new and independent countries, Indira's father, Jawaharlal Nehru, was elected as India's first independent Prime Minister. But the creation of India and Pakistan resulted in the immediate migration of hundreds of thousands of people as Hindus and Sikhs moved to India from Pakistan and Muslims moved from India to Pakistan, all seeking safety among others of their own religion. Indira flew into action and organized refugee camps for the dispossessed, providing shelter and medical aid. This experience gave her confidence that she too might one day become a great political leader.

It would take nearly twenty years, but she achieved her goal and became the first female Prime Minister of India in 1966. As a leader, she relied on the populist vote. Campaigning on an anti-poverty ticket, she focused on agricultural reform that would ensure that the people had at least enough to eat. But she was also accused of being dictatorial, ruthlessly suppressing dissent. She called elections in 1977 but lost and was forced from power and arrested on corruption charges. Determined to get back what she saw as her rightful position, she stood again at elections in 1979 and won in a landslide victory. Despite this success, her later years were darkened with violence and unrest as Sikh separatists fought for independence in the Punjab. She

ordered their leaders to be killed in a bloody battle in one of Sikhism's holiest shrine, the Golden Temple. This would prove to be a fatal mistake. In October 1984 two men, her own bodyguards, assassinated her in the gardens of her prime ministerial residence.

Although some of her actions while in power were questionable, her dedication to her country and the people was unwavering. The night before she died she is reported to have said, 'I don't mind if my life goes in the service of the nation. If I die today every drop of my blood will invigorate the nation.' She's a woman who changed the world, who stood up for what she believed in and was prepared to defend it to the end.

WOMEN WHO CHANGED THE WORLD

━━━━◆━━━━

Jane Goodall (b. 1934)

JANE GOODALL was born in London. Always fascinated by animals, she was the sort of girl who wanted to get really close to them and truly understand their nature. She once hid inside a henhouse for hours, just to discover how hens were able to lay eggs. Little did she realize that outside her hiding place all chaos was unleashed as her parents frantically searched for her!

So, when a friend invited her to visit her at her family farm in Kenya, Jane jumped at the chance. She knew that there she would see animals that she could only dream of at home in England. Once in Kenya she met palaeontologist and anthropologist Dr Louis Leakey who was looking for someone to go to the Gombe Stream National Park in Tanzania to

study wild chimpanzees. He saw the enthusiasm that Jane had for animals and decided that she would be an ideal candidate.

This was the turning point of Jane's life. It was unheard of for a woman to go into the African jungle alone so, accompanied by her mother, Jane, aged only twenty-three, took off for the adventure of a lifetime. What she discovered in Gombe would revolutionize science.

Once in the jungle, she realized that chimpanzees formed relationships with each other, had affection for each other and even seemed to assist each other purely for the sake of helping, rather than for any reward. But what was most crucial was her understanding of the way in which chimpanzees used tools

to help them fish termites out of a termite mound. They were the only animals, aside from humans, to use tools in this way. It was a remarkable discovery.

Jane has carried her work into the wider world by founding the Jane Goodall Institute for Wildlife Research, Education and Conservation. Originally set up to support projects like her own, observing wild chimpanzees, it now educates people about the environment and the importance of protecting it for both animals and humans. She's a remarkable woman whose life is an inspiration to girls everywhere. The little girl who once crawled into a henhouse is still travelling, still learning, still telling stories about how the world works, and still helping others to protect it.

PALM READING

◆

ANALYSING THE SHAPE of people's hands and the lines on their palms is a several-thousand-year-old tradition. Once the province of Gypsies and mysterious magicians versed in astrology and perhaps even the so-called 'black arts', *chiromancy* (from the Greek *cheir*, 'hand', and *manteia*, 'divination') is now more of a diverting amusement that can be performed for fun by anyone willing to suspend their disbelief and entertain, for a moment, the idea that a person's hand is an accurate indicator of their personality.

A palm reader usually 'reads' a person's dominant hand by looking at the hand's shape and the pattern of the lines on the palm. Often a palm reader will employ a technique called 'cold reading' – using shrewd observation and a little psychology to draw conclusions about a person's life and character. Good cold readers take note of body language and demeanour and use their insight to ask questions or make smart guesses about what a person is hoping to know. In this way, the reader appears to have knowledge the person whose palm is being read doesn't have, and may even seem to have psychic powers.

THE IMPORTANCE OF THE HAND

As with so many things we know today, palmistry has its roots in Greek mythology. Each part of the palm and even the fingers were associated with a particular god or goddess and the features of that area gave the palm reader clues about the personality, nature and future of the person whose palm was being read. The index finger is associated with Jupiter; clues to a person's leadership, confidence, pride and ambition are hidden here. The middle finger is associated with Saturn, originally a god of agriculture, and its appearance communicates information about responsibility,

accountability and self-worth. The ring finger is associated with the Greek god Apollo and its characteristics shed light on a person's abilities in the arts. The little finger is associated with Mercury, the messenger, and tells of a person's strengths and weaknesses in communication, negotiation and intimacy.

Another method of reading the hand is to take note of its shape. In one tradition, hand shapes are classified

by the elements: earth, air, water and fire. Earth hands are said to have a broad and square appearance, with coarse skin, a reddish colour and a palm equal in length to the length of the fingers. Air hands have square palms with long fingers, sometimes with prominent knuckles and dry skin; the length of the palm is less than the length of the fingers. Water hands have an oval palm with long, conical fingers and the length of the palm is equal to the length of the fingers but usually less than its width. Fire hands have square palms with short fingers and pink skin.

Other traditions classify the hands by appearance – a pointed hand, a square hand, a cone-shaped hand, a spade-shaped hand, a mixed hand – and assign personality traits to the various shapes. For instance, a person with a pointed hand appreciates art and beauty; a square hand indicates a grounded, practical, earthy person; a cone-shaped hand suggests an inventive, creative personality; a person with a spade-shaped hand is a do-it-yourself go-getter; and a mixed hand denotes a generalist who is able to combine creativity with a practical nature.

READING BETWEEN THE LINES

The four lines found on almost all hands are the heart line, the head line, the life line and the fate line.

The heart line lies towards the top of the palm, under the fingers, starting at the outer edge of the palm and extending towards the thumb and fingers. This line is said to indicate both metaphoric and literal matters of the heart, revealing clues about romantic life as well as cardiac health. The deeper the line, the stronger your emotions.

The head line begins at the inner edge of the palm beneath the index finger and extends across towards the palm's outside edge. The head line is often joined or intertwined with the life line at its start and the line itself is thought to indicate a person's intellect and creativity as well as attitude and general approach to life.

The life line starts at the edge of the palm above the thumb, where it is often joined with the head line, and extends in an arc towards the wrist. This line is said to reveal a person's vitality, health and general well-being. The life line is also said to reflect major life changes, including illness and injury – the one thing it doesn't indicate, contrary to popular belief, is the length of a person's life.

A fourth line found on most hands is the fate line, also called the line of destiny. It begins in the middle of the palm near the wrist and extends towards the middle finger. The deeper the line, the more a person's life is determined by fate. A line with breaks, changes of direction, or chains indicates a personality prone to change due to circumstances beyond a person's control.

THE HISTORY OF WRITING AND WRITING IN CURSIVE ITALICS

THE FIRST WRITING instrument resembled the first hunting instrument: a sharpened stone. These stones were used to etch pictures on cave walls depicting visual records of daily life. Over time, drawings evolved into symbols that ultimately came to represent words and sentences and the medium itself shifted from cave walls to clay tablets. Still, it wasn't until much later that the alphabet emerged to replace pictographs and symbols. Another milestone in the history of writing was the advent of paper in ancient China. The Greek scholar Cadmus, who was the founder of the city of Thebes and proponent of the Phoenician alphabet, was also the purported inventor of the original text message – letters, written by hand, on paper, sent from one person to another.

Some cultures lasted for many years before having a written language. In fact, Vietnamese wasn't written down until the 1600s. Two Portuguese Jesuit missionaries named Gaspar d'Amiral and Antonio Barboza romanized the language by developing a writing and spelling system using the Roman alphabet and several signs to represent the tonal accents of Vietnamese speech. This system was further codified in the first comprehensive Vietnamese dictionary (containing over 8,000 words) by Frenchman Alexandre de Rhodes in 1651. This is why its written language uses Roman letters instead of characters like the surrounding Asian countries do.

At first, all letter-based writing systems used only uppercase letters. Once the writing instruments themselves became more refined, lowercase letters became possible. And as writing instruments improved and the alphabet became more elaborate, handwriting became an issue. Today we have an incredible variety of things to write with – all manner of pens, pencils, markers, crayons – but the writing instrument most used in recent history was the quill pen, made from a bird feather. (See page 230 for instructions for making your own quill pen.)

Before we can discuss the art of writing with a quill pen, we must talk about penmanship. Even in the age of computers a clear handwriting style is a useful and necessary skill and drawing a row of tall and loopy As or Ps or quirky-looking Qs, twenty to a line and making them all look font perfect, can actually be a pleasurable

act. Nowadays, when we are more likely to type than to write with a pen, cursive might seem old-fashioned. But at the time of its invention, the notion of standardized handwriting was a revolutionary idea.

The first use of cursive writing was by Aldus Manutius, a fifteenth-century printer from Venice, whose name lives on today in the serif typeface 'Aldus'. Cursive simply means 'joined together' (the word has its roots in the Latin verb *currere,* to run) and one of the primary benefits of the 'running hand' was that it enabled the writer to write quickly and took up less space. But the uniform look of the script proved equally useful: in later centuries, before the typewriter was invented, all professional correspondence was written in cursive, and employees – men – were trained to write in 'a fair hand', so that all correspondence appeared in the exact same script. (Women were taught to write in a domestic, looping script.)

With the introduction of computers and standardized fonts, handwriting cursive documents is no longer seen as professional business etiquette – although for invitations, certificates and greeting cards, handwritten is still the sophisticated way to go.

Nowadays, there are several schools of thought about what nice cursive writing looks like and writing in 'a fair hand' is no longer entirely the province of men, as it originally was. Currently schoolchildren study a range of cursive, including D'Nealian, Getty-Dubay, Zaner-Bloser, Modern Cursive, Palmer and Handwriting Without Tears. All of

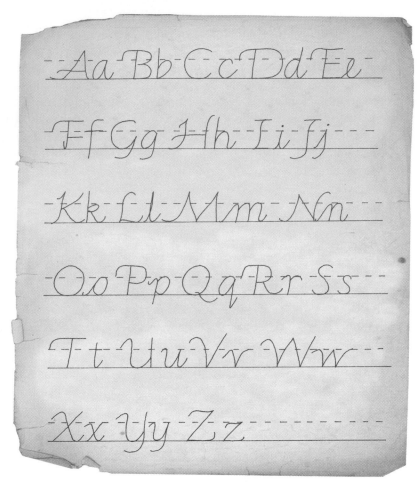

Cursive Italic

these styles are based on similar precepts about letter width and height and all are designed to bring some uniformity and legibility to the handwritten word. (The Getty-Dubay team even has a series of seminars specially designed for the sloppiest of handwriters – doctors.)

Cursive Italic is a fancier way of writing cursive that can dress up even the most mundane correspondence. Like regular cursive, the letters are connected, but Cursive Italic has a more decided slant and the rounded lowercase letters have more of a tri-angular shape to them. The form also lends itself to decorative flourishes, which is why you often see Cursive Italic used for wedding invitations, menus at fancy restaurants and the like.

Italic lettering is written at a slant of about 10 degrees from the vertical, with your pen held at about a 45-degree angle from the baseline.

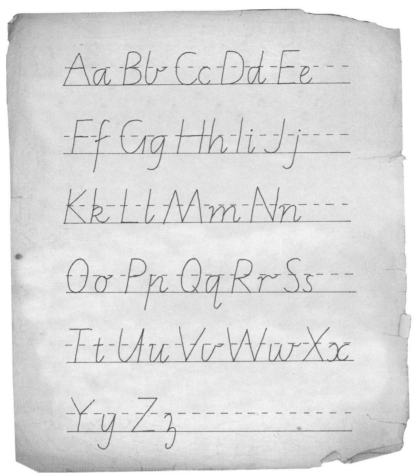

Victoria Modern Cursive

Adventure is worthwhile in itself.

In Victoria, Australia, a new style of handwriting was developed in the mid-1980s for primary schools. Now Victoria Modern Cursive is used across the country and is appreciated for its readability as well as its ease of elaboration – a few flourishes and the script is transformed from practical to fancy.

To practise, some writers like to write out their favourite poem as they work on perfecting their form. Here is a famous haiku from the eighteenth-century Japanese poet Issa that is a nice reminder of both the gradual evolution of human writing and the sometimes painstaking pace good penmanship requires.

Little snail
Inch by inch, climb
Mount Fuji!

SEVEN GAMES OF TAG

A GAME OF TAG can be as basic or as complicated as you like: you can revel in the pure straightforwardness of one person chasing another, or liven things up by adding rules and strategy. Either way, tag requires no equipment, no court, no uniform – just someone willing to be It, and others willing to run as fast as it takes to avoid getting tagged and becoming It themselves. Here are seven ways of playing tag.

1 **Chain/Chainey Tag.** In Chain Tag one person is It. But instead of being able to tag someone and no longer be It, the person who is It tags a player, and each player who is tagged then has to link arms with the tagger and join in as It. As more players are tagged, the link of taggers grows. No tags count if the chain separates. The game is over when the last player is finally tagged.

2 **Stuck in the Mud.** When a player is tagged in Stuck in the Mud, she must *freeze* in place immediately. Sometimes the game is played with the rule that other untagged players can *unfreeze* anyone who is frozen; the game can also be played so that the person who is It only wins when every single player is frozen.

3 **Shadow Tag.** This game is perfect towards the end of a sunny day when shadows are long, since the main rule of Shadow Tag is that whoever is It can tag a player by stepping on her shadow.

4 **Time Warp Tag.** This kind of tag is played just like normal tag, except that at any point during the game, any player (including whoever is It) can call out, 'Time Warp!' whereupon all players must move in slow motion. When 'Time Warp!' is called again, play returns to normal speed.

5 **Line Tag.** In Line Tag, which is played best on a playground or other surface with lines or painted areas on it, players are allowed to run or walk only on the lines. These can be hopscotch lines, netball court lines, or even lines on the pavement – if it's a line, you can step on it. Otherwise, you're out. If a player is tagged, she must sit down, and the only player who can move past her is the one who is It.

6 **Zombie Tag.** The person who is It must chase after the players 'zombie-style', staggering with her arms out in front of her and groaning like the undead. When the It zombie tags a player, that player also becomes a zombie. The game ends when all players have been transformed into moaning zombies.

7 **Hide and Seek Tag.** This is best played in woods with lots of places to hide. Everyone who is not It runs off while the seeker closes her eyes and counts to 100 next to a designated tree. The seeker calls, 'Ready or Not, Here I Come,' and begins searching for everyone else. The goal for those hiding is to get back to touch the tree before being tagged. Those who are tagged before touching the tree are also It and join the seeker. The last one to reach the tree or be tagged is the seeker in the next game.

MESSAGE IN A BOTTLE

◆

THE IDEA OF sticking a note in a bottle, throwing it out to sea and hoping it finds a friendly stranger at the other end may well seem an odd one, especially in today's world of mobile phones and email. But it seemed quite sensible to Theophrastus, a Greek philosopher living around 310 BC. Wanting to prove that the Mediterranean Sea flowed into the Atlantic Ocean, he concocted the first ever message in a bottle to prove his point. It was an idea that stuck, and we still love sending messages of friendship and hope across the seas to countries and people we can only imagine.

Often the most compelling stories of messages in bottles are those sent by explorers in distress. Christopher Columbus sent a note to the Queen of Spain that he hoped would reach her even if he himself did not make it home. And the great explorer David Livingstone used a message in a bottle to request aid and provisions from any passing ships. Indeed, during the Elizabethan era of exploration and discovery, messages in a bottle were so common that Queen Elizabeth I reportedly created the official position of 'Uncorker of Bottles' – and anyone else found opening bottles could be beheaded for their impudence.

The most unlikely story of a message in a bottle comes from the Normandy landings of the Second World War. Nine soldiers, all members of the 6th Border Regiment, were among one of the landing crews due to arrive first on the beaches of northern France and prepare the landing grounds for the battle to come. All friends, they had brought a bottle of champagne that they had bought back in 1940 and drank it together, knowing the sheer scale of the battle to come. Then, far from home yet desperate to get a message to their loved ones, they jotted down a note and thrust it into the empty bottle:

> If found, please put this paper in the post (with bottle) to The Castle, Carlisle, Cumberland, England.
>
> Signed,
> H J. Bartholomew, J. Westoll, C. Askew, B. Oliver, T. Heath, J. W. Triggs, T. Graham (M.O.), R.C. Troughton, T. Mackie.

The battle that followed proved to be one of the bloodiest of the war and yet, amazingly, not only did the bottle with its message find its way to Cumberland, via the Isle of Wight, but all nine soldiers also made it safely home to be reunited with their families. Their message is now kept in the Regimental Museum at Carlisle Castle.

Nowadays a modern girl has plenty of ways to get messages to her friends, but the fun of sending a message in a bottle is perhaps only bettered by the excitement of finding a message washed up on the shores near your house. Keep your eyes peeled – you never know what you might find.

SPANISH TERMS OF ENDEARMENT, IDIOMS AND OTHER ITEMS OF NOTE

TERMS OF ENDEARMENT

Mi chula
My pretty one

Querida
Darling

Hermanita
Little sister

Muñeca
Doll

FUN WORDS TO SAY

Chimichanga
(chim-ee-chahng-guh)
A crisp tortilla with a spicy meat filling.

Burro
(boo-row) (be sure to roll the 'R'!)
Donkey; stupid (*Como burro* means, 'like a donkey').

Tonto
(tahn-toe)
Silly or foolish.

Chistosa
(chee-stoh-sa)
Funny; a facetious attitude.

Parangaricutirimicuaro
(pahr-rahn-gahr-ee-koo-tee-ree-MEE-kwahr-row)
The name of a town in the southern part of Mexico; used as a nonsensical tongue-twister in much the same way as 'supercalifrag-ilisticexpialidocious'.

EXPRESSIONS

Este arroz ya se coció
'That rice has been cooked.' (Similar to our expression, 'That ship has sailed.')

De tal palo tal astilla
'Of such a stick is the chip.' (Like our phrase, 'A chip off the old block.')

No se puede tapar el sol con un dedo
'You can't cover the sun with one finger.'

Al mejor cocinero, se le queman los frijoles
'Even the best cook burns his beans.'

Porque naces en horno, ¡no quiere decir que eres una barra de pan!
'Just because you were born in an oven doesn't make you a loaf of bread!'

¡El mero, mero patatero!
'The real, real potato seller!' (Like 'The real McCoy', or 'It's the real thing!')

Spanish Food

Gazpacho

A cold uncooked bread soup usually made with stale bread, garlic, olive oil, salt, vinegar, tomato and peppers.

Paella

A rice dish made with saffron and olive oil and usually garnished with vegetables, meat or seafood.

Churros

Fried-dough pastry snacks, sometimes referred to as Spanish doughnuts, or Mexican doughnuts, that originated in Spain. The long fried stick, sometimes also dipped in chocolate, sugar or cinnamon, gets its name from its similarity to the horns of the Churro breed of sheep reared in the Spanish grasslands.

Spanish and Latin-American Books

Don Quixote
by Miguel de Cervantes

One Hundred Years of Solitude
by Gabriel García Márquez

Like Water for Chocolate
by Laura Esquivel

The House of the Spirits
by Isabel Allende

POEMS EVERY GIRL SHOULD READ

EVERY GIRL SHOULD FIND time to read some poetry. We have included just a few of our favourites here, but there is a world of poetry written by and for women out there. Find a quiet spot under a tree, and some time to yourself, and immerse yourself in words written long ago.

Because I Could Not Stop for Death

by Emily Dickinson (1830–86)

Because I could not stop for Death,
He kindly stopped for me;
The carriage held but just ourselves
And Immortality.
We slowly drove, he knew no haste,
And I had put away
My labor, and my leisure too,
For his civility.
We passed the school where children played,
Their lessons scarcely done;
We passed the fields of gazing grain,
We passed the setting sun.
We paused before a house that seemed
A swelling of the ground;
The roof was scarcely visible,
The cornice but a mound.
Since then 'tis centuries but each
Feels shorter than the day
I first surmised the horses' heads
Were toward eternity.

Emily Dickinson was a rather introverted and quiet person, living most of her life in the US town of Amherst, her family's home. She wrote several thousand poems, but only a handful were published during her lifetime. Since then she has become regarded as one of America's greatest poets.

Sonnets from the Portuguese

by Elizabeth Barrett Browning (1806–61)

Sonnet 43
How do I love thee? Let me count the ways.
I love thee to the depth and breadth and
*   height*
My soul can reach, when feeling out of sight
For the ends of Being and ideal Grace.
I love thee to the level of everyday's
Most quiet need, by sun and candlelight.
I love thee freely, as men strive for Right;
I love thee purely, as they turn from Praise.
I love thee with the passion put to use
In my old griefs, and with my childhood's
*   faith.*
I love thee with a love I seemed to lose
With my lost saints, – I love thee with the
*   breath,*
Smiles, tears, of all my life! – and, if God
*   choose,*
I shall but love thee better after death.

Elizabeth Barrett Browning's celebrated *Sonnets from the Portuguese*, of which 'Sonnet 43' is the best known, were written for her husband Robert Browning and named after his pet name for her. She is widely considered to be one of England's finest poets.

Remember
by Christina Rossetti (1830–94)

Remember me when I am gone away,
Gone far away into the silent land;
When you can no more hold me by the hand,
Nor I half turn to go yet turning stay.
Remember me when no more day by day
You tell me of our future that you plann'd:
Only remember me; you understand
It will be late to counsel then or pray.
Yet if you should forget me for a while
And afterwards remember, do not grieve:
For if the darkness and corruption leave
A vestige of the thoughts that once I had,
Better by far you should forget and smile
Than that you should remember and be sad.

Deeply religious, Christina Rossetti was an advocate of the rights of women, particularly young prostitutes, and animals, and an opponent of slavery and war. She was respected as a poet during her lifetime and moved in illustrious circles, counting among her friends the author of *Alice in Wonderland*, Lewis Carroll, the painter James McNeill Whistler and the poet Algernon Charles Swinburne.

SEVEN DARING WONDERS OF THE WORLD

◆

A DARING GIRL is always keen for adventure, and exploring the world is one of the most exciting things you can do. Here are seven daring wonders of the world, but they are just a starting point and you'll think of many more.

Fiordland National Park

One of the biggest national parks in the world, Fiordland is in the southern region of New Zealand. As you'd expect from its name, it is home to many fiords including Milford Sound and Doubtful Sound, considered by many to be two of the most amazing fiords in the world. It's a wet place with hundreds of waterfalls, rainforests and rivers. Here you'll see one of the highest waterfalls in the world, Sutherland Falls, which cascades from an amazing mile above sea level. Getting around this enormous park is an adventure in itself. Why not hire a horse, a boat, or even a helicopter, to get a close-up of this stunning area.

Mount Everest

We're not suggesting that you climb to the top of Mount Everest, but it's certainly an awesome sight to behold from afar. You'll find it on the border between Nepal and Tibet in Sagarmatha National Park. The world's highest peak, it has always been seen as a challenge to climbers and adventurers everywhere. It was first climbed by Edmund Hillary and Tenzing Norgay in 1953.

The first woman to climb Everest was Junko Tabei, a Japanese climber who reached the peak in 1975. It is possible for particularly daring girls to climb to the base camp but this is an expedition that requires preparation and good levels of fitness.

The Great Wall of China

Considered by many to be one of the seven wonders of the modern world, the Great Wall of China was built over centuries and is the longest man-made object on earth, measuring over 4,000 miles long, and is visible from space. It's staggering to behold and to comprehend that this was all built by hand. Those daring enough to undertake walks along some of its length will traverse mountains and valleys through impressive scenery. And if that's not daring enough for you, there's always the marathon. Held on the wall in May every year, it's not for the unprepared or unfit but it's a brilliant adventure and a fantastic way to see one of the world's most impressive sights.

Machu Picchu

Machu Picchu, in Peru, is often referred to as the Lost City of the Incas. Built around 1450, it was abandoned only 100 years later as Peru was invaded by the Spanish and the Inca residents fled for their lives. But the city was never discovered by the invading Spanish and so was not destroyed by the ravages of war. It remained abandoned, and the forests that surrounded it grew up and eventually encased the city, rendering it in effect 'lost' to the outside world. It was 'rediscovered' in 1911 and became a source of fascination to explorers from the rest of the world, many of whom speculated that it might have been the birthplace of the Incas. It is possible to visit it, either by a tourist train or, rather more adventurously, by going on an 'Inca trail' which involves a hiking trip of two to four days, camping in the mountains that surround the ancient city.

Paricutin Volcano

This is a volcano that exploded out of nothing – or out of a cornfield, to be more precise. In 1943 a farmer in the small Mexican village of Paricutin witnessed the birth of this volcano, an eruption of ash that marked the start of the growth of a volcano that is now over 400 metres high. It erupted for over ten years until it finally became still in 1952. It is the only time in living memory that volcanologists have been able to witness the birth of a volcano, although it must have been much more exciting for them than for the poor residents of the small town, all of whom lost their crops and land and had to move to vacant land nearby for safety. Nowadays it is possible to visit the volcano, heading up on horseback and then on foot. It's a strenuous hike but worth it if only to see the church that was half swallowed by the earth as the volcano erupted.

Northern Lights

Often described as a 'natural fireworks display', the Northern Lights are a naturally occurring phenomenon that can be seen from March to April and September to October. Formed by the collision of particles with atoms in the earth's upper atmosphere, they manifest as coloured lights which fill the night sky. Amazingly, it was discovered during what was described as a 'great geomagnetic storm' in 1859, when the lights were seen as far away as the United States, Japan and Australia. During this storm two telegraph operators found that they were able to communicate through the telegraph wires powered solely through the geomagnetically produced current. This level of geomagnetic activity is rare, however, so you'll need to travel to the northern countries to see these amazing light displays for yourself.

Mountain Railways of India

Compared to some of the other daring wonders of the world, this one is rather relaxing! The name refers to four of the railways built in the mountainous regions of India: the Darjeeling Himalayan Railway, the Nilgiri Mountain Railway, the Kalka-Shimla Railway and the Matheran Hill Railway. Located throughout India, the routes take you high into the mountains. They are an stunning way of seeing the country, all from the comfort of your own seat, the scenery passing by without your needing to lift a finger! They are some of the oldest railways in India and the carriages are deliciously old-fashioned.

HOW TO WHISTLE WITH
TWO FINGERS

◆

MAKE A TRIANGLE by putting the tips of your little fingers together, palms and fingers facing towards you. Stick out your tongue and put your little fingers right on the centre of it, pushing your tongue strongly against your fingers where they meet. Push your tongue back into your mouth with your fingers, so that your little fingers are inside your mouth up to the first knuckles. Angle your finger-tips slightly down, just behind your bottom teeth and keep your tongue pressing into your fingers. Purse your lips and blow. You may have to adjust the angle of your fingers to get that sound right, but just practise and before you know it you'll be hailing cabs with your piercing two-finger whistle!

ELASTICS

◆

ELASTICS IS SOMETIMES called French Skipping and is played with an elastic band looped around two players' legs, while a third player jumps around it and on it in a series of moves. If you don't have a large enough elastic band, you can make one by knotting together lots of normal-sized elastic bands.

To play, you'll need two people to control the elastic and a third to jump. (If you're by yourself and have a pair of sturdy chairs handy, those can fill in at a pinch.) The elastic-holders should stand several feet apart from one another with the elastic stretched around their ankles to form

a rectangular frame. The jumper begins by standing on the left side of the frame, and then jumping *in, out, over, on*:

* On *in,* the jumper jumps both feet inside the elastic frame.
* On *out,* the jumper jumps up and lands straddling the elastic, each foot to the outside.
* On *over,* the jumper jumps both feet to the left side outside the elastic, then both feet to the right side outside the elastic.
* On *on,* the jumper lands on the elastic with her left foot on the left side and her right foot on the right side.

Once the jumper has successfully completed this sequence, the elastic-holders raise the level of the elastic to the knees. The *in, out, over, on* jumps are repeated, and if the jumper makes it through, the elastic is raised to waist level. If the jumper is successful performing the sequence at that level, the elastic is raised to armpit level.

Some variations:

Washies Drysies

Start standing to the left of the elastic frame, which is at ankle level. With your right foot, lift the left side of the elastic (the side closest to you) and, with that elastic still against your right ankle, step across the other side of the elastic. Then put your left foot inside the elastic to make a diamond around your feet and jump left foot in front of right, feet side by side, right foot in front of left, then feet side by side. The elastic is raised by the elastic holders just as in *in, out, over, on.*

Diamonds

Begin as in Washies Drysies, standing outside to the left of the elastic with your feet together, and lifting the elastic with your right foot, bringing it over and stepping your left foot in to create a diamond shape. Jump up, freeing your feet from the diamond-shaped elastic, and land in the middle of the elastic. Jump to the right side (the side opposite from where you started) and repeat the steps on that side. Once you complete both sides, the elastic can be raised.

DOUBLE DUTCH

———— ◆ ————

DOUBLE DUTCH is a type of rope-skipping that uses two ropes. There are two rope-turners and usually one rope-jumper (though for added difficulty, there can be two jumpers). Each rope-turner holds the end of a rope in each hand. The ropes should be the same length, but they don't have to be the same colour – in fact, having two different-coloured ropes can help a jumper keep track of which rope is going where. The left-hand rope is turned clockwise and the right-hand rope is turned counter-clockwise, in an eggbeater motion. The jumper must clear both ropes as they hit the ground, jumping quickly so that it appears she is running on the spot.

What does this rope game have to do with the Dutch? Skipping lore has it that the game may have evolved from the twisting motions made by Dutch ropemakers as they wound ropes from hemp. With hemp around their waists and two strands attached to a wheel, ropemakers walked backwards, twisting the length of hemp into rope. The runners supplying hemp to the spinners had to jump quickly over the ever-twisting ropes as the ropemakers plied their craft, turning the hemp strand over strand. It is easy to imagine how this work might have evolved into a pastime for the ropemakers and their families. When Dutch settlers arrived in New Amsterdam (today's New York City), they brought the double-rope game with them, earning it the nickname 'Double Dutch'. The game grew in popularity, especially in urban areas, but sometime after the 1950s it fell out of practice. Then, in 1973, a New York City detective and his partner revived the skipping game by turning it into a competitive sport for city kids in fifth to eighth grades. Now Double Dutch is not just a playground game, but a competitive team sport played all over the world.

WOMEN WHO CHANGED THE WORLD

———— ◆ ————

Marie Stopes (1880–1958)

MARIE STOPES was a woman ahead of her time. Born in 1880, she grew up in a Britain where the role of women was changing rapidly. The Women's Suffrage movement was lobbying for votes for women, and soon women would experience far greater freedom than they ever had before. But education for women was still not encouraged, and attitudes were slow to change. Marie Stopes fought against these prejudices of her time. She not only went to university but received a double first in Botany and later a doctorate.

She married fellow scientist Reginald Ruggles Gates, and after a rather disastrous attempt to consummate their marriage it became clear that he was impotent. She annulled the marriage, and realized that she had been very naïve about what happened behind the bedroom door of a married couple. She felt strongly that other women should not have to suffer because of ignorance, so she set out to write a book intended to enlighten married women as to what to expect in the bedroom from their husbands, and how to enjoy what many still saw as a marital duty.

Married Love was always going to be a controversial book. It was condemned by the Church and the Establishment, but it was a huge hit with the woman on the street. Within two weeks of its publication it had sold over 2,000 copies.

But Marie Stopes knew that she needed to go further. She could see the effect that

unwanted pregnancies were having on women. Often poor and in ill health, they had no way of preventing pregnancies and found themselves expecting again and again, producing children that they could not afford to feed. Marie felt strongly that women should be allowed to have control over their bodies, so she set up the first ever birth control clinic in the UK – the Mothers' Clinic – amid great controversy and outcry, particularly from the Catholic Church.

Marie Stopes's legacy can be seen not only in the laws relating to birth control that we have in the UK, but also in the equality that now exists between men and women. Her pioneering work led to women questioning their position not only within their marriage, but also within society as a whole. Without her work we wouldn't enjoy the freedoms we have today.

HOW TO TIE A SARI
(And a Chiton)

◆

WE DON'T KNOW when the first sari was made, but stories and artistic renderings of saris have been around for roughly 5,000 years. Saris are still worn today all over India and around the world and the design, fabric, patterns and wrapping styles vary depending on the region and status of the wearer.

The contemporary sari is actually a three-piece garment: the sari itself (unstitched fabric 100–125 centimetres in width and 5–8 metres in length, usually with ornamental borders and an end piece called the *pallu*, which is the part draped over the shoulder); the petticoat, or underskirt; and the *choli*, a tight-fitting cropped shirt, also known as a sari blouse or sari jacket.

The underskirt is a fairly recent development in sari wear. It's not absolutely required, though it has practical applications: in addition to acting as a slip beneath sheer fabrics, the petticoat also provides the wearer with a waistband to tuck the cloth's edges and pleats into. Some modern sari-wearers use capri leggings instead. Most saris come with a matching piece of fabric for the *choli*, but a pre-made cropped top or tank top can be worn instead.

The most popular modern style of tying a sari is *nivi*, which is created most basically by wrapping the sari around the waist, tucking one end of it into the underskirt and then draping the *pallu* diagonally across the chest and over the shoulder. Here are some step-by-step instructions for wrapping a sari in the *nivi* style.

Choose your 8-metre length of fabric for the sari and put on the *choli* and petticoat, slip, or capri pants.

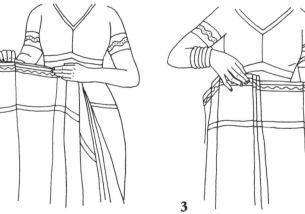

1 Tuck the inner top edge of the sari into the petticoat just to the left of where your bellybutton is. Wrap the sari from left to right so that it goes completely around you once, making sure that the bottom edge of the sari hangs evenly and touches the ground. Tuck that first wrap-around into the same left-of-bellybutton place where you made the first tuck.

1

2 Hold the tucked part of the fabric at your waist tightly and begin to make pleats. You'll be using about a metre of material for about seven to ten pleats of 10–13 centimetres in depth.

3 The first pleat should lie at the centre of your body, and as you continue to fold, take care to keep the pleats even and straight.

2

3

4 Hold the pleats together and make sure they line up evenly. Tuck the pleats into your waist to the left of your bellybutton, making sure the folds are turned towards the left. You can use a safety pin to fasten the pleats for more security.

5 Wrap the remaining material around your waist again from left to right.

6 Pull the sari up diagonally with your right hand so that it fits just beneath your right armpit, then drape the material over your left shoulder so that it hangs down your back. You can pleat the material and secure it with a safety pin if you wish by pinning from inside the *choli* along the shoulder seam. Or you can wrap the *pallu* over your left shoulder, bringing it behind your back and over your right shoulder to rest in front.

Now you have a beautiful *nivi*-style sari. It might take some getting used to to walk around in. But if you can't be bothered to master the art of wearing a sari as a dress, did you know that a sari can be tied as trousers?

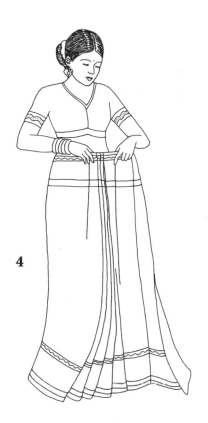

4

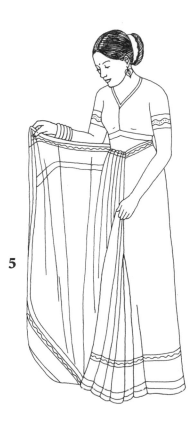

5

6

Kachha Style

This sari requires 5½ metres of cloth. Starting from your left hip, wrap the sari towards the right so that it goes around your waist. Tie a knot just under your bellybutton using the sari edge (held with your right hand) and bunched-up fabric (from the wrapping side, held with your left hand). Once you have made the knot snug, make a series of seven to ten pleats to the right of the knot. Wrap the *pallu* around yourself so that the end is centred on your back. Tuck it in all the way across your back to hold it in place. Pleat the rest of the fabric between the first pleats and the part of the sari tucked on your left hip. Tuck in the pleats at the waist, grab the bottom of your fabric and bring it back between your legs. Tuck that into your back, with or without securing it in a knot, and *voilà* – sari trousers!

The Chiton

The sari may remind you of another ancient style of dress involving what is essentially a large sheet – the toga. Togas were actually semicircular pieces of cotton or wool fabric measuring about 5 metres in diameter and worn wrapped around the body and draped over the shoulder. But togas were never worn by women – instead, women wore a similar but more flattering draped fabric called the *chiton* (KEE-ton).

The Doric *chiton* was a simple but elegant garment, the fabric of which depended on the season and the sensibility of the wearer. It could be worn as a dress or as an undergarment and was constructed by drawing a rectangular-shaped cloth around the body, pinning it at the shoulders and tying it about the waist. The most popular shade of fabric for the *chiton* was white, the better to display the elaborate embroidery or brightly coloured woven patterns often used to decorate the borders. Yellow was also a favourite colour, so common that the tunics were nicknamed 'saffrons'.

The *chiton* isn't complicated in terms of design – no sewing, no cutting – but it could be a little tricky to put on by yourself. So to assemble your own *chiton,* you'll need a length of fabric, a tie or sash to belt it, two safety pins and a friend to help you dress.

The piece of cloth used for a Doric *chiton* should be about 30 centimetres longer than the wearer is tall and as wide as the span of her outstretched hands. A single flat sheet will most likely do, or a nice gauzy curtain.

Place the fabric on the floor and fold the top over about two-thirds of the way down. Lift up the cloth, holding it so that the folded side is facing you and fold the fabric in half length-wise, keeping that first fold on the outside. Lay the fabric back on the floor so that the closed side of the fold is on the right and the open side of the fabric is on the left. Use a safety pin to pin the back and front sides together along the top of the fabric about one-third of the way in. Use a

second safety pin to fasten the front and back together about two-thirds of the way in. This creates two shoulder straps.

Here's where you might need a little help from your friend. Have her lift the cloth up and help you put your right hand all the way through the top, beneath the safety pins and out through the other side. Your right arm should be in the hole between the edge of the folded fabric and that first safety pin. Then put your head through the hole created between the two safety pins. The safety pins should now be resting on your shoulders. If you have a fair amount of cloth hanging open on your left side, you can wrap the back part against the left side of your body and put the front part on top of that. Then use your sash, rope or belt to tie around your waist for the girded *chiton* look.

HOPSCOTCH, SWINGBALL, SKIPPING

─────── ◆ ───────

Hopscotch

BELIEVE IT OR NOT, hopscotch got its start not as a playground game, but as a military exercise. During the early Roman Empire in ancient Britain, Roman soldiers ran through 30-metre-long rectangular courses wearing full armour to help improve their footwork. Roman children drew up their own version of these courses, shortening the length and adding a scoring system, and the game of hopscotch was born.

The word *hopscotch* comes from *hop*, of course, meaning to jump, and *escocher*, an Old French word that means 'to cut'. The game as we know it dates back to at least 1801, and now hopscotch is played all over the world. In France, the game is called *Marelle*. Germans play *Templehupfen*, and kids in the Netherlands play *Hinkelbaan*. In Malaysia hopscotch is called *Ting-ting* or *Ketengteng*, and in India it's called *Ekaria Dukaria*. In Vietnam it's known as *Pico*, in Chile it's *Luche*, and in Argentina and many Spanish-speaking countries, it's called *Rayuela*.

COURTS

Make your own court using chalk on a pavement or driveway, or by using masking tape on a floor or carpet indoors.

Traditional courts look something like this:

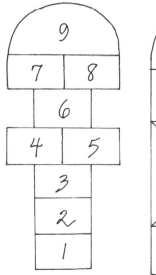 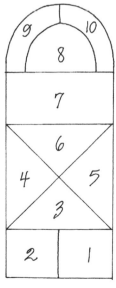 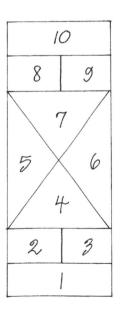 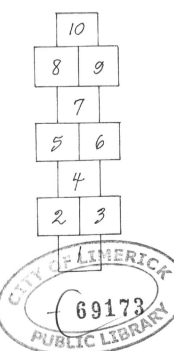

Super-old-fashioned courts had six boxes in a stack from one to six or three sets of two boxes:

Fancier versions include the Monte Carlo and the Italian:

Monte Carlo   **Italian**

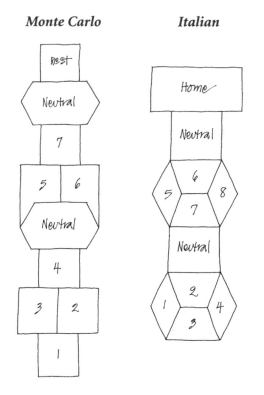

Or, you can always make up your own style of hopscotch court!

RULES

Nearly every girl knows the basic rules for hopscotch, but there are some interesting variations to liven things up.

In the most basic game, the first player stands behind the starting line to toss a marker (a rock, a penny, a beanbag, a button) in the first square. The marker must land in the correct square without bouncing out or touching a line. The player should hop over the first square to the second on one foot, then continue hopping all the way to the end of the court. Side-by-side squares can be straddled, with each foot on a square, but single squares must be hopped on with just one foot. A square with a marker in it must be hopped over, and any neutral, or safe, squares may be jumped through in any manner a player wishes.

When a player gets to the end of the court, she turns around and hops back through to the beginning, stopping to pick up her marker on the way. If she makes it to the end without jumping on a line or putting two feet down in a square, she can continue her turn by throwing the marker into square number two and trying again. If a player steps on a line, misses a square, falls, or puts two feet down, her turn is over. When it's her turn again, she starts where she left off. The winner is the first player to complete one course of hopping up and back for every numbered square.

VARIATIONS

A French version of hopscotch is played on a spiral court and called, because of its shape, *Escargot* (snail) or *La Marelle Ronde* (round hopscotch). The court is drawn as a big snail or shell-like spiral and then sectioned into squares, the number of which is limited only

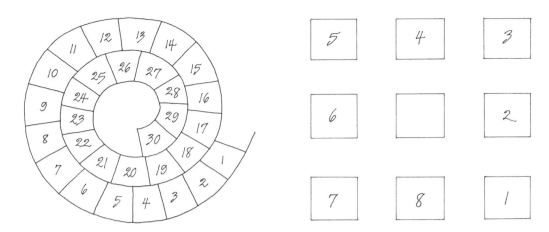

Escargot *(snail)* **or La Marelle Ronde**
(round hopscotch)

Toss-and-Reach Hopscotch

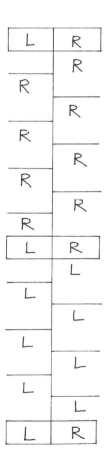

by the size of the spiral itself. In this version, each player hops on one foot to the centre of the spiral and back out again. When a player is able to complete the full circuit, she can mark one square with her initials, and from then on she is allowed to have two feet in that square. The other players must hop over it. The game is over when all squares are marked (or if no one can reach the centre), and the girl who wins is the one who has her initials in the most squares.

This variation, allowing the player to initial a square, can also be adapted for the traditional version of the game. After a player has completed one hopscotch sequence successfully, jumping all the way up and all the way back, she can throw her marker onto the court, and wherever the marker lands she can place her initials. Then that square is hers, and she is allowed to have two feet in it when hopping, while the other players must hop over it. In this version, each player is only allowed to initial one square per game.

Another variation, which can be used with traditional straight courts as well as with spiral courts, involves the player holding her marker between her feet and hopping from square to square on two feet without letting go of the marker or stepping on the lines.

In Toss-and-Reach Hopscotch, a player throws her marker into the centre square, then hops to each square in order. From each square, she must reach in to pick up her marker without losing her balance or stepping on any lines.

In Agility Hopscotch, the player must hop back and forth across the centre line without touching any lines or losing her balance. She must hop on her left foot in squares marked L and on her right foot in squares marked R. She may rest with both feet down where the L and R are marked opposite each other.

Agility Hopscotch

HOPSCOTCH, SWINGBALL, SKIPPING

Swingball

SWINGBALL REQUIRES a fast mind and equally fast hands to send the ball spiralling around the pole for a win. This was our favourite game growing up and we'd love to see more swingball courts – and maybe some day swingball as an Olympic event.

At its most basic, swingball involves a ball – similar to a volleyball but somewhat squishier – tied to the top of a 3-metre pole by a rope. Two players try to hit the ball in one direction so that the rope winds completely around the pole. (But swingball is also fun to play by yourself – in your garden when no one's around. You can practise and make up games for yourself, too. Like trying to duck before the ball hits you in the head.) Actual swingball courts have a circle drawn on the ground around the pole and are divided in half. A drawn circle isn't necessary, but you should expect to need about 2 metres of space all around the pole and each player should stay on her own side of the circle.

RULES

The rules of swingball are deceptively simple: two people stand opposite each other, one person serves by hitting the ball in one direction around the pole and the other tries to hit the ball in the opposite direction around the pole. The first player to get the rope wrapped completely around the pole is the winner.

Because the server has a big advantage (she gets to hit the ball first), players can decide to play matches instead of single games. The total number of games comprising the entire match is up to the players to decide, but the winner must win by at least two games. Another way to decrease the serving advantage is to have the player who doesn't serve choose which side of the circle she is on and which direction she is hitting.

FOULS AND VIOLATIONS

How seriously you take fouls is something that needs to be decided before the game. Fouls include:

* Stepping across the centre line.
* Server hitting the ball twice at the beginning before the opponent hits it once.
* Hitting the ball twice while it is still on your side of the circle.
* Hitting the ball with any part of the body other than the hand or forearm.
* Reaching around the pole and hitting the ball.
* Catching or holding the ball.
* Throwing the ball.
* Touching the pole with any part of your body.
* Hitting the rope with any part of your body.

If you only have a few players, you can treat these fouls as mere violations and resume the game by stopping the ball and returning it to where it was wrapped when the violation occurred. The non-violating player gets to serve, and then either player can hit the ball. If a player racks up three violations, the opponent automatically wins.

If the two players commit a violation at the same time, they must do a pole drop to start the game again. Both players hold the ball with one hand, lifting it about three feet away from the pole, directly over the line dividing their two halves of the circle and then let go of the ball at the same time. The ball should hit the pole and then either player can hit it to continue the game.

No matter how you decide to play, the only absolute game-ender is grabbing the pole. If a player does that, she immediately loses the game.

EQUIPMENT

The Ball

A swingball is the only piece of equipment that you must purchase specifically for the game and is similar to a volleyball, but softer. It will have either a loop sticking out of the surface or a recessed spot on the surface of the ball to attach the rope.

The Pole

The best pole for the job is a steel pipe 3 metres long and 5 centimetres in diameter sunk 30 centimetres into the ground, with an eyebolt run through the pole about 10 centimetres from the top for attaching the rope. This may be a good time to take a field trip to your local DIY shop. But with a good eye you might be able to spot a likely pole around town that will serve nicely for the game. Just remember to untie the ball and take it home with you when you are finished.

MAKING A SWINGBALL COURT IN YOUR GARDEN

Here's your shopping list:

* Steel pipe, 3 metres long, 5 centimetres in diameter
* Steel pipe, 50 centimetres long, slightly wider than 5 centimetres in diameter
* Eyebolt with nut (for attaching the rope to the top of the pole)
* Drill and bit capable of drilling through metal
* Concrete mix
* Swingball
* Rope (if not included with the swingball)

MAKING THE COURT

Drill a hole through the pole about 10 centimetres from the top for the eyebolt, and put the eyebolt in place.

Dig a hole in your lawn, gravel driveway or garden about 70 centimetres deep, with a 50-centimetre diameter.

Pour in 15 centimetres of concrete and let it set.

Stand the 50-centimetre-long pipe in the hole and add concrete around the pipe to fill the hole (it's a good idea to have something to keep the pipe in place while the surrounding concrete sets; also, the pipe should protrude just above ground level, but not so much that it sticks up enough to get nicked by a lawn mower).

Once the concrete is set, slide the pole into your concrete-and-pole base (this should be a solid, tight fit, but the long pole is removable).

Attach the rope and ball.

Skipping

IT'S SURPRISING to us now, since skipping is often thought of as a girls' game, but skipping actually began as a boys-only activity, prohibited for females. Nowadays, though, skipping is for everyone. It's even a competitive sport.

Skipping has been a favourite game through the ages. Medieval European paintings depict children rolling hoops and skipping along cobblestone streets. In Egypt in 1600, children used vines for skipping. In England, skipping was particularly popular around Easter, taking place in Cambridge and in several Sussex villages. Even today, every Good Friday in the East Sussex village of Alciston, children gather to skip.

CLASSIC SKIPPING RHYMES

From the streets of Manchester to the schoolyards of Wales these rhymes have been passed down and around for generations. As with handclap games, you may know different versions of these. Here are some of our favourites.

Down by the river, down by the sea,
Johnny broke a bottle and blamed it on me.
I told ma, ma told pa,
Johnny got a spanking so ha ha ha.
How many spankings did Johnny get?
One, two, three, four…
(Keep counting until the girl jumping makes a mistake.)

I love coffee, I love tea.
I want *(your friend's name)* to come in with me.
Two little dickie birds sitting on the wall
(You and your friend jump in)

One named Peter, one named Paul
(Each girl waves at their name)
Fly away, Peter, fly away, Paul
(Each girl exits the rope as her name is called)
Don't you come back 'till your birthday's called
January, February, March, April, May, June,
July, August, September, October, November, December
(Each girl jumps back in when the month of her birthday is called)
Now fly away, fly away, fly away all
(Girls both jump out of the rope)

Teddy Bear, Teddy Bear, turn around,
Teddy Bear, Teddy Bear, touch the ground
Teddy Bear, Teddy Bear, show your shoe
Teddy Bear, Teddy Bear, that will do!
Teddy Bear, Teddy Bear, go upstairs
Teddy Bear, Teddy Bear, say your prayers
Teddy Bear, Teddy Bear, turn out the lights
Teddy Bear, Teddy Bear, say goodnight!
*(The jumper acts out the actions as the words
come up in the rhyme.)*

I had a little puppy
His name was Tiny Tim
I put him in the bathtub, to see if he could
swim
He drank all the water, he ate a bar of soap
The next thing you know he had a bubble in
his throat.
In came the doctor *(one girl jumps in)*
In came the nurse *(the next girl jumps in)*
In came the lady with the alligator purse
(another girl jumps in)
Out went the doctor *(first girl jumps out)*
Out went the nurse *(second girl jumps out)*
Out went the lady with the alligator purse
(third girl jumps out)

Five currant buns in a baker's shop,
Round and fat with a cherry on the top,
Along came *(call a girl's name as she jumps in)*
with a penny one day
Bought a currant bun and took it away *(girl
jumps out).*

Four currant buns in a baker's shop,
Round and fat with a cherry on the top,
Along came *(call another girl's name as she
jumps in)* with a penny one day
Bought a currant bun and took it away *(girl
jumps out).*
(Repeat with three, two and one currant buns.)

QUEENS OF THE ANCIENT WORLD I

◆

Wise Artemisia

I T IS A MYSTERY what Queen Artemisia, who lived during the fifth century BC, looked like; no depictions of her survive. But the tales we know of her from the world's first historian, Herodotus, portray Artemisia as an intelligent and clever queen who bravely spoke her mind, even when no one else agreed with her. We also know she was a skilful and courageous sailor, who protected the Persian fleet during the ancient Greco-Persian Wars.

In the fifth century BC, Artemisia ruled Halicarnassus (today called Bodrum), a city nestled along a cove on the south-eastern coast of Turkey's Aegean Sea. Artemisia's father and her husband had ruled the city before her. When her husband died, she became queen, as their son was too young to rule.

At this time, in 480 BC, the Persian Empire was at its zenith. Xerxes (pronounced *Zerk-siz*), the fourth of the great Persian kings, was in power. He had already conquered much of Asia and turned his sights towards the Greek city-states and isles.

Xerxes narrowly won the battle of Thermopylae, capturing the pass to the Greek mainland, and then burned down its capital, Athens. He next headed south to take the island of Salamis, moving his battle to sea and relying heavily on the boats in his navy. He asked his allies around the Aegean Sea to send reinforcements. Loyal to Persia, Artemisia loaned five ships to Xerxes' war effort, large triremes, each with a grand sail, and powered by men from Halicarnassus rowing with long oars out the sides. She herself took command.

Yet Artemisia was different from many ancient queens (and kings), whom we are told

MAVSOLI A BVSTO CALIDOS HAVRIRE MARITI EXEMPLOQ POSVIT TVMVLVM, SPIRANTIA CVIVS
DEPOSCENS CONIVNX CINERES, PIETATIS ADVLTÆ ARTIFICES, SVMMI CÆLARVNT MARMORE SIGNA

wanted only to wage war. When Xerxes asked his general Mardonius to gather the commanders for counsel before storming Salamis, they all encouraged him to go ahead with the sea battle and assured him of victory. Except Artemisia. She warned Xerxes that the Greek ships were stronger than their own. She reminded him that he already held Greece's mainland with Athens and had lost many troops at Thermopylae. She contradicted all the other commanders in advising him to quit while he was ahead.

Xerxes admired Artemisia, but he decided, fatefully, to go with the opinion of the majority. The battle went wrong – terribly wrong – as Artemisia had predicted. Battle's end found the Persians watching from shore as their ships burned. Still, Artemisia kept her word to Xerxes and commanded her ship. She came under pursuit by an Athenian ship and faced a terrible decision either to be captured or to run into the Persian ships that were ahead of her.

Artemisia made the decision to save her crew, ramming one of her allies' ships and sinking it in the effort to escape from the Greek ship. Some have said that she had a long-standing grudge against its commander, King Damasithymos of Calyndia. The commander of the Greek vessel chasing her turned away, assuming perhaps she was a sister Greek ship, or even a deserter from the Persian navy. The Persians lost the battle at Salamis, all the men on the Calyndian ship died, but Artemisia and her crew escaped unharmed.

After that battle, Herodotus tells us, King Xerxes again sought advice from his commanders. And again all the commanders wanted to stay and fight for the Grecian islands, except Artemisia. Disagreeing with the group once more, the level-headed queen counselled Xerxes to consider another option: leave 300,000 soldiers behind to hold the mainland and return to Persia himself with the rest of his navy.

Artemisia reminded Xerxes for a second time that he had already torched Athens and taken the Greek city-states. It was enough. The king took Artemisia's wisdom more seriously this time, knowing she had been right before. He listened to the wise woman over the majority, choosing to leave a contingent of troops in Greece and turn towards home instead of fighting.

And after that? Herodotus makes a brief mention of Artemisia ushering Xerxes' sons from Greece to safety in the city of Ephesus, on the Turkish mainland. After that, we have no further information about Artemisia's life. Herodotus concerns himself with describing the next battle, and the next, and because Artemisia declines to fight, she disappears from his pages.

A small vase provides our last evidence of Artemisia: a white jar made of calcite that is now at the British Museum. Xerxes gave the jar to Artemisia, a gift for her loyalty and service, and he inscribed it with his royal signature. Artemisia must have bequeathed the jar to her son, and from there, it stayed a family treasure for generations. One hundred years later, another member of her royal line, also named Artemisia, built a burial monument to her husband – the Mausoleum of Halicarnassus, one of the Seven Wonders of the Ancient World. There, in the 1850s, the British archaeologist Charles Newton excavated Xerxes' gift to the first Artemisia and uncovered the final trace of the wise queen.

KNOTS AND STITCHES

———— ◆ ————

A GOOD KNOT ENSURES that your boat will be there when you return, your tyre swing will hold, and your dog won't run into traffic. Here are a few useful knots with many everyday uses, and a few words on stitches, which come in handy for small repairs.

A piece of rope is all you need to begin. In each of our directions, 'rope' means the stable or standing part of the rope. 'End' refers to the part you are working with to make the knot, the working end. Make sure it's always long enough to do the job. 'Bight' is another word worth knowing; it's the part of the rope that becomes the knot.

1. STOPPERS

A stopper knot keeps a rope from slipping through a hole; it is the bulge at the end of a line. The most ordinary kind is called the overhand knot, or half knot. It's the knot you use to keep a thread in place when you start to sew.

Half knots are not very strong, but they are perfect for making the swing part of a rope swing. Tie four or five loose half knots near the bottom of the rope. Push them together, and tighten. They'll form a larger bulb that's perfect for sitting on as you swing. If you like, tie a half knot every few feet up the rope, for climbing or for holding on to while you do an arabesque (twisting the rope slightly around one ankle, and lifting your other leg gracefully behind you, like they do at the circus).

Safety note: For rope swings, you'll want to attach the swing to a tree branch using a stronger clove hitch or a tautline hitch. Make sure you tie the rope to a branch that extends far enough from the trunk so you can swing safely.

An alternative to the half knot is the Flemish knot, which you can also use any time you need a knot at the end of a line. It's both strong and lovely.

1 Make a loop at the top.
2 Cross the end behind and over to the left.
3 Wrap the end over and into the eye of the initial loop. You should see a figure eight.
4 Pull the end into the eye, or centre, of that loop.
5 Pull tight.

2. LOOPS

Once you've mastered the Flemish figure eight, you can make a loop the same way. Double up the rope or string. For hauling, tie the loop around your object, and lift or drag with the rope.

3. BENDS

Bends link two ropes together. When you need to repair a string that's broken, add new length to a rope or for any reason tie two ropes together, the square knot is what you want. Also called the Hercules knot, it was used by the Greeks and Romans as a healing charm. In *Natural History,* the Roman writer Pliny the Elder advised people to tie off their bandages with this knot, since it would heal the wound more quickly. Simple and reliable, this knot works best on string or thinner rope, and with any ropes of equal size.

Square knot

The classic formulation for a square knot is this: Left over right, right over left. Don't worry: in our experience, that's the kind of

Square Knot

direction that makes more sense after you already know how to tie knots. So, try this: Loop A over loop B. Then wrap the ropes of B over the sides of, and into, loop A. Pull.

Sheetbend knot

If you're attaching the ends of a single rope, perhaps to tie off a friendship bracelet, try this: Make loop A. With loop B, thread the end into loop A, from the back. Then weave it out the bottom side, and under and across to the top of the loop. Next, bring rope A over the top side and through the loop, so it's next to the other side of rope B.

If you need something stronger, or your ropes are different sizes, use this variation, the sheetbend knot. The green one is the thicker rope.

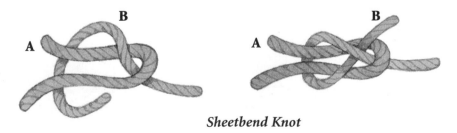

Sheetbend Knot

4. HITCHES

Hitches tie an object or animal to a post, whether it's your dog at a friend's house, your horse to a tree in the shade, or your kayak to a pole on the dock while you go for a swim.

The tautline hitch is incredibly useful on camping and boating trips. Here's how to make it:

1   Start from the back and bring the end around the pole to the front
2   then over and behind the rope
3   and into the centre, or eye, and out the front.
4   Pull the end over and behind and into the centre once again
5 & 6   and pull out the front.
7   Take the end past the first two loops,
8 & 9   and wind it over and behind and into the centre
10   and pull tight.

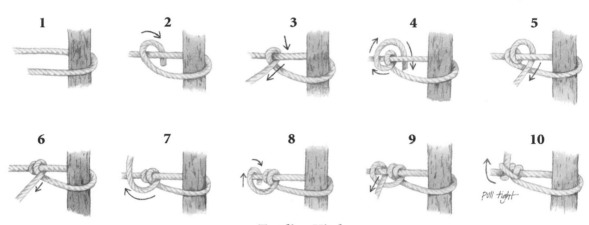

Tautline Hitch

The around-the-pole hitch moves around a pole. This is perfect for a dog who doesn't want to end up tangled, twisted, and stuck with a two-inch leash.

Loop the end one turn around the pole, front to back, and bring the end under and in front of the rope. Change course and lead it towards the top.

Wrap the end again around the pole, this time back to front, and then lead the end under and through the loop.

Finally, the timber hitch helps you drag a heavy object, like a log across a field. This knot is simple and also easy to untie, an important consideration in knots. It tightens in the direction you pull in, so make sure to use that to your advantage.

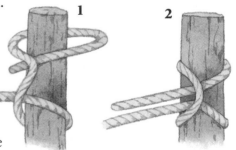

Around-the-Pole Hitch

Wrap one turn, top to bottom, back to front. At the top, loop the end around the rope, to the left (this loop is important; the end must be wrapped around the rope it just came from). Tuck the end over, back, and around three or four times, and pull tight. The tucks must sit flat against the object for this knot to stay tight, since it is held in place by the rope's pressure against the object as you pull.

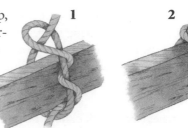

Timber Hitch

5. STITCHES

There will no doubt come a time when you need to mend your gloves, replace a button that's fallen off or sew the tear your trousers suffered while climbing rocks.

Cut your thread, push it through the needle, double the thread so it's extra strong, and place a knot – a gorgeous Flemish stopper knot – at the end. You're ready. The stitches below can help you quickly mend any rip or tear that will inevitably occur in a daring life.

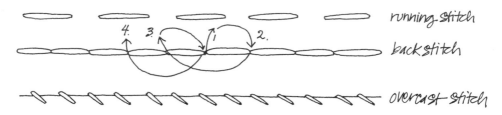

RULES OF THE GAME: ROUNDERS

ROUNDERS IS AN IMPORTANT part of every girl's school life. If she's lucky she'll continue to play it later in life. It has always been popular in the UK, with the first recorded game being played in Tudor times. Jane Austen, the grand-dame of all things English and female, even mentions it in *Northanger Abbey*, so all Austen fans really *ought* to know how to play rounders! And anyway, it's a great way to spend an afternoon in the park with some friends, and that should always be encouraged.

SOME THINGS TO KNOW

Rounders is played by two teams of between six and fifteen players, organized into batters and fielders.

The only equipment you need is a long, thin, round bat (although often we play with a cricket bat, and even sometimes a tennis racket – Miss Austen would be horrified!) and a small round ball (again, any ball will do if you don't have the proper rounders ball).

The pitch is made up of four bases, a bowling area and a batting area. Bases are traditionally poles which are placed in the ground but you can improvise, using long sticks or whatever you have to hand.

Batters have two 'good' balls (or 'innings') per game and the aim is to hit the ball as best they can and successfully run around the four bases on the pitch without being stumped or caught out. If you are stumped, you're out. Once the ball is returned to the bowler, you must stop at the base you are on and may not move again until the next ball is bowled to the next batter.

Fielders must aim to either catch the batter out or catch the ball and throw it to one of the fielders near the bases to touch the base before the running batter can reach it.

RULES OF THE GAME

A 'good' ball must be thrown underarm, aiming for the batter's striking side, between the knees and the shoulders. It should not hit the ground before it reaches the batter.

Once the batter has hit the ball, she must run around the bases aiming to reach fourth

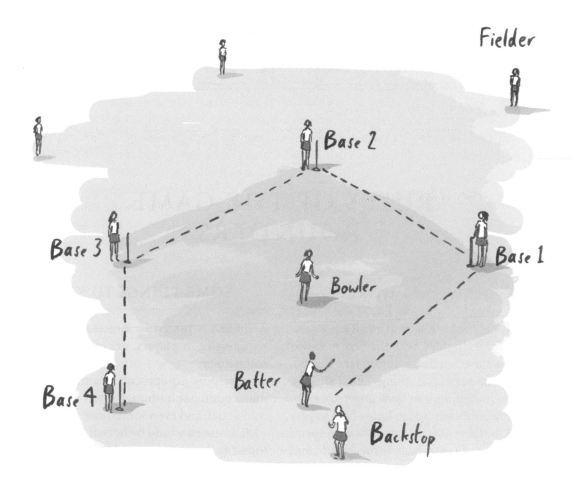

base before the ball is returned to the bowler and she must stop running.

A rounder (another name for a point) is scored if the batter manages to reach fourth base without being 'out'.

You can be out if a fielder catches the ball after you have hit it, or if a fielder 'stumps' the base you are running to before you can reach it. Once you are out you must sit out and you cannot score a rounder in that game.

Two innings make up a game, and each team can continue either until all their players are out or each player has played both of their innings. The team with the most rounders wins.

PLAYING CARDS: HEARTS AND GIN RUMMY

A Short History

EARLY PLAYING CARDS are believed to have originated in China, where paper was first invented, as a form of paper dominoes. The earliest references to playing cards in Europe featuring decks with four suits date from 1377. Cards back then were very expensive, as they were hand-painted, and they looked quite different from the design of cards today.

The earliest cards from China had designs recognizable to players of Mah Jong: coins, or circles; and bamboo, or sticks. On their way from China to Europe, cards passed through the Islamic empire, where they gained cups, swords and court cards. Once in Europe, the generic court cards evolved into depictions of actual kings, knights and other royalty – hence the name 'face cards'. The Italian, Spanish, German and Swiss cards did not include a queen – and in fact, even today, they still do not.

The basic familiar design of the cards – with hearts, diamonds, spades, and clubs, and court cards of Jacks, Queens and Kings – came from France, and with the invention of woodcuts in the fourteenth century, mass production became possible, making the French cards popular all across Europe.

There are hundreds of games that can be played with cards. Here are two popular and fun games for four or two people: Hearts and Gin Rummy.

HEARTS

Hearts is a trick-taking game for four players in which the object of the game is to avoid winning tricks (a set of cards) containing Hearts or the Queen of Spades. Hearts began its life in Spain around 1750 in a game called Reverse, the point of which was to lose tricks, not gain them. Eventually, about one hundred years later, Reverse fully morphed into the game we know today as Hearts.

'Tricks' are rounds of play in which each player puts a card face up on the table, and the player with the highest card wins all the cards – also called 'trick-taking'. But the real trick in this trick-taking game is that in Hearts players want to avoid winning tricks, because the lowest score wins.

Hearts uses a standard fifty-two-card deck. Aces are high, and there is no trump suit. To start, the dealer deals the cards clockwise so that all players have thirteen cards each. Each player then chooses three cards to pass: on the first hand, the cards are passed to the left; on the next hand, the cards are passed right; on the third hand, cards are passed across; and on the fourth hand, no cards are passed. Cards are passed stacked face down, and players must choose and pass their cards to the correct player before they can look at the cards passed to them.

The player who has the Two of Clubs goes first and must 'lead', or put down, that card. The play goes clockwise, with all the other players following suit (putting down a card of the same suit), if possible. That means each player must put down a Clubs card – if a player doesn't have any Clubs in this first hand, she can play any other card except for a Heart or the Queen of Spades. The player with the highest card takes the trick (stacking the cards face down next to her) and starts the next round. After the first trick, a Heart or the Queen of Spades can be used if a player doesn't have a card in the suit being led. Hearts can only be led (that is, be the first card in a trick) after a Heart has been 'broken' – played on a trick where a player couldn't follow suit.

Play continues until all the cards have been played. Then you add up the points for each player. Each Heart card gets one penalty point, and the Queen of Spades gets thirteen penalty points. The game is over when at least one person has one hundred points or more, and the winner is the player with the lowest score.

But there is one last 'trick' to be played in Hearts: a player can do something called 'Shooting the Moon'. That is when one player takes all the point cards (all Hearts and the Queen). The player who does this has her points reduced to zero, and everyone else automatically gets twenty-six points added to their score.

GIN RUMMY

This two-player card game is said to have been created by a man named Elwood T. Baker, who was inspired by an eighteenth-century game called Whisky Poker. Gin Rummy became popular in the 1930s, when Hollywood stars began playing the game in much the same way that celebrity poker is played today. Churchill even found time to play it.

To play the game, you need a standard fifty-two-card deck, and a pen and a pad of paper to keep score. You also need to know a bit of card talk to understand the game.

GIN VOCABULARY

Combination
Two cards of the same rank, such as Two-Two; or consecutive in the same suit, such as Two-Three of Clubs.

Count
The point value in a hand after deducting the total melded cards.

Deadwood
Cards that are not a part of any meld.

Gin
Ten melded cards.

Knock
To end the round.

Layoff
Getting rid of deadwood by incorporating it into the other player's melds, so that it is not counted.

Meld
Either a sequence or a set.

Sequences
A group of three or more cards of the same suit in consecutive order, such as Three-Four-Five of Spades, or Eight-Nine-Ten-Jack of Hearts.

Sets
A group of three or four cards of the same rank, such as Three-Three-Three or Jack-Jack-Jack-Jack.

TO PLAY

Decide who will be the dealer. The dealer then deals ten cards to each of the two players and places the remaining cards in a stack between the players. Another card is placed face up, next to the deck, to create a discard pile.

The goal of gin is to try to get your ten cards grouped in melds – sequences of cards (three or more cards of the same suit in order) or sets of cards (three or four cards of the same value). Before you take a turn, check to see if you have any melds, or any groups of cards that could easily turn into melds.

Each turn involves taking a card and discarding a card. The player who goes first draws a card from the deck. Now she must discard, choosing a card from her hand that is least likely to become part of a meld. High-point cards, like face cards, are good to discard if you can, since getting rid of them decreases your deadwood (the cards that are not part of any meld). Aces are low in this game: face cards are worth ten points each, Aces are one point and the other cards are equal to their numerical values (a Two card of any suit is worth two points, a Three card is three points, etc.).

When a player discards, the card must be placed face-up on the discard pile. The other player then has a turn, and she can draw from either the deck or the discard pile. Continue taking turns until a player 'knocks', or until only two cards remain in the deck (in which case the hand ends in a draw).

Knocking is when a player ends the round, and is signalled by a player literally making a knocking sound on the table. A player can only knock if she has ten points of deadwood or less. If you have zero points of deadwood, also known as 'going gin', you must knock. Otherwise, you don't have to knock unless you want to – even if you have ten points in deadwood or less, you can keep playing to try for gin or for a lower point count.

When you decide to knock, rap once on the table, lay down your cards face up, and add up your deadwood. The other player then lays down her hand and separates her deadwood from her melds. If she has any deadwood that can be incorporated into your melds, she can 'layoff' – that is, give them to you for your meld so they cannot be counted as her deadwood. After that, add up her total remaining deadwood. Subtract your deadwood from the other player's deadwood, and the answer you get is your score for this hand.

If you have zero points of deadwood, you must knock and call 'gin'. You get a twenty-five-point bonus for gin, on top of the points for the other player's deadwood (which she cannot layoff in this case).

If you knock and it turns out the other player has less deadwood than you, you get no points – but the other player scores not only the total of your deadwood minus hers, but twenty-five bonus points as well. That is called 'undercutting'.

After the cards have been counted and points totalled, gather up the cards, shuffle, and deal the next hand.

Keep playing until one of the players reaches one hundred points. Each player receives twenty-five points for each hand she won, and the player who reached one hundred points first gets an extra one-hundred-point bonus. The winner is the player with the most points after all the bonuses have been added.

EXPLORING: TOP FIVE ISLANDS

L IVING IN A COUNTRY surrounded by water, daring girls need look no further than their own shores to find exciting islands to explore. Here are our top five.

St Michael's Mount

St Michael's Mount can be found off the coast of Marazion, near Penzance in Cornwall. It's an island with a bloody and turbulent history but one that exudes a peace and calm today. Formed in 2000 BC when the sea rose to flood the surrounding marshlands, it's an island almost by accident. It's still possible to reach it by foot at low tide along the causeway that links it to the mainland. But be careful – the tide can rise quickly. Alternatively, it can be

reached by boat which will drop you at one of three landing points, depending on the level of the tide.

Once you are on the island you will be surrounded by living history. The island has fallen into many hands over the centuries and you'll find evidence of the French occupation of the eleventh century, the Lancastrian invasion during the Wars of the Roses in the fifteenth century, and the Civil War in the seventeenth.

The island now belongs to the National Trust which leases it to the St Aubyn family, who previously owned it for many generations. They still live in the impressive castle and maintain the island on behalf of the National Trust.

St Kilda

An archipelago of tiny islands perched precariously in the North Atlantic Ocean, St Kilda is known for its isolation. But, despite the harsh landscape, the islands were populated from the Bronze Age until very recently, 1930. A small community of St Kildans made their home in the only inhabitable area of the island, known as Village Bay. But if you visit now you'll find only the remains of life there, ruined buildings which lie crumbling in the face of constant bombardment by the elements.

The population of St Kilda had been gradually decreasing, from around 180 people at its highest point to around 37 in 1928. The First World War had taken its toll as young men had left to fight and had never come back. The women they left behind continued to farm and live on the islands, but, after being hit by bouts of influenza, successive crop failures and then a case of appendicitis, the islanders felt that they could not remain there. They chose to evacuate in 1930, and ever since the island's only population has been the wildlife.

It is a difficult place to get to: the crossing is rough and dangerous and there are very few landing points once you reach the islands. But persistence is rewarded with the amazing landscape that awaits visitors. It feels a world away from modern Britain, an island lost in time. Wild animals – gannets, Atlantic puffins, grey seals and the indigenous Soay sheep – now live undisturbed by human life. The remains of streets, houses, a shop, school and church point to how life might have been for the people who lived there. Not to be missed is the famous 'Mistress stone'. Martin Martin, a monk who visited the island in the seventeenth century, writes of the tradition around it:

> In the face of the rock, south from the town, is the famous stone, known by the name of the mistress-stone; it resembles a door exactly; and is in the very front of this rock, which is twenty or thirty fathom perpendicular in height, the figure of it being discernable about the distance of a mile; upon the lintel of this door, every bachelor-wooer is by an ancient

custom obliged in honour to give a specimen of his affection for the love of his mistress, and it is thus; he is to stand on his left foot, having the one half of his sole over the rock, and then he draws the right foot further out to the left, and in this posture bowing, he puts both his fists further out to the right foot; and then after he has performed this, he has acquired no small reputation, being always after it accounted worthy of the finest mistress in the world: they firmly believe that this achievement is always attended with the desired success. This being the custom of the place, one of the inhabitants very gravely desired me to let him know the time limited by me for trying of this piece of gallantry before I design'd to leave the place, that he might attend me; I told him this performance would have a quite contrary effect upon me, by robbing me both of my life and mistress at the same moment.

– Martin Martin, 'A Voyage to St Kilda',
in *A Description of the Western Islands of Scotland* (1703)

There are several ways of visiting St Kilda, but perhaps the most rewarding is to visit on a working trip, to help the National Trust of Scotland in its conservation work. It's difficult work and only for the fit and enthusiastic, but it can be a hugely satisfying way of exploring the island and experiencing a completely different way of life.

Brownsea Island

Brownsea Island is famous as the birthplace of the Scout and Guide movements. In 1907 Lord Baden-Powell, fresh from battle at the Siege of Mafeking, held the first camp for boys on Brownsea Island. It was meant as an experimental camp to test the ideas he was including in his handbook, *Scouting for Boys*. The camp was a huge success and so Baden-Powell pressed on with his scouting movement and published his handbook. But girls wanted to be part of this exciting new movement, and when several girls turned up to a Scout rally in Crystal Palace Baden-Powell realized that they were just as keen on adventure and activity as boys. He asked his sister Agnes to lead the new group, which called themselves the Girl Guides.

Nowadays a large portion of Brownsea Island is set aside for the Scouts and Guides, and jamborees and camps are still held there. If you're not part of the Guides, you can still visit, between March and October, by taking a ferry from Poole Harbour.

Farne Islands

The Farne Islands are a group of about fifteen to twenty islands off the coast of Northumberland. Today they are uninhabited, but before the modernization and automation of the lighthouses of the islands there were a few lighthouse-keepers who lived and worked there. The most famous of those is Grace Darling, daughter of the lighthouse-keeper on Longstone Island. Grace was only twenty-two when, on a stormy night in 1838, a ship carrying nine sailors ran into trouble close to Longstone Island and was wrecked on a nearby rock. Grace Darling and her father performed a daring rescue operation, and her bravery and courage that night made her a national heroine. Your mother may have told you her story and it's one that girls everywhere should know so they can continue to honour the memory of such a daring girl.

Visitors to the Farne Islands can take a boat trip to Longstone Island and can alight at the lighthouse to get a feel of what life must have been like for Grace Darling.

While in the Farne Islands, a trip to Holy Island, also known as Lindisfarne, is unmissable. The island is known as the place from which Christianity was spread in the seventh century, and is the site of the brutal Lindisfarne massacres as the monks of the islands were slaughtered by Viking raiders. The island is tidal so you should take care to read the tide charts carefully before you sct off.

Fota Island

Fota is located off the coast of Ireland, in Cork harbour, and is home to the only wildlife park in Ireland. Fota Wildlife Park opened in 1983 and was designed as a place where visitors could see animals in a more natural setting than a zoo, where animals wander freely with no obvious barriers to constrict them. You can get there from Cork by train and, once there, there's plenty to see: giraffes, zebras, gorillas, cheetahs and kangaroos, to mention just a few.

While you are on Fota, make time to visit Fota House and Gardens. This is a Regency-style house surrounded by beautiful gardens and an arboretum which contains many rare plants and trees.

HULA HOOPING

◆

THE REAL CRAZE FOR HULA HOOPING started in the 1950s in Britain, but the idea of spinning a hoop around your hips was not new. Children had been hooping with anything and everything from bamboo to grape vines to wood and metal for 3,000 years, all the way back to Egyptian times. But it wasn't until 1958 that the plastic hula hoop that we all know today was invented. A craze was born, and soon everyone was hooping!

DID YOU KNOW?

* The word 'hula' was added to 'hoop' after sailors visiting Hawaii in the eighteenth century noticed the similarity between hula dancing and hooping. The two have been linked ever since.
* The current world record for the longest hula hoop is held by Roxann Rose from America who managed to hoop for an amazing ninety hours in 1987. This was without a break, so no stopping to eat, drink or sleep.
* The greatest number of hoops used simultaneously to hula hoop is 100.
* The longest distance ever run while hula hooping is 100 metres.
* The largest hula hoop ever successfully hooped is a massive 15.3 metres.
* The strangest thing ever used as a hula hoop is a tractor tyre.

HOW TO HULA HOOP

It may seem obvious, but there is actually quite a skill to hula hooping. Here are some tips to get you started:

Stand with your legs about shoulder-width apart.

Start with the hoop against your back and spin it in whichever direction feels more comfortable. The trick now is not to try to rotate your hips with the hula hoop, but to move your hips up and down, shifting your weight from one foot to the other. It's trickier than it sounds but it will work! Then it's all about practice. Once you are comfortable with hooping around your waist, try to hoop around your wrist or your ankle. Or perhaps try adding another hoop for maximum effect.

CUSTOMIZING YOUR HULA HOOP

Hula hoops come in all different shapes and sizes, some even with flashing lights! But nothing is quite as satisfying as expressing your style and creativity and making a hoop your own. Here are just a few ideas; we're sure you'll come up with lots more.

* Try tying lengths of ribbon around the hoop at regular intervals. When you hoop, they'll spin out impressively.
* Grab some coloured sticky tape and wind it around the hoop, creating a spiral effect that will look even better once you're spinning.
* A slightly more fiddly option is wrapping your hoop in decorative paper, sticking it down with glue so it doesn't catch when you're hooping.

MAKING YOUR OWN HULA HOOP

You can go one stage further and make your own hula hoop from scratch. This way you'll end up with a hoop exactly the right size for you.

* Start off with a length of tubing, around 2 centimetres in diameter. Hosepipe is good and can be found in most garden centres.
* Cut a length that, when in a hoop shape, comes to above your bellybutton.
* Using an inserted connector (available from DIY shops), push one end of the tube onto the connector. At this stage you can fill the tube with sand if you want to weigh it down. Then connect the other end of the tube to the connector, making sure it is securely fastened.
* Decorate to your taste, and then you are ready to impress your friends.

Happy hula hooping!

WEATHER

◆

Signs, Clouds, Vocabulary and Famous Poems about the Weather

Weather Signs

METEOROLOGISTS USE DOPPLER RADAR, weather balloons, satellites and computers to give fairly accurate predictions of what the weather will be like in the near future. But even before we had computerized weather forecasts, we had ways to interpret and predict the weather. Generations ago, people passed down their knowledge about weather signs through rhymes and sayings they taught to their children. As it turns out, those rhyming proverbs based on the observations and wisdom of sailors, farmers and other outdoors people are grounded not only in experience but also in science. So if you're out camping, or hiking, or travelling on foot in nature, far away from technology, you can use some of that lore to determine a fairly reliable reading of the weather. Here are some of the most well-known rhymes about weather signs.

'Red sky at night, shepherd's delight. Red sky in morning, shepherd's warning'
The various colours of the sky are created by rays of sunlight that are split into colours of the spectrum as they bounce off water vapour and dust particles in our atmosphere. When the atmosphere is filled with lots of dust and moisture, the sunlight coming through it makes the sky appear

reddish. This high concentration of particles usually indicates high pressure and stable air coming in from the west, and since weather systems usually move from west to east, that means you'll have good weather for the night. When the sun rises in the eastern sky looking red, that indicates a high water and dust content in the atmosphere, which basically means that a storm system may be moving in your direction. So if you notice a red sky in the morning, pack your umbrella.

'Ring around the moon, rain or snow soon'
You may have noticed some nights it looks like there's a ring around the moon. That halo, which can also form around the sun, is a layer of cirrus clouds composed of ice crystals that reflect the moon's light like prisms. These clouds are not rain- or snow-producing, but they sometimes show up as a warm front and low-pressure area approaches, which can mean inclement weather. The brighter the ring, the greater the chance of rain or snow.

'Clear moon, frost soon'
When the moon sits in a clear, cloudless sky, lore has it that frost is on its way. The weather science behind the saying explains that in a clear atmosphere, with no clouds to keep the heat on earth from radiating into space, a low-temperature night without wind encourages the formation of frost. When clouds cover the sky, they act as a blanket, keeping in the sun's heat absorbed by the earth during the day.

'A year of snow, a year of plenty'
This one seems a bit counter intuitive, but in fact a season of continuous snow is better for farmland and trees than a season of alternating warm and cold weather. When there's snow throughout the winter, that delays the blossoming of trees until the cold season is fully over. Otherwise, the alternate thawing and freezing that can come with less stable winter weather destroys fruitbearing trees and winter grains.

'Rainbow in the morning gives you fair warning'
Rainbows always appear in the part of the sky opposite the sun. Most weather systems move from west to east, so a rainbow in the western sky, which would occur in the morning, signifies rain – it's giving you 'fair warning' about the rainstorm that may follow. (A rainbow in the eastern sky, conversely, tells you that the rain has already passed.)

Clouds

THE TERMS FOR CATEGORIZING CLOUDS were developed by Luke Howard, a London pharmacist and amateur meteorologist, in the early 1800s. Before this, clouds were merely described by how they appeared to the viewer: grey, puffy, fleece, towers and castles, white, dark. Shortly before Howard came up with his cloud names, a few other weather scientists started devising cloud terminology of their own. But it was ultimately Howard's names, based on Latin descriptive terms, that stuck.

Howard named three main types of clouds: cumulus, stratus and cirrus. Clouds that carried precipitation he called 'nimbus', the Latin word for rain.

Cumulus

Cumulus is Latin for 'heap' or 'pile', so it makes sense that cumulus clouds are recognizable by their puffy cotton-ball-like appearance. These types of clouds are formed when warm and moist air is pushed upwards, and their size depends on the force of that upward movement and the amount of water in the air. Cumulus clouds that are full of rain are called cumulonimbus.

Stratus

Stratus clouds are named for their layered, flat, stretched-out appearance, as 'stratus' is the Latin word for layer. These clouds can look like a huge blanket across the sky.

Cirrus

Cirrus clouds are named for their wispy, feathery look. 'Cirrus' means 'curl of hair' and looking at cirrus clouds you can see why Luke Howard thought to describe them that way. These clouds form only at high altitudes and are so thin that sunlight can pass all the way through them.

Nimbus

Nimbus clouds, the rain clouds, can have any structure or none at all. If you've seen the sky on a rainy day and it looks like one big giant grey cloud, you'll know what we mean.

Weather Vocabulary

Air pressure

Here's a fun fact: air is actually a fluid. Like other fluids, it has internal pressure due to the force of earth's gravity. Measured at sea level, the air weighs 14.7 pounds per square inch. Air pressure gets lower with increasing altitude.

Barometer

An instrument measuring atmospheric pressure, which can predict weather changes.

Humidity

The amount of moisture in the air. You've probably heard the expression, 'It's not the heat, it's the humidity' – meant to convey that the oppressive moisture in the air is what makes hot weather so uncomfortable. But even in the driest, hottest desert, there is always some water vapour in the air. There are two ways to measure humidity: Absolute humidity and relative humidity. Absolute humidity is the percentage of moisture actually present in the air, while relative humidity is absolute humidity divided by the amount of water that could be present in the air. Relative humidity is what people are complaining about when they say, 'It's not the heat, it's the humidity' – because relative humidity indicates the amount of sweat that can evaporate from the skin.

Mean Temperature

The average of temperature readings taken over a specified amount of time.

Wind

Wind is the air in natural motion, a current of air moving along or parallel to the ground. We can feel the wind, and see the effects of wind, but we can't see the wind itself – except as it appears in meteorological pictures, as in the swirling spirals we see on weather maps when a hurricane is present. The way the wind blows depends on the atmosphere around it: in the presence of high and low pressure, the wind blows in a circular pattern, clockwise around a high-pressure cell and counterclockwise around a low.

Famous Poems about Weather

Who has seen the wind?
by Christina Rossetti (1830–94)

Who has seen the wind?
Neither I nor you:
But when the leaves hang trembling
The wind is passing thro'.

Who has seen the wind?
Neither you nor I:
But when the trees bow down their heads
The wind is passing by.

Fog
by Carl Sandburg (1878–1967)

The fog comes
on little cat feet.

It sits looking
over harbour and city
on silent haunches
and then moves on.

I Wandered Lonely as a Cloud
by William Wordsworth (1770–1850)

I wandered lonely as a cloud
That floats on high o'er vales and hills,
When all at once I saw a crowd,
A host, of golden daffodils;
Beside the lake, beneath the trees,
Fluttering and dancing in the breeze.

Continuous as the stars that shine
And twinkle on the milky way,
They stretched in never ending line
Along the margin of a bay:
Ten thousand saw I at a glance,
Tossing their heads in sprightly dance.

The waves beside them danced; but they
Out did the sparkling waves in glee:
A poet could not but be gay,
In such a jocund company:
I gazed and gazed but little thought
What wealth the show to me had brought:

For oft, when on my couch I lie
In vacant or in pensive mood,
They flash upon that inward eye
Which is the bliss of solitude;
And then my heart with pleasure fills,
And dances with the daffodils.

The Cloud
by Percy Bysshe Shelley (1792–1822)

I bring fresh showers for the thirsting flowers,
From the seas and the streams;
I bear light shade for the leaves when laid
In their noonday dreams.
From my wings are shaken the dews that
    waken
The sweet buds every one,
When rocked to rest on their mother's breast,
As she dances about the sun.
I wield the flail of the lashing hail,
And whiten the green plains under,
And then again I dissolve it in rain,
And laugh as I pass in thunder.

I sift the snow on the mountains below,
And their great pines groan aghast;
And all the night 'tis my pillow white,
While I sleep in the arms of the blast.
Sublime on the towers of my skiey bowers,
Lightning, my pilot, sits;
In a cavern under is fettered the thunder,
It struggles and howls at fits;

Over earth and ocean, with gentle motion,
This pilot is guiding me,
Lured by the love of the genii that move
In the depths of the purple sea;
Over the rills, and the crags, and the hills,
Over the lakes and the plains,
Wherever he dream, under mountain or stream,
The Spirit he loves remains;
And I all the while bask in Heaven's blue
    smile,
Whilst he is dissolving in rains.

The sanguine Sunrise, with his meteor eyes,
And his burning plumes outspread,
Leaps on the back of my sailing rack,
When the morning star shines dead;
As on the jag of a mountain crag,
Which an earthquake rocks and swings,
An eagle alit one moment may sit
In the light of its golden wings.
And when Sunset may breathe, from the lit
    sea beneath,
Its ardors of rest and of love,

And the crimson pall of eve may fall
From the depth of Heaven above,
With wings folded I rest, on mine aery nest,
As still as a brooding dove.
That orbed maiden with white fire laden,
Whom mortals call the Moon,
Glides glimmering o'er my fleece like floor,
By the midnight breezes strewn;

And wherever the beat of her unseen feet,
Which only the angels hear,
May have broken the woof of my tent's thin
    roof,
The stars peep behind her and peer;
And I laugh to see them whirl and flee,
Like a swarm of golden bees,
When I widen the rent in my wind built tent,
Till the calm rivers, lakes, and seas,
Like strips of the sky fallen through me on
    high,
Are each paved with the moon and these.

I bind the Sun's throne with a burning zone,
And the Moon's with a girdle of pearl;
The volcanoes are dim, and the stars reel and
    swim
When the whirlwinds my banner unfurl.
From cape to cape, with a bridge like shape,
Over a torrent sea,
Sunbeam proof, I hang like a roof,
The mountains its columns be.
The triumphal arch through which I march
With hurricane, fire, and snow,
When the Powers of the air are chained to
    my chair,
Is the million coloured bow;
The sphere fire above its soft colours wove,
While the moist Earth was laughing below.

I am the daughter of Earth and Water,
And the nursling of the Sky;
I pass through the pores of the ocean and
    shores;
I change, but I cannot die.
For after the rain when with never a stain
The pavilion of Heaven is bare,
And the winds and sunbeams with their
    convex gleams
Build up the blue dome of air,
I silently laugh at my own cenotaph,
And out of the caverns of rain,
Like a child from the womb, like a ghost from
    the tomb,
I arise and unbuild it again.

LEMON-POWERED CLOCK

◆

A PAIR OF LEMONS and a quick trip to the DIY shop is all you need to convert natural chemical energy into electric power.

Alessandro Volta invented the battery in Italy, in 1800, combining zinc, copper and an acid to create energy. A common lemon can provide acid (as do potatoes, which you can use if there's no lemon around), and you can rig one to run your own digital clock.

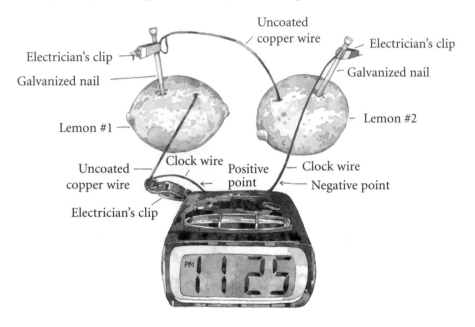

WHAT YOU NEED

1 A battery-operated digital clock without a plug. It can use two AA batteries, or a round battery. Depending on the connections, you have to rig the wires in different ways, but that's where the fun starts.

2 Two fairly large galvanized nails. Nails are measured in length and in diameter (with designations of 3d, 6d, 8d, 10d, and the like). We used a 16d, 3½-inch solid nail. Galvanized nails are a must and we'll explain why below.

3 Copper wire. Uncoated wire is easier. If your wire comes with a coating, use a wire stripper to remove an inch or two of the covering.

4 Three electrician's clips.

5 Two lemons, or one very large lemon, cut in half.

WHAT YOU DO

In five simple steps, here is how you run a digital clock on a lemon.

Step One

Place the lemons on a plate, or any flat surface that can serve as the base for the clock. Push one nail into each lemon and then, as far away from the nails as possible, also push in a strand of copper wire. Label your lemons one and two. What you're going to do now is create a closed circuit, so energy can flow from the lemon into the clock and back again.

Step Two

Open up the clock's battery compartment. Depending on your clock, there are two AA batteries, or a single battery that looks like a button. Remove the battery (you'll be replacing its energy, believe it or not, with the lemon, nail and copper concoction you've just created). Notice that the positive and negative points are marked as such.

Step Three

On lemon number one, use the electrician's clip to connect the copper wire to the positive point in the clock. This may be a challenge; in some cases it is easier said than done.

If you can't connect your wire to the positive point in the battery compartment, you'll need to remove the clock's plastic backing and open up the clock. An adult should help with this, and remember, once you take the clock apart it may not go back together. You'll see that the positive and negative points are connected to wires on the inside of the clock. You can remove the wires from the back of the battery compartment, and then use them to make your connections. If you have a two-AA-battery clock, and inside you find two positive wires, make sure you connect your copper wire with both. Once you've figured this out, the rest is a breeze.

Step Four

On lemon number two, connect the nail to the clock's negative point. You may need to move the lemon into a new position so you can clip the nail to the clock.

Step Five

Link the copper wire from lemon number two to the nail sticking out of lemon number one. You'll see now that you've made an entire electrical circuit, from clock to lemon to the next lemon, and back to the clock. If all has gone well, the clock now works, because just under one volt of electricity is coursing around the circuit.

If the clock does not work, make sure all connections are secure, and then double-check the directions. If several months from now the clock stops, replace the lemons, or the nails, and it should begin ticking once again.

1 The nail has been galvanized, which means it was coated with zinc to help resist rust. The lemon contains acid. This acid dissolves the zinc on the nail. In chemistry terms, this means that the zinc loses an electron and becomes a positive force. (If you haven't already read the chapter about the Periodic Table of the Elements, now's a good time to do so.) The moisture in the lemon functions as an electrolyte, a fluid that conducts electrons – if you will, a swimming pool for electrons.

2 The electron shoots out of the zinc, through the lemon, to react with the copper on the wire. The copper gains an electron and becomes a negative force. The exchange of electrons is a chemical reaction. It creates chemical energy, or charge. All that charge needs is a circuit.

3 The electron exchange buzzes around the circuit you built – zinc/nail to copper wire to clock to copper wire to nail to lemon to copper to zinc/nail to lemon, and so on. That's the transfer from chemical energy to electricity, and it gets the clock going as well as any manufactured battery.

SNOWBALLS

SNOWBALLS MAY NOT BE allowed in playgrounds, but this shouldn't stop you from holding a neighbourhood snowball fight when school gets cancelled because of a big storm. When a snowball fight breaks out, everyone must agree to some ground rules, such as no ice, and all snowballs must always be aimed well below the neck.

There are four basic kinds of snow.

Powder

Likely to be seen on very cold days. It has low moisture content and lots of air. Skiers love it, but not snowball fighters, because it's too dry to pack well.

Slush

No one likes slush; this mushy, melty water-logged snow is horrid for snowballs.

Ice

Snow that has melted and refrozen. Leave it alone. You don't want to be hit by it, and you don't want to throw it. Ice hurts, and it wrecks the fun.

Snowball Snow

Made in weather that hovers around the freezing mark. You know it when you see it. The snow is airy yet firm, and when you roll some between your hands it sets into a ball that nearly leaps into the air.

To make a snowball, scoop enough snow to fill your hands. Push in, and rotate both hands around your snowball. Pack it. Smooth it. Add more to make it bigger. It's your choice to stockpile, or make them as you go.

After hours playing in the snow, head inside to warm up with a mug of hot chocolate with, if you're lucky, plenty of marshmallows.

EVERY GIRL'S TOOLBOX

◆

WITH TOOLS you can make stuff, and that is a powerful feeling. You can help your grandfather finish that doll's house he's been tinkering with for years. You can make a swing for the garden, a bench for your den – or make the whole den.

Experiment with wood, nails, screws, hammers, screwdrivers and drills. After a while, you'll start to think in tools and materials, and you'll see how screws and nails hold wood together. Then you'll begin to come up with your own projects. Trial and error are the best teachers, and it doesn't take long to feel comfortable.

Visiting the DIY shop

Before we turn to the basic tools, a word on DIY shops. You might be intimidated by them, as many people are. Especially those antiquated-looking, small DIY shops, with their dusty shelves filled to the brim with unfamiliar, scary-looking objects, usually guarded by men who are burly and possibly gruff.

Fear not, we are here to tell you. Said shops mark the entrance to a world in which you can create and repair anything imaginable. And the shops' burly guardians? The truth is, they may look gruff, but usually they're very nice, and they love to problem-solve and to find the perfect nail or wire for you. Ask for help when you're matching bolts and nuts. Get their advice on what kind of drill bit will attach a wood plaque to the stone wall outside your house. They'll show you where to find DIY shop exotica, and they know fix-it secrets you'll never learn in books.

Besides, many of them have daughters, too, and you can bet they've taught their girls a thing or two about what to do with a hammer and a box of nails.

Creating your toolbox

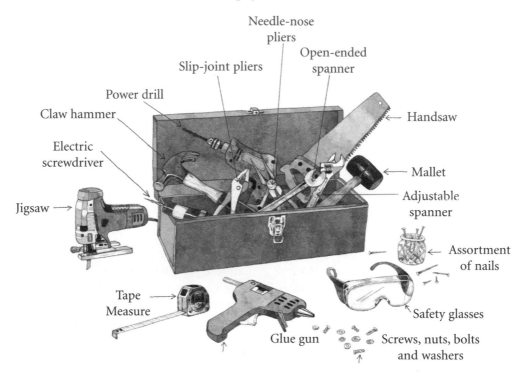

Needle-nose pliers

Open-ended spanner

Slip-joint pliers

Power drill

Claw hammer

Handsaw

Electric screwdriver

Mallet

Adjustable spanner

Jigsaw

Assortment of nails

Tape Measure

Safety glasses

Glue gun

Screws, nuts, bolts and washers

Every girl needs her own toolbox. You can get a decent toolbox, with a latch and an organizing tray, for as little as ten pounds. Here are the basics to fill it with.

1 **Safety Glasses.** These are an absolute must when hammering, drilling or sawing.

2 **Claw Hammer.** The flat side of the hammer bangs nails into wood; the V-shaped claw side pulls them out.

To hammer, grip the handle solidly, near the bottom. Hold a nail with your thumb and forefinger, and tap it into the wood, gently, until it stands on its own. Then move your fingers away and hammer harder, from your forearm (that is, don't use your entire arm), and keep your wrist straight. Keep your eye on the nail, and trust your eye-hand coordination.

3 **Nails.** The measurements for nails derive from the custom of selling 100 nails for a certain number of pennies. Nails are thus described in pennyweights, except the

resulting abbreviation is not p, but, oddly enough, d, in reference to an ancient Roman coin, the denarius.

Once upon a time you could walk into a store in Yorkshire and purchase 100 1½-inch nails for fourpence, and because of that, they are now labelled 4d nails after the old money. Much of the world, it must be said, uses the metric system for an easier and more reasonable way to measure nails.

4 **Screwdriver.** The screwdriver not only gets screws where they're going and takes them out; it can be used in a bazillion creative ways to do almost anything. Try a six-in-one screwdriver (which has six changeable heads). To get jobs done faster, we recommend a battery-operated screwdriver.

5 **Screws.** Screws and bolts live in those mysteriously thin cabinets in the back aisle of the hardware store, along with their friends, bolts, nuts and washers. Tighten a nut on a bolt to keep things ultra-secure. A washer – that's a flat circular object that slips on the bolt between the nut and the surface – protects the surface and helps tighten the nut.

Remembering the saying 'righty-tighty, lefty-loosy' will help you recall which direction to turn a screw.

6 **Spanner.** Spanners tighten and untighten the nuts that go at the end of bolts. They come in the open-end (fixed size) variety, and the adjustable. A small set of open-ended spanners, or one adjustable spanner, should start you off well.

7 **Pliers.** For gripping objects, like a stuck tap, get versatile slip-joint pliers. Also handy are needle-nose pliers to grab small objects, like wire. They often have a little wire cutter built in (peek at the intersection of the handles and you'll find it).

8 **Glue Gun.** When you can't use screws, bolts or nails, a glue gun saves the day, and is quite fun to operate. A small one should do, and don't forget plenty of glue sticks to melt in it.

9 **Tape Measure.** A 5-metre retractable tape measure that can lock in place is a good start.

10 **Saw.** A saw is not for the very young, of course, but it's a necessity for cutting wood to size and making shapes. A handsaw is a flat hand tool. A modern jigsaw is a power tool, activated by a trigger. All power tools are extremely dangerous if they are not used exactly as specified in their instructions, and you should always have adult supervision when operating them.

Hold long strips of wood on a sawhorse (a beam connected by four legs); cut small pieces of wood off the edge of a work table. Be careful, ask for help and, as always, use your safety glasses.

11 **Drill.** To drill, start with an awl or centre punch (hand tools that look like small spikes) to make an indentation in your surface so the drill bit won't slip.

A battery-operated power drill is very handy. It will come with a basic set of bits, or you can get a set if it doesn't. There's an art to matching up the right drill bit to the size of the hole you'll need for the screw. If you know the size of the bolt or screw, that helps. Otherwise, the best we can tell you is to peer closely at the sizes and when in doubt try the smaller bit first. Experience will make it all the more clear.

Once you have your own toolbox, you might begin to truly love the DIY shop. You'll stand for hours looking at the display of unique drill bits to make holes in metal, brick, plastic or stone; at the sander attachment that can remove paint or brush wood's rough edges clean; at the buffer that smooths it to perfection. You'll handle each one carefully, and after much deliberation with the burly bloke behind the counter about the pros and cons of each, take some home to try out on a project of your own imagination.

A SHORT HISTORY OF WOMEN INVENTORS AND SCIENTISTS

EVEN THOUGH IT'S SAID that 'necessity is the mother of invention', women's contributions to inventing and science have been, in the past, often overlooked. It's likely women have been using their creativity and intelligence to engineer new ideas and products since the beginning of human experience, but nobody really kept track of such things until a few hundred years ago. Below we've assembled some of our favourite daring women inventors, scientists and doctors – from Nobel Prize winners to crafters of practical devices, from women who revolutionized the way nappies were changed to women whose revolutionary ideas changed the world.

1902

Ida Henrietta Hyde is named the first female member of the American Physiological Society. She was also the first woman to graduate from the University of Heidelberg and the first woman to do research at the Harvard Medical School. She went on to invent the microelectrode in the 1930s, which revolutionized the field of neurophysiology.

Marie Curie

1903

Scientist **Marie Curie** is awarded the Nobel Prize in Physics for her discovery of the radioactive elements radium and polonium. She is awarded the Nobel Price for Chemistry in 1911, making her the first person to win two Nobel prizes.

1932

Hattie Elizabeth Alexander, an American paediatrician and microbiologist, develops a serum to combat *Haemophilus influenzae*, which at that time had a fatality rate of 100 per cent in infants. In 1964, she is the first woman to be elected president of the American Paediatric Society.

1935

Irène Joliot Curie, the French scientist and daughter of Marie Curie, is awarded the Nobel Prize for Chemistry with her husband, for their discovery of radioactivity, making the Curies the family with most Nobel laureates to date.

1938

Katherine Blodgett, American physicist, invents a micro-thin barium stearate film to make glass completely nonreflective and 'invisible'. Her invention has been used in spectacles, camera lenses, telescopes, microscopes, periscopes and projector lenses.

1941

The actress **Hedy Lamarr** invents (along with George Anthiel) a 'Secret Communications System' to help combat the Nazis in World War II.

1957

Rachel Fuller Brown and **Elizabeth Lee Hazen**, researchers for the New York Department of Health, develop the anti-fungal antibiotic drug nystatin. The scientists donated the royalties from their invention, totalling over $13 million dollars, to the nonprofit Research Corporation for the Advancement of Academic Scientific Study. They were inducted into the National Inventors Hall of Fame in 1994.

1958

Helen Free, a biochemist and expert on urinalysis, invents the home diabetes test. She and her husband were inducted into the National Inventors Hall of Fame in 2000.

1964

Dorothy Crowfoot Hodgkin, a British biochemist and crystallographer, wins the 1964 Nobel Prize in Chemistry for using X-ray techniques to determine the structures of biologically important molecules, including penicillin, vitamin B-12, vitamin D and insulin.

1964

Chemist **Stephanie Louise Kwolek** invents Kevlar, a polymer fibre that is five times stronger than the same weight of steel and is now used in bulletproof vests, helmets, trampolines, tennis rackets, tyres and many other common objects.

1966

Lillian Gilbreth becomes the first woman to be elected to the National Academy of Engineering. This inventor, author, industrial engineer, industrial psychologist and mother of twelve children patented many kitchen appliances, including an electric food mixer, shelves inside refrigerator doors, and the foot-pedal, lid-opening bin. In her work on ergonomics, she interviewed over 4,000 women to design the proper height for stoves, sinks and other kitchen fixtures.

1975

Physicist **Betsy Ancker-Johnson** becomes the fourth woman elected to the National Academy of Engineering, one of the highest honours an engineer can receive.

1975

Dr Chien-Shiung Wu is elected the first woman president of the American Physical Society. The nuclear physicist studied beta-decay, worked on the Manhattan Project and helped develop more sensitive Geiger counters.

1988

Gertrude Belle Elion is awarded the Nobel Prize in Physiology or Medicine. The bio-chemist invented many life-saving drugs, now commonly used to fight leukaemia and other diseases.

1995

Physical chemist **Isabella Helen Lugoski Karle** receives the National Medal of Science for her work on the structure of molecules.

1997

Dr Rosalyn Sussman Yalow wins the Nobel Prize in Medicine for her 1959 invention of RIA, a revolutionary way to diagnose illness at the molecular level.

BANDANA TYING

◆

THE WORD *BANDANA* has a global history. It comes from the Sanskrit *bhandhana*, which means tying. The word was absorbed first into Portuguese (in the sixteenth century, Portugal had conquered the cities of Goa and Bombay, now called Mumbai, on the western coast of India). From Portuguese, the word entered English. We can thank Indian languages for an assortment of English clothing words, such as cashmere (from the northern region of Kashmir), cummerbund, bangle, khaki, pyjamas and dungarees.

Bandanas are often also called kerchiefs or headscarfs. A bandana can be a belt or a blindfold for Blind Man's Bluff. With a needle and thread, two or more can be sewn together to make a shirt or skirt.

You can wrap it loosely around your neck, cowboy style, pull it up over your nose and mouth for a disguise or use it to dress up your pet. Best of all, you can wrap treasures or lunch in a bandana, then attach it to a long stick and sling it over your shoulder when you head out to see the world.

Bandanas are an excellent way to cover your hair, too, while playing lacrosse or hiking on a hot day, and they make perfect headbands.

To tie a bandana around your head, fold it in half to make a triangle. Place the long edge on your forehead, however low or high you want (you'll most likely experiment with this, and try different possibilities). The cloth will fall lightly over your hair. With your hands, smooth it towards the back, push the tip of the triangle towards the nape of your neck. Then draw the ends over it, and tie (use your square knot).

You'll probably want to pull the triangle portion of the bandana into place, so it's smooth against your head, and so the corners don't stick out the sides.

If your head is larger, or if your mother or father wants to wear one, instead of folding the cloth in half, merely fold one corner towards the opposite corner, and go from there.

To turn a bandana into a headband, fold in half to make a triangle. Start folding in, from the tip of the triangle towards the long edge, till you're left with the size headband you want to wear. Wrap around your head and tie in the back.

FIVE KARATE MOVES

KARATE BEGAN in the fifth century BC as a set of mind-strengthening exercises. Legend says that it was brought to a small forest temple in China by a Zen Buddhist monk named Bodhidharma (Bo-dee-darma) who, amazingly, had walked there all the way from India. Below are five basic moves that are fun to do with friends. To learn more and to take karate more seriously, look for a professional teacher in this and other martial arts.

Front Kick

The front kick is Karate's most powerful kick. Bring your left knee up to waist level, then extend the rest of the leg straight out. Your right leg should be firmly grounded to balance the kick, and your arms should be held close to your chest. Try the quick-surprise front kick, and then try a slower but more forceful variation.

Front Kick

Back Kick

Stand in a comfortable position facing forward. Your right leg is your kicking leg. Bend your left non-kicking leg just a little bit to give your body extra support and balance. Look over your right shoulder. Find your target. Bend your right knee, aim your heel in a straight line towards your target and kick your foot high behind you. Your eyes are very important in this kick. Keep looking at your target while you kick back, extending your leg. Pull your leg back in the same path you used for your kick. Alternate kicking leg.

Punch and Pull

Face forward with your feet shoulder-width apart. Keeping your right leg straight, lunge forward with your left leg, bending at the knee. Push your right arm forward in front of your body, with your hand in a downward-facing fist. Your left arm stays back, at your side, with your left hand in an upward-facing fist. Now, punch forward with the left arm and twist the wrist so that when this arm fully extends, your fist faces down. While the left arm punches, the right arm comes to rest at your side, with hand in an upward-facing fist. Alternate punches.

Back Kick

Punch and Pull

Knife Hand, or Classic Karate Chop

Open your hand and turn it so your thumb faces the ceiling and your little finger faces the floor. Extend your fingers forward and away from you. The fingers should lightly touch. Let your thumb fall into the palm of your hand, and bend the top of the thumb downwards. Arch the hand slightly backwards. Raise your hand above your shoulder. Swing diagonally downwards across to the other side of your body aiming to strike your target with the part of your hand that's just below your little finger.

Lunge Punch

Face forward, with your feet shoulder-width apart. Place your left leg in front of the right, and bend your knee into a lunge. Keep your right leg straight. This is called front stance. Step forward with your right foot into a powerful lunge, and as your right foot lands, punch forward with the right hand. To add power, at the same time as you punch the right fist forward, pull your left hand back to your left side in an upward-facing fist. Pull your punching hand back to lunge again, alternating sides, or to change to another move.

Knife Hand

Lunge Punch

PUTTING YOUR HAIR UP WITH A PENCIL

PERFECT FOR WHEN you're on the run, in the midst of a project, or otherwise adventuring and too busy to fuss with your hair. This skill is best practised on hair that is at least shoulder-length long; otherwise, a quick ponytail with a rubber band is your best bet.

We're using a pencil, but you can really use anything that's handy and stick-shaped – a toothbrush, a fork, a chopstick. Just make sure to have the sharp side of the implement pointing up, and you'll be good to go. (We're also assuming a righty here, so if you're a lefty, reverse the rights and lefts in the directions.)

First, find a pencil.

Gather your hair into a tight, high ponytail with your hands – you don't need to use a rubber band.

Hold your hair with your left hand, and with the right, grab your pencil, sharp side pointing down.

Turn the pencil sideways, then slide it, end side first, through your hair just next to your left hand that's creating the base of your ponytail.

Change your grip with your right hand so that you are grabbing both the pencil and your hair, and with your left hand, pull the ponytail down, loop it behind the pencil, and pull the end of the ponytail straight up.

Shift the pencil, turning it clockwise so that the sharp end is down and the eraser end is up. Push the end side of the pencil down a bit so that just a small part of it sticks out.

Flip the pencil over by lifting the sharp side up and pushing the end side down. Keep pushing until the end part pokes through the underside of your hair.

PUTTING YOUR HAIR UP WITH A PENCIL

FRENCH TERMS OF ENDEARMENT, EXPRESSIONS AND OTHER ITEMS OF NOTE

---◆---

TERMS OF ENDEARMENT

Ma petite chou
'My little cabbage.' Can be used romantically to mean 'my darling', or said to a younger person 'my little one'.

Bonjour, ma petite chou, t'as passé une bonne journée?
'Hello, my little cabbage, did you have a good day?'

Ma puce
'My flea'

Bonne nuit, ma puce!
'Goodnight, my flea!'

FUN WORDS TO SAY

Pamplemousse
(Pom-pel-moose)
Grapefruit

Chantilly
(Shan-tee)
Whipped cream (or a kind of lace)

Gros
(Grogh)
Big

Dodo
(Doe-doe)
A baby's naptime

Coucou
(Coo-coo)
Hello there!

EXPRESSIONS

Avoir un chat dans la gorge
To have a cat in your throat. (Like the expression 'I have a frog in my throat.')

Revenons a nos moutons
Let's get back to our sheep. (Meaning, return to the subject at hand.)

Oui, quand les poulets auront des dents
Yes, when chicken have teeth. (Like the expression 'When pigs fly!')

What to order at a restaurant

Bonjour, Monsieur. Puis j'avoir un croque monsieur avec une salade verte? Et aussi un coca s'il vous plait?
Hello, sir. May I have a grilled ham and cheese sandwich with a green salad? And a cola, please.

Books with a French setting

Madeline
by Ludwig Bemelmans

The Little Prince
by Antoine de Saint-Exupéry

Eloise in Paris
by Kay Thompson

The Hunchback of Notre Dame
by Victor Hugo

The Count of Monte Cristo
by Alexandre Dumas

JOAN OF ARC

◆

*'One life is all we have and we live it as we believe in living it.
But to sacrifice what you are and to live without belief, that is
a fate more terrible than dying.'*

JOAN OF ARC

JOAN WAS BORN around 1412 in the small town of Domrémy in France, on the border of the provinces of Champagne and Lorraine, to Jacques d'Arc and Isabelle Romée. She grew up helping her father and brothers work the land and helping her mother, a devout woman, look after the house.

The year she turned twelve, she became convinced that there was something special about her – a destiny she alone could fulfil. She began hearing the voices of St Michael, St Catherine and St Margaret, whom she believed had been sent by God to inform her of her divine mission to save France. So compelled was she by the urgency of these voices that by the time she was fifteen she cut her hair, began dressing in a man's uniform and took up arms.

France and England were deep into the Hundred Years War at this point. At that time in history, the two nations were not as separate as they are now and there was a battle raging over who should be king of the general area. By 1429, King Henry VI was claiming the throne and the English occupied Paris and all of northern France. Joan had two missions, thanks to the voices that guided her: to recover her homeland from English domination and reclaim the besieged city of Orléans; and to see the dauphin of France, Charles VII, crowned king. She left her home, without telling her parents, and appealed to the captain of the dauphin's army, telling him of her divine mission. He initially dismissed the notion of a fifteen-year-old girl having the leadership capacity to head his forces. However, her persistence and clarity of vision ultimately convinced

him, and she went on to convince the dauphin as well that she was on a mission from God meant to save him and restore France. After being examined by a board of theologians, she was given the rank of captain and allowed to lead men into battle.

She was seventeen when she led her troops to victory over the English at the battle of Orléans in May 1429. She rode in white armour and carried a banner bearing the likenesses of her three saints. It wasn't all that unusual at that time for women to fight alongside men; indeed, throughout the Middle Ages women had, when necessary, worn armour, led armies, ridden horses and defended castles and lands. Joan was an excellent leader. Through her self-assured confidence, her courage and her determination, she was able to effectively command soldiers and captains alike. She organized her army of men into professional soldiers and even required them to attend mass and go to confession. So formidable was her leadership that it was said when her troops approached, the enemy fled the battlefield. But by far her most innovative act was instilling among her people a sense of nationalism and patriotic pride: she was one of the first leaders to consider England and France as separate countries, with separate cultures and traditions that were worth fighting to preserve.

Due in great part to Joan's leadership on the battlefield, Charles VII was crowned king of France on 17 July 1429 in Reims Cathedral. Her victory, however, was short-lived: she was captured by the Burgundians in 1430 while defending Compiègne, near Paris, and was sold to the English. The English turned her over to the court at Rouen to be tried for witchcraft and crimes against the church. Though the witchcraft charge was dismissed (on the grounds that she was a virgin), she was accused of perpetrating crimes against God by wearing men's clothing. After a fourteen-month trial, during which she never strayed from her insistence on the divinity of her voices and the absolute rightness of her calling, Joan was convicted and burned at the stake in the Rouen marketplace on 30 May 1431. Her last words were 'Jesus! Jesus!' She was nineteen years old.

Almost twenty-five years after her death, Pope Callixtus III reopened the case at the request of Inquisitor-General Jean Brehal and Joan's mother Isabelle Romée. Joan was vindicated as a martyr and declared an innocent woman on 7 July 1456. It was nearly 500 years after her death that she was canonized as a saint, on 16 May 1920, by Pope Benedict XV. Joan of Arc is now recognized as the patron saint of France.

The story of a girl guided by voices to change the world has proved irresistible to storytellers and artists from the time of her death to the present day. She continues to serve as an inspiration to daring girls everywhere.

MAKING A WILLOW WHISTLE

You will need

- ∗ A 20-centimetre straight, smooth, round willow twig
- ∗ A Swiss Army knife
- ∗ Water

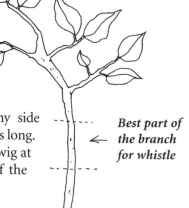

Best part of the branch for whistle

Find a willow twig that is straight and round, without any side branches, less than 3 centimetres thick, and about 20 centimetres long.

Using your Swiss Army knife, cut one end of the willow twig at an angle to make the mouthpiece. Then cut just the end of the pointy tip off to make it a little blunt.

On the top side of the twig, the side opposite your angled cut, carve a small notch in the willow, starting just past the point where your angled cut ends.

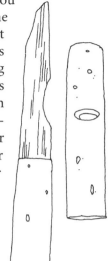

Just more than halfway down, cut a ring around the twig, taking care to cut just the outer layer of bark and not all the way through the wood.

Wet the twig (from the ring to the mouthpiece) with water, tap it gently with your knife to loosen the bark, and then carefully twist and pull the bark off. Try not to rip, tear or break the bark, because you'll need to put it back on the twig. Dip it in water to keep it moist until you need it again.

Go back to the notch you made on the top side of the twig, make it deeper and cut it some more so that it extends down the length of the twig towards the end that still has bark on. The length and depth of this notch is what determines the pitch of your whistle. Carve off just a sliver of wood from the upper surface of the mouthpiece to make it completely flat.

Dip the barkless end of your twig into a glass of water and slip the bark back on.

Now all you have to do is blow! It may take a few tries or alterations to get it right, but keep at it and you'll have your willow whistle blowing.

A dried-out willow whistle can be revived with a thorough soaking in water, but you might want to keep it wrapped in a damp towel so that it doesn't dry completely.

PERIODIC TABLE OF THE ELEMENTS

❖

THE MYSTERIOUS Periodic Table of the Elements holds up to 118 squares with numbers and abbreviations that are, really, the secret code to how the universe works. In these squares rests the true story of how elements combine to create chemical reactions and electricity and the tantalizing mechanisms of life itself.

A scientist named Dimitri Mendeleev of Siberia published *The Periodic Table of the Elements* in 1869 (beating another European scientist to fame by just a few months). Mendeleev listed all the elements that scientists knew at that time – sixty-three, but he had

KEY

Relative atomic mass — Symbol — Atomic number

1.0		
H		
Hydrogen		
1		

Those numbers within brackets are the mass numbers of common isotopes
Those elements underlined are radioactive

N — Element is a gas
Hg — Element is a liquid
Li — Element is a solid
} at room temperature and pressure

Periodic Table of the Elements:

Group	1	2	3	4	5	6	7	8	9	10	11	12	13	14	15	16	17	18
1	1.0 H 1																	4.0 He 2
2	6.9 Li 3	9.0 Be 4											10.8 B 5	12.0 C 6	14.0 N 7	16.0 O 8	19.0 F 9	20.2 Ne 10
3	23.0 Na 11	24.3 Mg 12											27.0 Al 13	28.1 Si 14	31.0 P 15	32.1 S 16	35.5 Cl 17	39.9 Ar 18
4	39.1 K 19	40.1 Ca 20	45.0 Sc 21	47.9 Ti 22	50.9 V 23	52.0 Cr 24	54.9 Mn 25	55.8 Fe 26	58.9 Co 27	58.7 Ni 28	63.5 Cu 29	65.4 Zn 30	69.7 Ga 31	72.6 Ge 32	74.9 As 33	79.0 Se 34	79.9 Br 35	83.8 Kr 36
5	85.5 Rb 37	87.6 Sr 38	88.9 Y 39	91.2 Zr 40	92.9 Nb 41	95.9 Mo 42	(99) Tc 43	101.1 Ru 44	102.9 Rh 45	1.6.4 Pd 46	107.9 Ag 47	112.4 Cd 48	114.8 In 49	118.7 Sn 50	121.8 Sb 51	127.6 Te 52	126.9 I 53	131.3 Xe 54
6	132.9 Cs 55	137.3 Ba 56	138.9 La 57 *	178.5 Hf 72	181.0 Ta 73	183.9 W 74	186.2 Re 75	190.2 Os 76	192.2 Ir 77	195.1 Pt 78	197.0 Au 79	200.6 Hg 80	204.4 Tl 81	207.2 Pb 82	209.0 Bi 83	(210) Po 84	(210) At 85	(222) Rn 86
7	(223) Fr 87	(226) Ra 88	(227) Ac 89 †	(261) Rf 104	(262) Db 105	(263) Sg 106	(262) Bh 107	(265) Hs 108	(266) Mt 109									

* 58-71 Lanthanide series

140.1 Ce 58	140.9 Pr 59	144.2 Nd 60	(147) Pm 61	150.4 Sm 62	152.0 Eu 63	157.3 Gd 64	158.9 Tb 65	162.5 Dy 66	164.9 Ho 67	167.3 Er 68	168.9 Tm 69	173.0 Yb 70	175.0 Lu 71

† 90-103 Actinide series

232.0 Th 90	(231) Pa 91	238.1 U 92	(237) Np 93	(244) Pu 94	(243) Am 95	(247) Cm 96	(247) Bk 97	(251) Cf 98	(252) Es 99	(257) Fm 100	(258) Md 101	(259) No 102	(260) Lr 103

worked out the pattern of those elements, which had gaps, and predicted there were actually ninety-two.

Mendeleev was correct in his prediction of elements in the gaps. And we now know, in fact, that there are 111 natural elements, along with 7 (slightly controversial) elements made in the laboratory. Our chart shows 109 of them.

Some elements – like silver, gold, tin, sulphur, copper and arsenic – were known in classical antiquity, and native peoples of the Americas knew about platinum. Others were discovered during Europe's Age of Science or more recently. Six elements are the core of life as we know it: phosphorous and sulphur (the main components of DNA), carbon (the most abundant element in the universe), hydrogen, oxygen and nitrogen. Women scientists have discovered several elements:

Element	Abbreviation/ Atomic Number	Discovered by	Date
Polonium	Po/84	Marie Sklodowska Curie	1898
Radium	Ra/88	Marie Sklodowska Curie with her husband Pierre Curie	1898
Rhenium	Re/75	Ida Tacke-Noddack with her colleagues Walter Noddack and Otto Carl Berg	1925
Francium	Fr/87	Marguerite Catherine Perey	1939

What is an element?

Elements are basic pieces of matter, composed of a single unique kind of atom. There is nothing that's not made of elements.

What is an atom?

An atom is the basic structure of everything. A group of atoms is called a molecule, and molecules form everything we know, sense, live in and touch.

What is in an atom?

Protons, neutrons, electrons, quarks and gluons, none of which are visible to our eyes, unfortunately. Protons are in the atom's nucleus and carry a positive charge. Each element has a unique number of protons. In fact, the protons determine the order of the elements in the chart. Os, or Osmium, is not the random seventy-sixth element, it has seventy-six protons – hence its place on the chart. The number of protons in an atom never changes. Hydrogen, H, always has one proton. Aluminum, Al, always has thirteen. The proton number distinguishes one element from the others and accounts for each element's character and behaviour. Neutrons also are in the nucleus and carry a neutral charge. Both protons and neutrons break down into quarks, and quarks are held together by gluons.

Electrons have a negative electrical charge and they orbit around the nucleus. The sharing of electrons between atoms creates bonds. In metals, the movement of electrons can generate electrical current.

What do the abbreviations and numbers in each box mean?

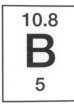

* The top number is the relative atomic mass, or how heavy the element is. This is measured in atomic mass units, or amus. One amu weighs about one trillionth of a trillionth of a gram.
* The letters are the atomic symbol, or abbreviation, of each element. B stands for Boron.
* The atomic number, at the bottom, tells how many protons are in the nucleus.

What do the columns and rows stand for?

Mendeleev observed that some of the elements behave similarly. He organized the elements into columns, according to eighteen family groups, such as gas or metal. He organized the rows according to the pattern of atomic numbers, or number of protons, known as the seven periods.

VINEGAR AND BAKING SODA

◆

SCIENTISTS ACROSS THE GLOBE have studied and debated the concept of acid-base reactions since the 1700s. This chemical reaction can get quite complicated, but it's easy to understand the basic idea and use your knowledge straightaway for everyday projects. All you need is a trip to the supermarket (or your own kitchen cupboard) for two ingredients: vinegar and baking soda.

ACID-BASE BASICS

Acids corrode and dissolve things. They work by releasing hydrogen bubbles. Vinegar is a medium acid. On the pH scale, which measures the 'potential of Hydrogen', it ranks three or four on a scale of one to seven.

Bases cancel out acids. Another word to know, science-wise, is alkali, which is a base that can be dissolved in water. Baking soda is a base, or at least it acts like a base, which is good enough for us. Together vinegar and baking soda, acid and base, can tackle many a small task – and some bigger projects, too.

EVERYDAY VINEGAR USES

Vinegar corrodes and dissolves, it has a repellent smell and it counteracts things that act as a base. Use it to:

Treat skin irritations. Certain itches, like poison ivy and mosquito bites, and pains like jellyfish stings and sunburn, act as bases, so vinegar will counteract them. Mix vinegar half and half with water and spray directly on skin, or soak in towels for compresses. (Cider vinegar smells a bit better than white, if you prefer.)

Get rid of rust. Take rusty hand shovels and other items, dip them in a bowl filled with vinegar, and leave overnight. You can do this to shine pennies, too.

Remove sticky goo. For stubborn stickers or the like, soak a cloth in vinegar, then drape it over the sticky area for a few hours.

Repel mosquitoes and ants. Apply it to your body with a cotton ball as a mosquito repellent. Leave a cup of it open to persuade ants to camp somewhere other than your family kitchen.

Counteract stink. Put smelly things in a half-and-half mixture of water and vinegar overnight. Or, if something stinky happens in your family car, leave a bowl of vinegar in there overnight to capture the smell.

EVERYDAY BAKING SODA USES

Baking soda neutralizes acidic things, and can act as an abrasive for scrubbing. You can use it to:

Soothe bee stings. Apply a baking soda and water paste to a bee sting (which acts as an acid) to neutralize it. Now, if your sting is from a wasp (which actually act as bases), you'll want to treat those stings with vinegar on a cotton ball.

Remove stains. If you get food colouring on your hands, scrub them with baking soda and water. However, if that food colouring gets onto your clothes, you'll want to soak those in vinegar.

Calm animal smells. If you're sprayed by a cat, mix hydrogen peroxide (available at all pharmacies) with baking soda and some washing-up liquid – that works like a charm. Similarly, if your dog smells, sprinkle her all over with baking soda, rub it in and brush through her hair.

Brush teeth. Mix baking soda with water into a thick paste (without the unnecessary extras in toothpaste).

Extinguish fires. Baking soda, when heated, emits carbon dioxide, which can smother small flames.

That said, if you see fire, shout quickly for the nearest adult and call 999 immediately.

Washing the car

You can forgo expensive non-eco-friendly shop-bought cleaners for our two wonder products instead.

Before you start washing, sprinkle baking soda through the car's interior to remove odours. Vacuum it up when the outside washing is done.

For the car body, grab a bucket, and pour in 100 millilitres of vinegar for every four litres of water; scrub car with a big sponge.

For windows, mirrors and interior plastic, mix 400 millilitres of water and 100 millilitres of vinegar in an empty spray bottle. You can add up to 50 millilitres of rubbing alcohol and, to make it look fancier, one drop each, no more, of blue and green food colouring. Instead of rags, use newspapers to clean and shine windows.

Volcano Project

In an old lemonade bottle, pour a little more than 100 millilitres of vinegar and a little more than 100 millilitres of washing-up liquid. Add red food colouring, if you wish, for a lava effect.

Make a foundation from a piece of cardboard. Stick the bottle onto that with tape. Then build up a volcano around it. Mound up old newspapers, leaves or whatever material you have on hand. Once it attains a mountain shape, cover the whole thing with a large sheet of foil, crimping it a bit so it looks volcano-like.

For the eruption, measure one heaped tablespoon of baking soda. Wrap it in a small piece of paper towel or pour it straight in. Either way, when you deposit the baking soda, the concoction will erupt before your eyes. It's always fun, no matter what your age.

Here's the chemistry behind the volcano: vinegar is acetic acid, baking soda is sodium bicarbonate, a base. When they react together they produce carbonic acid and that decomposes very quickly into water and carbon dioxide. The foaming bubble explosion is the carbon dioxide gas escaping.

RULES OF THE GAME:
BOWLING

I N THE 1930s, a British archaeologist named Sir Flinders Petrie discovered items in an Egyptian grave that appeared to have been used in an ancient version of the game we know today as bowling. By his estimation, bowling is a 5,000-year-old game. In the Middle Ages in Britain, bowling was so popular – and distracting – that King Edward III was said to have outlawed it, so that his men could keep focused on honing their archery skills for battle. Bowling has a famous sister sport – Lawn Bowling – perhaps made most famous by Sir Francis Drake who insisted on completing his game of Bowls before he would set sail for battle with the Spanish Armada.

Today ten-pin bowlers all over the world compete and play for fun with friends. Here are some rules for playing and scoring the game.

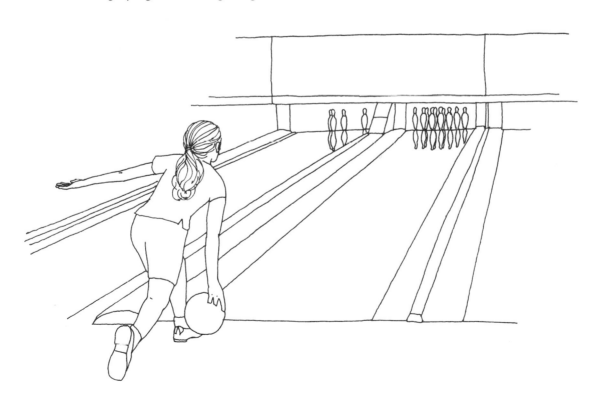

Bowling Terminology

Approach This 5-metre-long area is where bowlers start. The approach ends at the foul line, which marks the start of the bowling lane. Your feet cannot cross the foul line, or even touch it, not even after you've released the ball.

Average This is the sum of all a bowler's games divided by the number of games played.

Bowling Shoes These are shoes with special soles to help a bowler glide across the floor during her approach. Street shoes are not allowed on bowling alleys.

Clean Sheet This means making all the spares in the game.

Dutch 200 Scoring spare-strike-spare-strike for the entire game, resulting in a score of 200.

Foul The foul line separates the approach from the start of the lane. When a bowler steps on or over the foul line, she doesn't get the score for that attempt. A foul is marked on the score sheet with an 'F'.

Frame Each game of bowling consists of ten frames for each bowler, who has two chances to knock down the ten pins in each frame.

Lane The narrow stretch where the ball rolls towards the pins. Lanes are usually about 20 metres long and 1 metre wide. Gutters, two lower rounded areas alongside the lane about 25 centimetres wide, are there to catch balls that stray to the left or right. When a ball rollsinto the gutter, it's called a 'gutter ball' and gets zero points.

Open Frame This is when a bowler fails to knock down all ten pins in both tries.

Perfect Game A perfect game is when a bowler scores twelve strikes in a row in the same game. The resulting score is 300, the highest possible score for a bowler in any one game.

Pin Deck The place where bowling pins are set at the end of the lane. The pins are set just over 30 centimetres apart from each other to form a 1-metre triangle. Pins, which are 40 centimetres tall, are usually made of wood and plastic, and weigh about $1\frac{1}{2}$ kilos. The widest part of the pin is called the belly.

Sleeper When you have a spare with one pin standing directly behind another, the back pin is called a 'sleeper'.

Spare If one or more pins are standing after a bowler's first try, the bowler gets a second chance to knock all the pins down – a 'spare' shot. If the bowler knocks the rest of the pins down on her second try, she has made a spare. A spare is marked on the score sheet by a slash (/).

Split This is when two or more pins remain standing with a gap between them. A split that is left can be marked on the score sheet by drawing a circle around the pin-count for that frame.

Strike This is when a bowler knocks down all ten pins on her first try. When a bowler gets a strike, her score goes up by ten, and in addition the score of her next two turns gets added to the strike score. A strike is marked on the score sheet by an 'X'.

Turkey Getting three strikes in a row. Each 'turkey' (group of three strikes in a row) is worth thirty pins a frame.

HOW TO KEEP SCORE

There are ten frames in the game, and each bowler is given up to two opportunities to try to knock down all ten bowling pins in each frame. The object of the game is to have the highest

score. The pins knocked down on a player's first attempt are counted and recorded on a score sheet. (The score sheet has a place for each player's name, and next to that, ten boxes, one for each frame of the game. At the top of each box are two squares, which is where the scores for each of the two balls thrown per frame are recorded. At the far right is a larger box, which is where the total score for all ten frames should go.) If there are still pins left standing, the bowler then has a second try at knocking them down, and the number of pins knocked down on her second try is recorded. Her score is the pins from the first roll, plus the pins from the second roll; the resulting amount is then added to any previous score. Scores continue to accumulate as each bowler takes her turn until all ten frames have been played by each of the bowlers.

BONUS SCORING

When a bowler rolls a strike or a spare, she gets bonus points. Both a spare and a strike are worth ten pins, but how they are scored actually depends on what the bowler does in the next frame. With a spare, marked by a '/' on the score sheet, you add ten to the number of pins knocked down in your next attempt. With a strike, marked by an 'X' on the score sheet, you add ten to the number of pins knocked down in your next *two* attempts as a bonus for knocking all the pins down.

If you bowl a spare in the tenth frame, you get an extra ball. If you bowl a strike in the tenth frame, you get two extra balls. If you happen to bowl a strike in the tenth frame and then score a spare with your two extra balls, you're awarded a score of twenty for the tenth frame and your game is over. If you bowl a spare in frame ten and then a strike with your additional ball, you get a score of twenty for frame ten and your game is over. If you bowl a strike in the tenth frame and then get two additional strikes with your two extra balls, you get a score of thirty for the tenth frame and your game is over.

QUEENS OF THE ANCIENT WORLD II

◆

Salome Alexandra of Judea

SALOME'S STORY is a tale of diplomacy, of managing the constant challenges of royal leadership, and of resisting attacks from outside armies as well as from members of her own family. She is remembered as the last independent ruler of her country, Judea, during the period just before the countries of the Mediterranean were conquered by Rome.

Salome Alexandra was born in 140 BC. Not much is known of her girlhood. Her Judean name was Shelamzion, which is translated as Salome. Her Greek name was Alexandra, after Alexander the Great, who had brought his Greek armies to the region nearly 200 years earlier. Like many people of her time, Salome lived amid her family and clan and spoke their language, Aramaic. She was also versed in the Hellenistic culture and Greek language that united the many lands around the Mediterranean Sea, including the nearby empires of Egypt and Syria.

From what historians can piece together, it seems Salome Alexandra first married in her late twenties. Her choice of husband – Aristobulus, the eldest son of the native ruler of Judea – led her both to royal life and to the beginning of her family problems. Aristobulus was intensely ambitious. When his father the king died in 104 BC, he willed the country to Aristobulus' mother. But his eldest son would have none of it. He imprisoned his mother, starved her to death and jailed three of his brothers.

In this brutal way, Judea became his, and Salome became the reigning queen. Just a year later, though, Aristobulus died of a mysterious disease. As Salome performed the proper funeral rites over him, she learned that he had bequeathed the kingdom to her.

Salome was faced with another complicated decision: should she rule by herself or share the throne? She released the three royal brothers from jail and chose the eldest of them to be king and high priest. His name was Alexander Janneus. She married him and continued her life as queen.

Her second husband, Alexander, was a tough man to live with. He was bad-tempered and he drank too much. He was fond of raiding and pillaging nearby cities and he was cruel to his own people. He reigned for twenty-seven years. The historian Josephus tells us that as much as the people hated Alexander, they adored Salome, and considered her wise, kind, strong and reliable, decent, fair and a person of good judgement. It's possible that during Alexander's long rule, the people didn't rise to overthrow him because they loved Salome so much.

In 76 BC, Alexander was on his deathbed. He called Salome close and bequeathed the kingdom to her, returning the favour she had granted him twenty-seven years before.

Alexander presented Salome with a plan: 'Conceal my death until, under your command, the soldiers will have won this battle we are now fighting. March back to the capital Jerusalem and hold a Victory. I have oppressed many people, and they now hate me. Make peace with them. Tell them you will include their leaders as advisers in your government. Finally, when you return to Jerusalem, send for the leading men. Show them my dead body and give it over to them. Let them defile it, if they wish, or honour me with a proper burial. The choice will be theirs. And then, they will support you.' Quite a beginning for the new reigning queen.

As queen, ruling from her palace in Jerusalem, Salome faced immediate challenges from her family once more, this time from her two grown sons. Salome anointed her oldest son, Hyrcanus, a quieter and more private sort of man, to be high priest. Hebrew religious law forbade women from overseeing the Temple and performing the animal sacrifices, so

although she was queen, she couldn't be high priest, as her husband had been. Her younger son, named Aristobulus after Salome's first ruthless husband, was a much bigger problem. Like his father, he was very ambitious. He wanted Salome's throne from the start. Soon he would rise against her.

True to her promises and King Alexander's plan, Salome delegated the domestic affairs and a good deal of the power over the nation's religious life to the elders of Judea. This helped to end the civil war that had simmered under her husband's rule, during which he had killed a great many of the elders' group. Still, the remaining elders wanted revenge. Before Salome could stop them, they slit the throat of one of Alexander's ringleaders, Diogenes, and set out to find more.

The ambitious son Aristobulus used the growing violence to threaten his mother's reign. After the revenge killings, Aristobulus led a delegation of men to Salome's throne. They demanded she put a stop to the killings. If she could do so, they promised they would not avenge the recent murders. They would keep the country from descending into a spiral of violence. In return for keeping the peace, Aristobulus demanded his mother give him several of the family fortresses strung throughout the desert from Jerusalem to the Jordan River.

Salome negotiated a deal. She kept the majority of the fortresses for herself, including those that housed her royal treasure, but she gave a few to Aristobulus. Seeking to push him far from her capital, she dispatched him on a small military mission to Damascus.

As Salome dealt with the situation at home, another problem was brewing outside Judea. The country's northern neighbour, Syria, was very weak. The Seleucid dynasty that had once controlled the entire region was in its last days. Taking advantage of this weakness, King Tigranes of Armenia descended on Syria with a massive army of half a million soldiers, quickly taking over Syria's cities. Tigranes trapped the Syrian queen, Cleopatra Selene, in the city of Ptolemais, on the Mediterranean coast.

Ptolemais was not far from Salome's city of Jerusalem. Terrible news of the siege reached Salome quickly, as did the rumour that Tigranes planned to march on Judea next. Salome knew that despite her large army of mercenaries and native soldiers, she could not beat Tigranes.

Rather than ready her troops for war, Queen Salome took a different stance. She sent her ambassadors to meet King Tigranes, and sent along with them many camels loaded with extraordinary treasure. Tigranes agreed not to attack. Luck was on Salome's side, because another army had begun to attack Armenia. Instead of marching south towards Jerusalem, Tigranes had to turn north to defend his own people back home.

That episode, and the years of strife leading up to it, wore Salome down. She was over seventy and her health was beginning to fail. She had outlived two husbands, she faced attacks from outsiders and her youngest son continued to undermine her authority from within.

Sensing her final frailty, Aristobulus planned a coup. He had been angry that Salome negotiated a peace with King Tigranes. Had it been up to him, he would have led their soldiers to battle. He knew she was near death and he suspected that she would bequeath the throne to his older brother, who was already the high priest.

Secretly, Aristobulus left the family palace in Jerusalem. He rode his horse through the countryside, and at each city and village he asked the people to forswear their allegiance to Queen Salome and pledge their loyalty to him.

Salome gathered her last ounce of strength and decided to take harsh action against her son. She imprisoned his wife and children – much as her first husband had done to his relatives. She stashed them in a fortress next to the Temple where Hyrcanus was high priest, but she knew her time was running out. She gave Hyrcanus the keys to the treasury and directed him to take command of her army.

Salome Alexandra died soon thereafter, in 67 BC, before Aristobulus could strike against her. She was seventy-three, had reigned for nine years as her people's only independent queen and she died a natural death. Salome took part in no great battles. She commanded no stunning ships on the sea. She merely did her best to keep the peace at home and to keep stronger armies at bay.

Queen Salome was so admired that for many generations, hers was one of the two most popular names that Judean people would give to their baby daughters (including one infamous Salome who appears in the New Testament). She couldn't have known that she would be the only Judean queen and that this era of independent states was about to end.

In the year Salome died, across the sea in Italy an empire was growing. The Roman general Pompey was fighting the pirates who controlled the Mediterranean. He cleared them out and made it safe once again to cross the vast waters by boat. By 64 BC, Pompey forged his soldiers into battalions and started his eastward trek. He took control of Syria later that year and of Judea the year after. Soon, all of western Asia was under Rome's hand and the era of Queen Salome the diplomat was a distant memory.

ORIGAMI

———◆———

ORIGAMI IS THE ART of folding paper, originating in Japan. The name is made up of two Japanese words: 'oru', which means 'fold', and 'kani', which means 'paper'. In Japan origami is not only a popular art form, it also holds a deeper cultural significance. The crane is one of the most frequently made objects and it is said that anyone who manages to make 1,000 paper cranes will have their dreams or desires come true. The crane has come to symbolize peace and hope in Japan, and Japanese children often make cranes to release onto lakes and rivers as a symbol of their desire for peace.

As with all things, it is best to start with a simple project and work up to more complicated objects. The origami box is very easy to make and yet satisfying and useful too.

Start with a square of coloured paper. You can find traditional origami paper in craft shops – there is a wide range of colours and patterns to choose from. Or you can use normal paper, and perhaps colour it yourself to create a really original look.

3 Then bring the right edge and the left edge in so they meet in the middle.

1 Fold the square in half, straight edges to straight edges, with the coloured side of the paper on the inside of the fold. Then fold it in half again the other way. Unfold the paper and place in on the table in front of you so the coloured side is face down and the folds are pushing the middle of the paper up in the middle slightly.

4 Repeat this with the top and bottom edges. Now you need to go back a little. Undo the last two steps.

2 Keeping the coloured side down and using the folds you have just made as guides, fold each corner into the middle of the paper (in our picture we are using the darker side of the paper as the coloured side).

5 Then fold out the top and bottom corners. Your paper should look like this:

6 Now this is the tricky bit. Put your finger behind the top left-hand corner of the paper and push it in so you are doing a reverse fold. Do the same on the right-hand side.

7 Then pull the top flap in and over and fold down.

8 Then repeat this step on the bottom. That's it. You should have an origami box.

9 We like to keep our jewellery and bits and bobs in ours. You could also make several and fill them with sweets or cakes to give away as presents for your friends and family.

Now you have had a chance to practise, you should be ready to move on to the crane. It's a little tricky in places so be patient and keep trying until you get it right. It really is satisfying.

1 Start by folding the square in half, corner to corner, with the coloured side of the paper on the inside of the fold. Unfold and repeat with the other sides to create the mountain as before.

2 Now bring the straight sides together, unfold and repeat.

5 Bring the opposite corners of the square together to meet in the middle.

3 This bit is tricky, so pay attention. Bring the top left hand corner down to meet the bottom left hand corner.

6 Now undo the last step, turn the square over and repeat on the other side, remembering to unfold on the other side too.

Fold the top corner down and then unfold.

4 Now bring the top right hand corner down to the bottom left hand corner, pulling in the bottom right hand corner at the same time. You will end up with a square.

7 Now pull the top layer up and away.

8 Fold the sides together to make a diamond shape.

11 Repeat on the other side and then turn the tip down and inside itself to form a beak.

9 Now turn it over and repeat on the other side.

Once again, fold the corners into the middle.

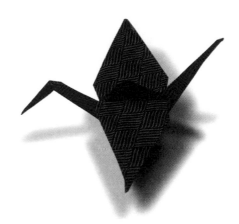

12 Fold the top triangle down horizontally to form wings, and you're finished.

Now only another 999 to go…

10 And turn it over and repeat on the other side. Once you have done this, take the bottom right part of the shape and fold it up and back to look like the picture below.

SLEEPOVER PARTY GAMES

◆

THERE IS USUALLY not much sleep involved in your typical sleepover party. Instead, pyjama-clad girls stay up into the small hours talking, watching films, playing games, telling stories, having pillow fights and giggling. It's a chance for girls to enjoy the bonding element of playing together as a group and revel in subverting the normal evening routine – sleeping in the living room together instead of in bed, alone; staying up well past bedtime; being awake in the dark telling scary stories. It's a time for mystery and daring, as illustrated by some of the most popular slumber party games played by girls over the years.

Bloody Mary

WHO WAS BLOODY MARY?

There are many different stories of who the real 'Bloody Mary' was. The Bloody Mary of sleepover fame has been linked to Queen Mary Tudor, who gained the nickname of 'Bloody Mary' when she had more than 300 people burned at the stake during her reign because they would not follow her Roman Catholic faith. She is also sometimes confused with Mary Queen of Scots (Bloody Mary Tudor's cousin), who in fact may have been instead the subject of a much more benign children's tradition: the nursery rhyme 'Mary, Mary, Quite Contrary'. In other versions, Bloody Mary is thought to be the ghost of Mary Worth, a supposed witch killed in the Salem witch trials, though no historical record of a person by that name exists. The most far-fetched version of the story is rooted in the legend of a woman named Elizabeth Bathory, a sixteenth-century countess who was rumoured to have killed girls and then bathed in their blood to retain her youth. Her name wasn't Mary, obviously, but the nickname she earned, 'The Blood Countess', may contribute to her confusion with the Bloody Mary of countless sleepovers. The most mundane story associated with the Bloody Mary myth is that Mary was a local woman who was killed in a car accident;

Mary Tudor

her ghostly visage features a horrible facial disfiguration she received in the crash. No matter which story you decide to go with – and there are merits to each of them – the basic method of summoning the restless spirit of Bloody Mary is the same: a darkened room, a mirror and the chanting of her name.

Why the mirror? 'Mirror, mirror on the wall, who is the fairest one of all?' is probably the most familiar rhyme about the magical divination possibilities of your own reflection. Indeed, girls in ancient times were encouraged to eat a red apple and brush their hair at midnight in front of a mirror, whereupon they would be rewarded with a glimpse of their future husbands (the red apple and the mirror both figure prominently in the Snow White story we know today). Other rituals involving a mirror required spinning around a certain number of times or looking over your shoulder, the end result being, again, the revelation of whom you might marry. Even today we have less binding versions of these chanting rituals and superstitions – think 'he loves me, loves me not' to see if someone likes you, or twisting an apple stalk until it breaks while chanting the alphabet to discover the first initial of the person you like best. What does this have to do with Bloody Mary? One of the variations of the Bloody Mary chant was 'Bloody mirror, bloody mirror'. This, combined with the idea that you were supposed to discover who you were going to marry by looking in the mirror, plus the gruesome legends of various Marys who were bloody themselves, easily evolved into the 'Bloody Mary' game.

HOW TO PLAY

Go into the bathroom, or another room with a mirror. Holding a torch beneath your chin so that it lights up your face in a ghostly way, close the door and turn off all the lights. Stand in front of the mirror and chant 'Bloody Mary' thirteen times to summon the spirit of Bloody Mary. Ideally this should be done alone, but you can take your friends in there with you for moral support – which you may indeed require, since the legend is that if you get to the thirteenth chant of her name, Bloody Mary will appear in the mirror and either reach out to scratch your face, pull you into the mirror with her, or scare you to death. However, some people believe Bloody Mary isn't always cruel: they say if you're lucky, you'll just see her face in the mirror or she'll appear and answer your questions about the future. And even if no face appears in the mirror, there are other ways Bloody Mary can make her presence felt – a scar or cut that wasn't there before, a window slamming shut, or other eerie happenings. Ultra-daring girls can play this game with one crucial variation: turning off the torch and summoning Bloody Mary completely in the dark.

Truth or Dare

HOW TO PLAY

Truth or Dare, the essential sleepover party game, goes by several different names. Sometimes it is called 'Truth, Dare, Double-Dare', and there is also a variation called 'Truth, Dare, Double-Dare, Promise to Repeat'.

In its most basic version, 'Truth or Dare', players take turns choosing between a truth or a dare, and must either answer a question or perform a dare determined by the other players. The questions can be as embarrassing as you like, and the dares as risky as you can imagine – but neither should ever be harmful. First, because the game is supposed to be fun, and second, because what you ask or dare may come back to haunt you when it's your turn to choose. In 'Truth, Dare or Double-Dare', the players have a choice between telling the truth when asked a question, performing a minor dare and performing a bigger dare. In 'Truth, Dare, Double-Dare, Promise to Repeat', there is the added choice of promising to repeat something – usually embarrassing – in public later.

It's a good idea to set some ground rules before you play so that nobody gets her feelings hurt or gets in too much trouble: nothing that would get a girl in hot water with her parents, nothing that requires going outside or bothering people not involved in the game. The other basic rule is that once you agree to tell the truth, perform a dare or double-dare or promise to repeat, there is no chickening out. If you refuse to do what's asked of you, you're out of the game.

Examples

* **Truth:** You have to answer a personal question. This can be something like: What's your deepest darkest secret? What was your most embarrassing moment? When was the last time you brushed your teeth? What superpower do you wish you had?

* **Dare:** You have to do an easy dare, such as: Act like a chicken for thirty seconds. Wear your underwear on your head the rest of the night. Do ten push-ups. Act out a dramatic death scene.

* **Double-Dare:** You have to do a bigger or more embarrassing dare, such as: Kiss a stuffed animal with sound effects. Try to pick your nose with your big toe and then wipe it on somebody. Sing the national anthem at the top of your lungs.

* **Promise to Repeat:** If you don't want to tell the truth or perform a potentially humiliating dare, you can choose 'Promise to Repeat', which requires you to promise to repeat something embarrassing in public later, like agreeing to include the word 'stultifying' in every sentence you say to your mother the next day.

Light as a Feather, Stiff as a Board

HOW TO PLAY

One person lies on the ground while four to six others gather around her. The players should place the index fingers of both hands underneath the person lying down and then, with eyes closed, everyone begins to chant, 'Light as a feather, stiff as a board'. After twenty chants or so (or whatever number of chants you agree upon ahead of time), the players start raising their arms, lifting the person and seemingly levitating her above the ground.

One variation is to play this game as a call-and-response story. The player next to the person's head begins the story with, 'It was a dark and stormy night.' Each player (except the one lying on the ground) repeats the phrase one at a time, and then the player at the head continues, 'It was cold and the road was icy.' Everyone repeats, then the head player says, 'The car she was in spun out of control.' Everyone repeats, then: 'And when they found her.' Everyone repeats, then: 'She was light as a feather.' Everyone repeats, then: 'And stiff as a board.' These last two sentences are repeated by the group several times and then the entire group begins chanting, 'Light as a feather, stiff as a board' and lifting up the person who is lying down.

IS YOUR FRIEND REALLY LEVITATING?

The Light as a Feather, Stiff as a Board game has its roots in a long tradition of unexplainable, seemingly miraculous feats of weightlessness. Levitation, from the Latin word *levis*, or 'light', means to float into the air, and numerous religions, from Christianity to Islam, have stories of levitation by shamans, mediums, saints, and those demonically possessed.

Saints who levitated were said to possess a luminous glow. Among the reported levitators was Saint Teresa of Avila, who levitated while in states of rapture in the 1680s and is usually painted with a bird, signifying her ability to fly; St Edmund around 1242; St Joseph of Cupertino who astonished the Church with his flights in the 1600s; Catherine of Siena in the late fourteenth century; and St Adolphus Liguori in 1777. Reports of levitation in more recent times include Father Suarez in 1911 in southern Argentina, and, also at the beginning of the twentieth century, the Passionist nun Gemma Galgani. The Christian saints, priests and nuns generally attributed their levitation to states of rapture or ecstasy that were beyond their control, while in Hinduism, Buddhism and other Eastern traditions, levitation was presented as a skill that could be accomplished through spiritual and physical training. Levitation, like all things otherworldly, turned demonic in the Middle Ages, where rather than being a signal of a person's divinity and proximity to God, it was seen as a manifestation of evil generated by demons, ghosts or witchcraft. The nineteenth-century Spiritualism movement, with its interest in séances, ghosts, poltergeists and other spooky things, helped give levitation a boost once again. But in modern times it's mostly understood to be a magic trick, a phenomenon based in real-world explanations and techniques. Still, as anyone who has seen David Blaine – or played Light as a Feather, Stiff as a Board at sleepover parties – can attest, it's entertaining, even when you're pretty sure it's not real.

MAKING A CLOTH-COVERED BOOK

◆

You will need

* Two pieces of 22 × 15.5 centimetre cardboard
* A needle or embroidery needle and thread
* Fabric (about 30 × 35 centimetres) – an old dress, T-shirt or pillowcase works well
* Eight pieces of A4 (21 × 29.5 centimetre) plain white paper (for a longer book, you can use more paper)
* 1 piece of fancy or coloured A4 (29.5 × 21 centimetre) paper
* Wide packing tape and regular tape
* A ruler
* Fabric glue
* 30-centimetre ribbon
* Scissors

Fold the plain paper and the fancy paper in half. If the fancy paper looks different on the front than it does on the back, fold it so that the 'front' side is on the inside. Put the folded plain paper inside the folded fancy paper, like a book. Then use your needle and thread to sew the papers together in two places, about 3 centimetres from the top and 3 centimetres from the bottom.

Cut your fabric to about 30 centimetres by 35 centimetres and lay it out, wrong side facing up. Place the two pieces of cardboard in the middle of the fabric, leaving about a centimetre between each piece. Tape the cardboard pieces together and maintain the centimetre separation. Coat the back of the cardboard lightly with fabric glue and then glue the cardboard to the cloth. Fold and glue each of the corners first and then fold and glue the fabric on each side. You can use tape to secure the fabric if necessary; just make sure the tape doesn't stick up close to the outer edge. Now you've made the fabric book cover.

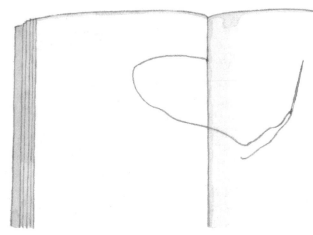

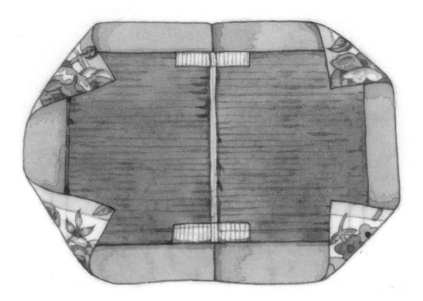

Cut your 30-centimetre ribbon in half. Use your ruler to find the centre of the left side of your fabric cover and glue the end of one ribbon there (starting about 5 centimetres from the end of the ribbon). Try not to over-glue, but also try to make sure you glue right to the very edge so that the ribbon is firmly attached. Secure with tape. Do the same thing on the right side of the cover with the other ribbon.

Open your pages and place them in the middle of the cardboard and fabric so that the fold of the paper is right in the centre of the tape between the cardboard pieces. Using the fabric glue, glue the outer paper (the fancy paper) to the inside of the cover and let it dry. Once dry, tie the ribbon to close your book. It's not as secure as a lock and key, but it's a pretty way to keep safe your handmade journal, should you choose to use it as a secret diary.

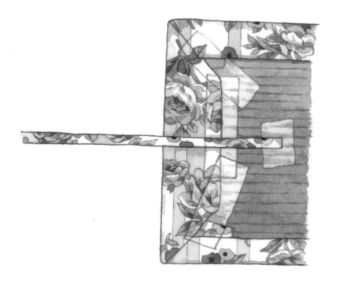

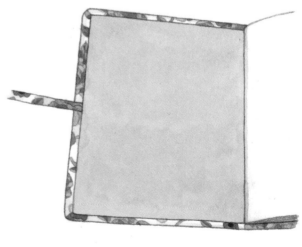

PIRATES

◆

THERE HAVE BEEN women pirates throughout the ages, from Queen Artemisia to female Vikings to modern-day women pirates in the Philippines. Many of the stories about female pirates are just that: stories made up showcasing women pirates who are merely fictional. But there are several women pirates whose stories are verifiable, and who really did live and (in some cases) die a pirate's life on the high seas.

Charlotte Badger

Charlotte Badger was a convicted felon when she was sent to Australia from England. She was found guilty of the crime of breaking and entering when she was eighteen years old and sentenced to seven years' deportation. She sailed to Port Jackson, Sydney, aboard the convict ship *The Earl of Cornwallis* in 1801 and served five years of her sentence at a factory, during which time she also gave birth to a daughter.

With just two years of her sentence left, she was assigned to work as a servant to a settler in Hobart Town, Tasmania, along with fellow prisoner Catherine Hagerty. In April 1806, Charlotte, her daughter, Catherine, and several male convicts travelled to Hobart Town on a ship called *Venus*. When the *Venus* docked at Port Dalrymple in June, the convicts mutinied and Charlotte and her friend Catherine joined in with the male convicts to seize control of the ship. The pirate crew headed for New Zealand (even though nobody aboard really knew how to navigate the ship) and Charlotte, her child, Catherine, and two of the male convicts were dropped off at Rangihoua Bay in the Bay of Islands.

Charlotte and her compatriots built huts and lived on the shore of the island, but by 1807, Catherine Hagerty was dead and the two men had fled. The *Venus* had long since been overtaken by South Sea islanders, who captured the crew and then burned the ship. Charlotte and her child stayed on at Rangihoua Bay, living alongside the Maori islanders.

Twice she was offered passage back to Port Jackson and twice she refused, saying that she preferred to die among the Maori.

What happened to Charlotte after 1807 isn't entirely clear. Some stories have her living with a Maori chieftain and bearing another child; in other stories the Maori turned on her, prompting her and her daughter to flee to Tonga; still other stories eventually place her in America, having stowed away on another ship. Whatever happened to her, she was quite possibly the first European woman to have lived in New Zealand and one of New Zealand's first women pirates.

Anne Bonny and Mary Read

Anne Bonny, born in Ireland around 1700, is by all accounts one of the best-known female pirates. She was disowned by her father when, as a young woman, she married a sailor named James Bonny; the newlyweds then left Ireland for the Bahamas. There, James worked as an informant, turning in pirates to the authorities for a tidy sum. While James confronted pirates,

Anne Bonny

Anne befriended them: she became especially close to Jack Rackam, also known as 'Calico Jack'. Jack was a pirate who had sworn off pirating so as to receive amnesty from the Bahamian governor, who had promised not to prosecute any pirate who gave up his pirating ways. In 1719, however, Anne and Jack ran off together and Jack promptly returned to pirating – this time with Anne by his side. She donned men's clothing in order to join the crew on his ship, the *Revenge*, and was so good at the work that she was accepted as a crewmate even by those men who discovered she was actually a woman.

When the *Revenge* took another ship during a raid and absorbed its crew, Anne discovered she was no longer the only woman on board: a woman by the name of Mary Read had also disguised herself as a man to be accepted as a pirate. Mary, born in London in the late 1600s, had spent nearly her whole life disguised as a man. Mary's mother had raised her as a boy almost from birth to keep the family out of poverty. (Mary's father died before she was born and her brother, who would have been the only legal heir, also died. Back then, only men could inherit wealth, so baby Mary became baby Mark.) As a young girl living as a boy, Mary worked as a messenger and eventually enlisted in the infantry, fighting in Flanders and serving with distinction. She fell in love with another soldier (to whom she revealed her true gender) and they soon married, leaving the army to run a tavern called The Three Horseshoes. Sadly, her husband died in 1717 and Mary once again had to disguise herself as a man to earn a living. She put on her dead husband's clothes, enlisted in the army and went to Holland. She found no adventure there, so she boarded a ship for the West Indies. That was when her ship was captured by the *Revenge* and her life intersected with those of Calico Jack and his mistress, Anne Bonny.

Mary Read

the Crown. Calico Jack, along with nearly the entire crew, was drunk at the time and the men quickly retreated to hide below deck and wait out the attack. Only Anne and Mary stayed above, fighting for the ship. It is said that Anne shouted to the crew, 'If there's a man among ye, ye'll come out and fight like the men ye are thought to be!' Enraged by the crew's cowardice, Anne and Mary shot at them, killing one man and wounding several others, including Calico Jack.

Anne and Mary became close friends and once Anne knew the truth about Mary, she swore that she would never reveal Mary's true identity. But Calico Jack, jealous of Anne's attention, grew suspicious of their friendship and demanded an explanation. Soon the secret was out, but, luckily for Mary, Jack was relieved and not angered to discover she was a woman. He allowed her to continue on the crew, and just as Anne had been accepted by her crewmates despite being female, Mary was accepted too. Unfortunately for the crew of the *Revenge,* the Bahamian governor was not so accepting of pirates who flouted amnesty agreements by returning to pirating after promising not to, and he issued a proclamation naming Jack Rackam, Anne Bonny and Mary Read as 'Pirates and Enemies to the Crown of Great Britain'.

In 1720, the *Revenge* was attacked by a pirate-hunter eager to capture an enemy of

Despite the women's efforts, the ship was captured.

The crew was taken to Jamaica and tried for piracy in November of 1720. All of them were hanged, save for Anne and Mary, who were granted stays of execution due to the fact that they were both pregnant. Mary was brave in the face of her punishment, telling the court, 'As to hanging, it is no great hardship. For were it not for that, every cowardly fellow would turn pirate and so unfit the sea, that men of courage must starve.' But as it turned out, Mary never had to face the gallows: she died in prison of a fever. As for Anne, after the piracy trial, the historical record is silent. Rumours say alternately that she was hanged a year later; that she was given a reprieve; that she reconciled with the father who disowned her, or with her first husband, whom she had left; that she gave up the pirate's life and became instead a nun. We may never know for sure what happened to her.

Ching Shih

Ching Shih – also known as Shi Xainggu, Cheng I Sao, Ching Yih Saou, or Zheng Yi Sao – ruled the South China Sea in the early nineteenth century, overseeing about 1,800 ships and 80,000 male and female pirates.

She became the commander of the infamous Red Flag Fleet of pirates after her husband Cheng Yi, the former commander from a long line of pirates, died in 1807; she went on to marry Chang Pao, formerly her husband's right-hand man. To say that Ching Shih ran a tight ship was an understatement: pirates who committed even innocuous offences were beheaded. Her attitude in battle was even more intense, with hundreds of ships and thousands of pirates used to engage even a small target.

Ching Shih was also a ruthless businesswoman. She handled all business matters herself, and pirates not only needed her approval to embark on a raid, they were also required to surrender the entire haul to her. She diversified her business plan by expanding beyond the raiding of commercial ships, working with shadowy businessmen in the Guangdong salt trade to extort the local salt merchants. Every ship passing through her waters had to buy protection from her and Ching Shih's fleet of mercenaries torched any vessel that refused to pay up.

The Red Flag Fleet under Ching Shih's rule could not be defeated – not by Chinese officials, not by the Portuguese navy, not even by the British. But in 1810, amnesty was offered to all pirates and Ching Shih took advantage of it, negotiating pardons for nearly all her troops. She retired with all her ill-gotten gains and ran a gambling house until her death in 1844.

Books about Pirates

Granuaile: Ireland's Pirate Queen, 1530–1603 by Anne Chambers
This book was made into a Broadway musical called *The Pirate Queen*. It tells the story of Grace O'Malley, also called Granuaile, a remarkable and notorious Irish pirate.

The Pirate Hunter: The True Story of Captain Kidd by Richard Zacks
A vivid account of the often brutal nature of pirate life and politics in the seventeenth century.

Under the Black Flag: The Romance and the Reality of Life Among the Pirates
by David Cordingly
A look at the realities of the oft-romanticized pirate life through stories of real and fictitious pirates between 1650 and 1725

The Pirates' Own Book: Authentic Narratives of the Most Celebrated Sea Robbers
by Charles Ellms
Originally published in 1887, this book features pirates reporting in their own words.

Booty: Girl Pirates on the High Seas by Sara Lorimer
Stories of twelve women pirates from the ninth century to the 1930s.

Rachel Wall

Rachel Schmidt was born in Carlisle, Pennsylvania, in 1760. When she was sixteen, she met George Wall, a former privateer who served in the Revolutionary War; against the wishes of her mother, she married him. The two moved to Boston, where George worked as a fisherman and Rachel worked as a maid in Beacon Hill. George, whom Rachel's mother had considered more than slightly shady to begin with, fell in with a rough crowd and gambled away what money they had. Unable to pay the rent, and lured by the fun of his fast-living fisherman friends, he hit upon pirating as the answer to their financial woes and convinced Rachel to join in.

George and Rachel stole a ship at Essex and began working as pirates off the Isle of Shoals. They would trick passing ships by having the blue-eyed, brown-haired Rachel pose as a damsel in distress, standing at the ship's mast and screaming for help as ships floated by. Once the rescuing crew came aboard to help, George and his men would kill them, steal their booty and sink their ship. Rachel and George were successful as pirates, capturing a dozen boats, murdering two dozen sailors and stealing thousands of dollars in cash and valuables.

Their evil plan was cut short in 1782, when George, along with the rest of his crew, was drowned in a storm. Rachel, who really did need rescuing in that situation, was saved, brought ashore and taken back to Boston, but it was hard to leave her pirating ways. She spent her days working as a maid, but by night she broke into the cabins of ships docked in Boston Harbor, stealing any goods she could get her hands on.

Her luck ran out in 1789, when she was accused of robbery. At her trial, she admitted to being a pirate but refused to confess to being a murderer or a thief. She was convicted and sentenced to death by hanging. She died on 8 October 1789, the first and possibly the only woman pirate in all of New England, and the last woman to be hanged in Massachusetts.

SECRET GARDEN

❖

IN *THE SECRET GARDEN* by Frances Hodgson Burnett, the orphaned Mary is sent to live with her recently widowed uncle at Misselthwaite Manor. Mary takes to roaming the grounds, and one day she finds a mysterious, ivy-covered wall. A robin leads her to the key that reveals, behind the wall, an abandoned garden. The late mistress of the manor loved the garden dearly, and her husband, unable to enter its walls since her death, has neglected it and let it fall into disrepair. But Mary can see that the flowers still show signs of life and she determines to revive it with the help of the local boy, Dickon. One night Mary hears someone crying somewhere in the house and finds Colin, a young boy hidden away out of shame by his father, Mary's uncle. She shares her secret about the garden with him and together they tend it back to life.

The garden in the book is based on a real garden. Frances Hodgson Burnett was born in Manchester but lived most of her life in America. She did come back to England in the late 1890s and lived at Great Maytham Hall in Kent. It was here that she discovered a real secret garden, much in the same way as her heroine, Mary. Burnett's garden dated from the eighteenth century and had been neglected and become overgrown. She nurtured it back to life and restored its traditional walled garden, filled with roses and hollyhocks. She spent several years happily writing there. When Burnett returned to America, the next owners of the house retained the walled gardens, looking after them until the outbreak of the Second World War. Then, as part of the government's campaign for people to 'Dig for Victory', Burnett's garden was dug up to make space for vegetables. After the war the house

was left empty and the garden deteriorated once again. Now the house has been converted into apartments and the gardens are restored once more to their former glory.

GOING TO AFRICA

◆

TRAVELLING TO DISTANT COUNTRIES and experiencing different cultures is extremely daring. It can sometimes be disorienting at first, as you adjust to the language barriers and foreign foods and customs, but the rewards often more than make up for the challenges. A well-planned trip to Africa offers incredible history, mind-blowing sights, and once-in-a-lifetime adventures. Before you go, make sure to read up on the facts, like the ones overleaf.

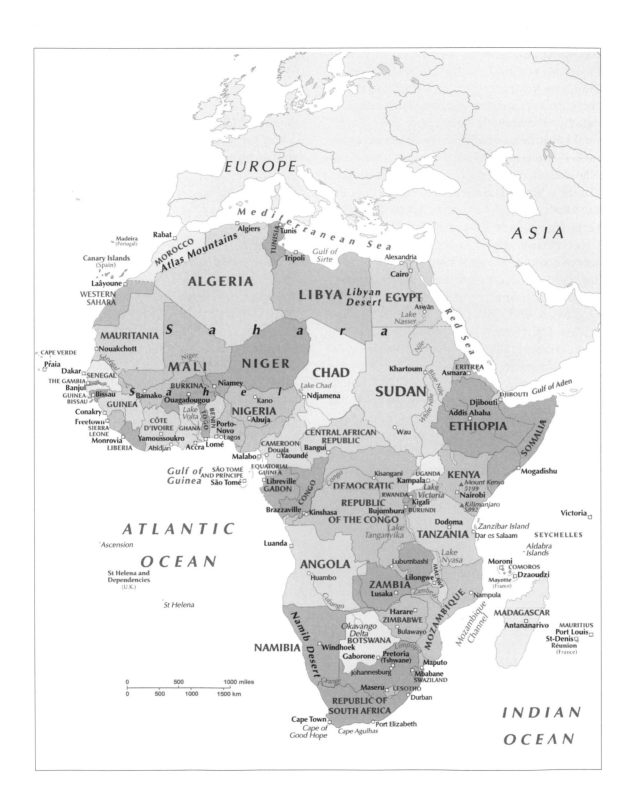

ALGERIA
Declared independence in 1962 from France
Languages: Arabic, French, Berber dialects
Adventures: The 400,000 palm trees of the Sahara oasis town of Timimoun, and El-Oued, the Town of a Thousand Domes

ANGOLA
Declared independence in 1975 from Portugal
Languages: Portuguese, Bantu, and other African languages
Adventures: The Calendula waterfalls

BENIN
Declared independence in 1960 from France
Languages: French, Fon, Yoruba, and six other tribal languages
Adventures: Elephants and baboons at the Pendjari wildlife park

BOTSWANA
Declared independence in 1966 from the United Kingdom
Languages: English, Setswana, Kalanga, Sekgalagad
Adventures: Chobe game park

BURKINA FASO
Declared independence in 1960 from France
Languages: French, African languages
Adventures: Wild elephants at Nazinga Reserve

BURUNDI
Declared independence in 1962 from Belgium
Languages: French, Kirundi, Swahili
Adventures: Drumming in Gitega, Bujumbara, a port on Lake Tanganyika

CAMEROON
Declared independence in 1960 from French administration of a United Nations trusteeship
Languages: English, French, twenty-four African languages
Adventures: The Royal Palace at Foumban

CAPE VERDE
Declared independence in 1975 from Portugal
Languages: Portuguese, Crioulo
Adventures: The fishing village of Tarrafal

CENTRAL AFRICAN REPUBLIC
Declared independence in 1960 from France
Languages: French, Sangho, African languages
Adventures: The rainforest surrounding M'Baïki

CHAD
Declared independence in 1960 from France
Languages: French, Arabic, Sara, over 120 languages and dialects
Adventures: Prehistoric cave paintings in the Ennedi desert

COMOROS
Declared independence in 1975 from France
Languages: French, Arabic, Shikomoro
Adventures: The active volcano at Mount Karthala

REPUBLIC OF CONGO
Declared independence in 1960 from France
Languages: French, Lingala, Monokuluba and Kikongo
Adventures: Hundreds of gorillas, elephants and monkeys at Odzala National Park

DEMOCRATIC REPUBLIC OF THE CONGO

Declared independence in 1960 from Belgium

Languages: French, Lingala, Kinguana, Kikongo, Tshiluba

Adventures: Pygmy chimp orphanage at the Chutes de Lukia

CÔTE D'IVOIRE (IVORY COAST)

Declared independence in 1960 from France

Languages: French, sixty native dialects, of which Dioula is most widely spoken

Adventures: Stained-glass windows at the Cathédrale Notre-Dame-de-la-Paix

DJIBOUTI

Declared independence in 1977 from France

Languages: French, Arabic, Somali, Afar

Adventures: Tadjoura, Djibouti's oldest town

EGYPT

Declared independence in 1922 from the United Kingdom

Languages: Arabic, English and French

Adventures: Ancient Egyptian pyramids

EQUATORIAL GUINEA

Declared independence in 1958 from Spain

Languages: Spanish, French, pidgin English, Fang, Bubi, Ibo

Adventures: Beaches with black volcano sand

ERITREA

Declared independence in 1993 from Ethiopia

Languages: Afar, Asmara, Tigre, Kunama, Tigrinya, other Cushitic languages

Adventures: The ruins of the old town of Koloe, in Qohaito

ETHIOPIA

Ethiopia has been independent for at least 2,000 years.

Languages: Amharic, Tigrinya, Oromigna, Guaragigna, Somali, Arabic, other local languages, English

Adventures: The caves of Sof Omar

GABON

Declared independence in 1960 from France

Languages: French, Fang, Myene, Nzebi, Bapounou/Eschira, Bandjabi

Adventures: The river rapids in the Okanda region

THE GAMBIA

Declared independence in 1965 from the United Kingdom

Languages: English, Mandinka, Wolof, Fula

Adventures: Cruise through the Abuko Nature Reserve and see crocodiles, monkeys, birds and antelopes

GHANA

Declared independence in 1957 from the United Kingdom

Languages: English, African languages such as Akan, Moshi-Dagomba, Ewe, Ga

Adventures: 600 butterfly species at Kakum National Park and a walkway 30 metres above the forest floor

GUINEA

Declared independence in 1958 from France

Languages: French, and each ethnic group has its own language

Adventures: Malinke music on the streets of Conakry, and Les Ballets Africains

GUINEA-BISSAU
Declared independence in 1973 from
Portugal
Languages: Portuguese, Crioulo, African
languages
Adventures: Winding streets of the old
Portuguese quarter of Bissau

KENYA
Declared independence in 1963 from the
United Kingdom
Languages: Kiswahili, English, African
languages
Adventures: The Gede Ruins, a Swahili
village abandoned in the twelfth century, and
baobob trees

LESOTHO
Declared independence in 1966 from the
United Kingdom
Languages: Sesotho, English, Zulu, Xhosa
Adventures: Ancient rock shelter paintings in
Malealea

LIBERIA
Settled in 1847 by freed African slaves from
the United States of America
Languages: English and about twenty ethnic-
group languages
Adventures: Firestone Plantation, the world's
largest rubber plantation; and the forest
elephants and pygmy hippos at Sapo

LIBYA
Declared independence in 1951 from Italy
Languages: Arabic, Italian, English
Adventures: The ancient Greek architecture
of Cyrene

MADAGASCAR
Declared independence in 1960 from France
Languages: Malagasy and French
Adventures: Parc National de Ranomafana
and its twelve species of lemur

MALAWI
Declared independence in 1964 from the
United Kingdom
Languages: Chichewa, Chinyanja, Chiyao,
Chitonga
Adventures: Mount Mulanje for some of the
best hiking in Africa

MALI
Declared independence in 1960 from France
Languages: French, Bambara, numerous
African languages
Adventures: The Mosques of Timbuktu

MAURITANIA
Declared independence in 1960 from France
Languages: Arabic, Pulaar, Soninke, French,
Hassaniya, Wolof
Adventures: Chinguette is the seventh holiest
city of Islam

MAURITIUS
Declared independence in 1968 from the
United Kingdom
Languages: Creole, Bhojpuri, French
Adventures: Tamarin Waterfalls

MOROCCO
Declared independence in 1956 from France
Languages: Arabic, Berber dialects, French
Adventures: Fès el-Bari, the largest living
medieval city in the world

MOZAMBIQUE
Declared independence in 1975 from Portugal
Languages: Emakhuwa, Xichangana, Portuguese, Elomwe, Cisena, Echuwabo, other Mozambican languages
Adventures: Wimbi beach and its spectacular coral reefs

NAMIBIA
Declared independence in 1989 from South Africa
Languages: English, Afrikaans, German, Oshivambo, Herero and Nama
Adventures: Bubbling hot springs at Fish River Canyon

NIGER
Declared independence in 1960 from France
Languages: French, Hausa, Djerma
Adventures: Climb the minaret of the Great Mosque for a view of Agadez

NIGERIA
Declared independence in 1960 from the United Kingdom
Languages: English, Hausa, Yoruba, Igbo (Ibo), Fulani
Adventures: Visit the Shrine of Oshuno, the River Goddess, in the sacred forest

RWANDA
Declared independence in 1962 from Belgium
Languages: Kinyarwanda, French, English, Kiswahili
Adventures: Rare mountain gorillas at the Parc National des Volcans

SÃO TOMÉ AND PRÍNCIPE
Declared independence in 1975 from Portugal
Languages: Portuguese
Adventures: Snorkel at Logoa Azul and see the giant baobob trees

SENEGAL
Declared independence in 1960 from France
Languages: French, Wolof, Pulaar, Jola, Mandinka
Adventures: Three million birds migrate from Europe to the Parc National des Oiseaux du Djoudj

SEYCHELLES
Declared independence in 1976 from the United Kingdom
Languages: Creole, English
Adventures: At Valée de Mai, the Seychelles black parrot and the rare *coco de mer* palm trees

SIERRA LEONE
Declared independence in 1961 from the United Kingdom
Languages: English, Mende, Temne, Krio
Adventures: Dive to underwater shipwreck sites and coral in the Banana Islands

SOMALIA
Declared independence in 1960 from the United Kingdom
Languages: Somali, Arabic, Italian, English
Adventures: Las Geel has Neolithic rock art paintings in caves and shelters

REPUBLIC OF SOUTH AFRICA

Declared independence in 1910 from the United Kingdom, and again in 1994 from minority white rule

Languages: Afrikaans, English, IsiNdebele, IsiXhosa, IsiZulu, Northern Sotho, Sesotho, Setswana, SiSwati, Tshivenda, Xitsonga

Adventures: Cable cars to the top of Table Mountain; Robben Island, where Nelson Mandela was once imprisoned, now a national monument

SUDAN

Declared independence in 1956 from Egypt and the United Kingdom

Languages: Arabic, Nubian, Ta Bedawie, Nilotic dialects, Nilo-Hamitic, English

Adventures: Ancient hieroglyphics and pyramids in Meroe

SWAZILAND

Declared independence in 1968 from the United Kingdom

Languages: English, SiSwati

Adventures: Safari through the Mlilwane Wildlife Sanctuary to see zebras and giraffes

TANZANIA

Declared independence in 1964, as the merger of Tanganyika and Zanzibar

Languages: Kiswahili or Swahili, English, Arabic

Adventures: Scale mysterious Mount Kilimanjaro, the tallest peak in Africa

TOGO

Declared independence in 1960 from France

Languages: French, Ewe and Mina (South), Kabye and Dagomba (North)

Adventures: The Grand Marché in Lome with its famous female merchants; the fortified villages in the Tamberma Valley, built in the 1600s by people fleeing the slave traders

TUNISIA

Declared independence in 1956 from France

Languages: Arabic, French

Adventures: The ruins of ancient Carthage

UGANDA

Declared independence in 1962 from the United Kingdom

Languages: English, Ganda, Luganda, Swahili, Arabic

Adventures: The bustling city of Kampala, and the mountain gorillas of the Impenetrable Forest

ZAMBIA

Declared independence in 1964 from the United Kingdom

Languages: English, Bemba, Kaonda, Lozi, Lunda, Luvale, Nyanja, Tonga, seventy other African languages

Adventures: Victoria Falls

ZIMBABWE

Declared independence in 1980 from the United Kingdom

Languages: English, Shona, Sindebele, numerous dialects

Adventures: The ruins of Great Zimbabwe, near Masvingo

CAMPING OUTDOORS

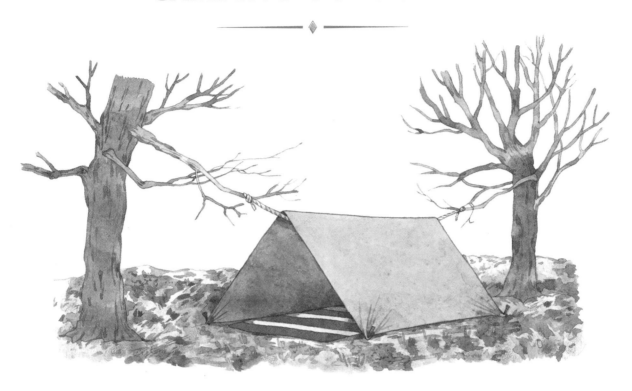

A QUICK TENT can be made with just a rope, some stakes and two tarpaulins – big plastic, waterproof sheets essential to camping. First, string a rope between two branches on two different trees. Then stretch one tarpaulin out on the ground and hang the second over the rope. Lastly, stake the four corners of the hanging tarpaulin to the ground, using a hammer or a rock.

Shop-bought tents are much larger than ever before, and come with flexible poles that fold into short lengths and stow away in a bag, making tent-pitching relatively simple. They also better protect us from the number one evil scourge of camping: insects. (The number two evil scourge, should you ask, is nettles.) This leads to the prime rule of tents: Keep the zip shut, because it's nearly impossible to shoo a mosquito out of your tent once it's in.

Before you pitch your tent, you may want to lay down an additional tarp to keep things extra clean and dry. (If you do, tuck the edges under so the tarp is slightly smaller than your tent.) Then set out the tent and follow directions for inserting the poles. The fly, which protects from rain and dew, goes over the top of the tent and usually clips on, is staked to the ground, or both. Finally, bang the tent pegs into the ground, lest large gusts of wind send your tent soaring towards Kansas.

You've just made your home outdoors. Here are the basic furnishings:

* The sleeping bag. To make things a bit more comfortable, add a sleeping pad underneath and bring along a pillow or just a pillow case you can stuff with clothes. Sleeping pads have become softer, longer and more elaborate, and can even involve air pumps, which your parents will undoubtedly appreciate if you invite them to sleep out with you.
* Torch and insect spray. Enough said.
* A coolbox. Filled with lots of drinking water and camping food staples like fresh apples and dried fruit. Marshmallows are a necessity, too, if a campfire's involved.

The anti-litter mantra for sleeping and camping outdoors is: take it in, take it out. Since there are no bins in the wilderness, bring a bag for your wrappers and other rubbish.

Once you've learned to pitch a tent and roll out the sleeping bag in your garden, you can graduate to the full-on camping experience where the fridge and indoor toilet are not close at hand.

Camping is gear-intensive and takes careful planning, especially if you're hiking a few miles out. You must carry several days' food and water in your backpack, not to mention a camping stove and mess kit, soap and a toothbrush and so much more. When you're ready for a first experience at a wilderness campsite, find a friend whose family are pros, and learn from them.

Whether you are in your garden or the wildest part of the Pennines, remember the whole point of sleeping outdoors is to breathe in the night air, listen to nature's songs and drift off to sleep under the stars.

Building a Campfire

Sitting around a campfire is probably one of the oldest human activities. Nowadays, unless you're on a solo wilderness hike, a campfire is less a tool of survival than a social event – a chance to sing songs and tell stories and be out in the dark in nature with friends.

A fire needs three things: fuel, heat and air. The most common fuel is wood – main fuel such as logs cut from trees, and smaller fuel like tinder (twigs, strips of paper, or anything small that burns well) and kindling (branches and twigs about the size of a pencil and no thicker than a finger). Heat, which comes in the form of a flame or spark generated from matches, lighters, friction or even focused sunlight, should be generated from the smaller fuel, which will then ignite the larger fuel. And of course, fire needs oxygen, so make sure that your fuel is packed loosely enough to allow for air circulation. When there's not enough oxygen present, the fire goes out, which is why dousing flames with water or smothering a small fire with sand extinguishes the flames.

What you'll need to build your own campfire

* A fire ring, a fire pit, a fire pan, or other temporary fire site
* Water or sand to extinguish the fire
* Tinder
* Kindling
* Main fuel (thick, dry wood and logs – the thicker the wood, the longer the fire will burn)
* Matches or a lighter

BUILDING THE FIRE

The first item of business when building a fire is deciding where to make it. Find a spot away from tents, trees with low-hanging branches, or other flammable elements. Once you've determined your location, you can begin to assemble your fire. Ideally, you can use an existing fire pit or fire ring. If there isn't one handy, you can create a fire site yourself. One way is to clear away a space on the ground, dig a pit, line it with small rocks and then cover that area about half an inch deep with sand or aluminium foil. Otherwise you can use a fire pan, either a store-bought metal pan for the purpose of making fires, or any round metal surface, such as a pizza pan or a metal dustbin lid.

Once you have your site established, place your tinder (the small pieces you collected) in a small pile in the middle of the fire site. Around that, place the kindling, taking care not to pack it too tightly, as your fire will need air in order to burn. Arrange the kindling in a kind of 'teepee' format, as though you are creating a small tent around your tinder. Leave an opening so that you can light the tinder and keep some of your kindling in reserve, so you can add more to the fire as it takes hold.

Using a match, lighter, or your preferred method of ignition, light the tinder and gently fan or blow on it until it becomes a strong flame and ignites the kindling around it. Once the kindling is burning, you can add your main fuel – those large, thick logs that will burn long and bright. Add more kindling to the fire to keep it burning, but take care to keep the fire manageable. Also make sure to place your wood carefully and not just throw it onto the fire.

Once the fire is dwindling and it's time to put it out, use water to douse the flames completely. You can also use sand, if that is available, to smother the fire. Water is the most thorough method of putting out a fire and, when it comes to extinguishing fires, you definitely want to be thorough. Check to make sure there's nothing still smouldering, even when it seems like the fire is out. Everything – the fire site, the burned fuel, the area around the fire – should be cool to the touch before you leave. A fire that is carelessly put out, or not put out thoroughly enough, can flare up again.

WHAT TO DO AROUND THE FIRE

If you have some long sticks and a bag full of marshmallows or some bread or crumpets, you can cook over the open fire. Skewer a marshmallow with a stick and hold it over the flames to toast it. Or toast your bread or crumpets to perfection. A campfire is also the perfect setting for singing songs and telling ghost stories. Once you've had your fill of marshmallows, crack open your copy of this book (which you of course packed with you on your camping trip) and check out the following pages for campfire song lyrics. Also, see our tips on telling spooky ghost stories later in this book.

Precautions and tips

* Check to see if campfires are permitted.
* Clear the fire site before you start and after you're done. You don't want to leave a mess behind – or anything that could potentially start another fire.
* Never use flammable liquid or aerosols on a fire.
* Build your campfire far enough from your tent and trees and low-hanging branches so that stray sparks won't start a fire outside the pit.
* Do not build your fire on peat or grass.
* Don't pick up burning wood.
* Wind can spread fire quickly, so make sure to build your fire in a place shielded from gusts.

Campfire Songs

Singing songs together is a fun way to pass the time around a campfire, on the school bus or in the car. Here are some of our favourites.

Darling Clementine

In a cavern, in a canyon,
Excavating for a mine,
Dwelt a miner, forty-niner,
And his daughter Clementine.

Refrain:
Oh my darling, oh my darling,
Oh my darling Clementine
You are lost and gone forever,
Dreadful sorry, Clementine.

Light she was, and like a fairy,
And her shoes were number nine,
Herring boxes without topses,
Sandals were for Clementine.

Refrain

Walking lightly as a fairy,
Though her shoes were number nine,
Sometimes tripping, lightly skipping,
Lovely girl, my Clementine.

Refrain

Drove she ducklings to the water
Ev'ry morning just at nine,
Hit her foot against a splinter,
Fell into the foaming brine.

Refrain

Ruby lips above the water,
Blowing bubbles soft and fine,
But alas, I was no swimmer,
Neither was my Clementine.

Refrain

In a churchyard near the canyon,
Where the myrtle doth enstring,
There grow rosies and some posies,
Fertilized by Clementine.

Refrain

Then, the miner, forty-niner,
Soon began to fret and pine,
Thought he oughter join his daughter,
So he's now with Clementine.

Refrain

I'm so lonely, lost without her,
Wish I'd had a fishing line,
Which I might have cast about her,
Might have saved my Clementine.

Refrain

In my dreams she still doth haunt me,
Robed in garments soaked with brine,
Then she rises from the waters,
And I kiss my Clementine.

Refrain

Sweet Chariot

Swing low, sweet chariot
Comin' for to carry me home
Swing low, sweet chariot
Comin' for to carry me home
I looked over Jordan and what did I see
Comin' for to carry me home
A band of angels comin' after me
Comin' for to carry me home
Swing low, sweet chariot
Comin' for to carry me home
Swing low, sweet chariot
Comin' for to carry me home
If you get to heaven before I do
Comin' for to carry me home
Tell all my friends I'm comin' there too
Comin' for to carry me home
Swing low, sweet chariot
Comin' for to carry me home
Swing low, sweet chariot
Comin' for to carry me home
I'm sometimes up and sometimes down
Comin' for to carry me home
But still I know I'm heavenly bound
Comin' for to carry me home
Swing low, sweet chariot
Comin' for to carry me home
Swing low, sweet chariot
Comin' for to carry me home
If I get there before you do
Comin' for to carry me home
I'll cut a hole and pull you through
Comin' for to carry me home
Swing low, sweet chariot
Comin' for to carry me home
Swing low, sweet chariot
Comin' for to carry me home

Mulberry Bush

Here we go round the mulberry bush,
The mulberry bush, the mulberry bush,
Here we go round the mulberry bush,
On a cold and frosty morning.
This is the way we wash our hands,
Wash our hands, wash our hands,
This is the way we wash our hands,
On a cold and frosty morning.
This is the way we wash our clothes,
Wash our clothes, wash our clothes,
This is the way we wash our clothes,
On a cold and frosty morning.
This is the way we go to school,
Go to school, go to school,
This is the way we go to school,
On a cold and frosty morning.
This is the way we come out of school,
Come out of school, come out of school,
This is the way we come out of school,
On a cold and frosty morning.

One Man Went to Mow

One man went to mow,
Went to mow a meadow,
One man and his dog,
Went to mow a meadow
Two men went to mow,
Went to mow a meadow,
Two men, one man and his dog,
Went to mow a meadow
Three men went to mow,
Went to mow a meadow,
Three men, two men, one man and his
    dog,
Went to mow a meadow
Four men went to mow,
Went to mow a meadow,
Four men, three men, two men, one man and
    his dog,
Went to mow a meadow
Went to mow a meadow

How Much is That Doggy in the Window?

How much is that doggy in the window?
Woof, woof
The one with the waggily tail
Woof, woof
How much is that doggy in the window?
Woof, woof
I do hope that doggy's for sale
Woof, woof
How much is that doggy by the telly?
Woof, woof
The one with the waggily tail
Woof, woof
How much is that doggy by the telly?
Woof, woof
I do hope that doggy's for sale
Woof, woof
How much is that doggy in the playhouse?
Woof, woof
The one with the waggily tail?
Woof, woof
How much is that doggy in the playhouse?
Woof, woof
I do hope that doggy's for sale
Woof, woof
How much is that doggy chasing Jakey?
Woof, woof
The one with the waggily tail
Woof, woof
How much is that doggy chasing Jakey?
Woof, woof
I do hope that doggy's for sale
Woof, woof

Row, Row, Row Your Boat

Row, row, row your boat
Gently down the stream
Merrily, merrily, merrily, merrily
Life is but a dream
Dance, dance, dance your dolly
Gently down the stream
Merrily, merrily, merrily, merrily
Life is but a dream
Gallop, gallopy, gallop your horse
Down beside the stream
Merrily, merrily, merrily, merrily
Life is but a dream
Roll, roll, roll your hoop
Wobbly by the stream
Merrily, merrily, merrily, merrily
Life is but a dream
Bounce, bounce, bounce your ball
Down beside the stream
Merrily, merrily, merrily, merrily
Life is but a dream

She'll Be Coming Round the Mountain

She'll be coming round the mountain
   when she comes
She'll be coming round the mountain when she
   comes
She'll be coming round the mountain

Coming round the mountain
Coming round the mountain when she comes
Singing eye-yai-yippee-yippe-yai
Yippe-yai
Singing eye-yai-yippee-yippe-yai
Yippe-yai
Singing eye-yai-yippee
Eye-yai-yippee
Eye-yai-yippee-yippe-yai
She'll be wearing pink pyjamas when she comes
She'll be wearing pink pyjamas when she comes
She'll be wearing pink pyjamas
Wearing pink pyjamas
Wearing pink pyjamas when she comes
Singing eye-yai-yippee-yippe-yai
Yippe-yai
Singing eye-yai-yippee-yippe-yai
Yippe-yai
Singing eye-yai-yippee
Eye-yai-yippee
Eye-yai-yippee-yippe-yai
She'll be riding six white horses when she comes
She'll be riding six white horses when she comes
She'll be riding six white horses
Riding six white horses
Riding six white horses when she comes
Singing eye-yai-yippee-yippe-yai
Yippe-yai
Singing eye-yai-yippee-yippe-yai
Yippe-yai
Singing eye-yai-yippee
Eye-yai-yippee
Eye-yai-yippee-yippe-yai

EXPLORERS

Amelia Earhart

Amelia Mary Earhart, born in 1897, was a pilot who received the Distinguished Flying Cross – and worldwide fame – for being the first woman to fly solo across the Atlantic Ocean. During World War I, she trained as a nurse's aide through the Red Cross and worked in a hospital in Ontario, Canada, until after the war ended in 1918. Around that time she saw her first flying exhibition, and she was captivated. She stood her ground when one of the pilots flew low to buzz the crowd and later said of the experience, 'I did not understand it at the time, but I believe that little red airplane said something to me as it swished by.' The next year, she visited an airfield and was given a ride; a few hundred feet in the air and she was hooked. She began working odd jobs, including driving a truck and working at a telephone company, to earn money for flying lessons with female aviator Anita 'Neta' Snook. After six months of lessons, she bought her own plane, a used yellow biplane that she nicknamed 'The Canary' and in October 1922 she flew it to an altitude of 14,000 feet, setting a world record for women pilots. In May 1923, Earhart became the sixteenth woman to be issued a pilot's licence by the Fédération Aéronautique Internationale (FAI). She not only broke aviation records, she also formed a women's flying organization (The Ninety-Nines) and wrote bestselling books. She was the first woman to fly across the Atlantic, the first woman to fly across the Atlantic alone and the first person, man or woman, to fly across the Atlantic alone twice. Earhart was also the first woman to fly an autogyro (a kind of flying craft) and the first person to cross the United States in an autogyro; the first person to fly solo across the Pacific between Honolulu and Oakland, California; the first person to fly solo non-stop from Mexico City to Newark, New Jersey; and the first woman to fly non-stop coast to coast across the United States. Her final accomplishment was becoming an enduring mystery: at the age of thirty-nine, in 1937, Amelia Earhart disappeared over the Pacific Ocean during an attempt at making a circum-navigational flight. The official search effort lasted nine days, but Amelia Earhart was never found.

Amelia Earhart

In 1921, Bessie Coleman became the first woman to earn an international pilot's licence and the first black woman to earn an aviator's licence. One of thirteen children, Coleman discovered aeroplanes after graduating from high school, but she couldn't find an aviation school that would teach a black woman to fly. She went to Paris, where she was able to train and earn her licence.

Jacqueline Cochran, who in 1953 became the first woman to break the sound barrier, holds more distance and speed records than any pilot, male or female. She was the first woman to take off from and land on an aircraft carrier; to reach Mach 2; to fly a fixed-wing jet aircraft across the Atlantic; to enter the Bendix Trans-continental Race; and to pilot a bomber across the north Atlantic. She was the first pilot to make a blind landing, the first woman in Ohio's Aviation Hall of Fame and the only woman ever to be president of the Fédération Aéronautique Internationale.

Alexandra David-Néel

Alexandra David-Néel, born Louise Eugénie Alexandrine Marie David (1868–1969), was the first European woman to travel to the forbidden city of Lhasa, Tibet, in 1924, when it was still closed to foreigners. She was a French explorer, spiritualist, Buddhist and writer, penning over thirty books on Eastern religion, philosophy and the experiences she had on her travels. By the time she was eighteen, she had already made solo trips to England, Spain and Switzerland, and when she was twenty-two, she went to India, returning to France only when she ran out of money. She married railway engineer Philippe Néel in 1904 and in 1911 she returned to India to study Buddhism at the royal monastery of Sikkim, where she met the Crown Prince Sidkeon Tulku. In 1912 she met the thirteenth Dalai Lama twice and was able to ask him questions about Buddhism. She deepened her study of spirituality when she spent two years living in a cave in Sikkim, near the Tibetan border. It was there that she met the young Sikkimese monk Aphur Yongden, who became her lifelong travelling companion, and whom she would later adopt. The two trespassed into Tibetan territory in 1916, meeting the Panchen Lama, but were evicted by British authorities. They left for Japan, travelled through China and in 1924 arrived in Lhasa, Tibet, disguised as pilgrims. They lived there for two months. In 1928, Alexandra separated from her husband and settled in Digne, France, where she spent the next ten years writing books about her adventures. She reconciled with her husband and travelled again with her adopted son in 1937, at the age of sixty-nine, going through the Soviet Union to China, India, and eventually Tachienlu, where she continued her study

of Tibetan literature. It was an arduous journey that took nearly ten years to complete. She returned to Digne in 1946 to settle the estate of her husband, who had died in 1941, and again wrote books and gave lectures about what she had seen. Her last camping trip, at an Alpine lake in early winter, 2,240 metres above sea level, was at the age of eighty-two. She lived to be one hundred, dying just eighteen days before her one hundred and first birthday.

Freya Stark

Dame Freya Madeleine Stark (1893–1993) was a British travel writer, explorer and cartographer. She was one of the first Western women to travel the Arabian deserts and was fluent in Arabic and several other languages.

Alexandra David-Néel

Freya Stark

Women Explorer Timeline

1704	Sarah Kemble Knight journeys on horseback, solo, from Boston to New York.
1876	Maria Spelternia is the first woman to cross Niagara Falls on a high wire.
1895	Annie Smith Peck becomes the first woman to climb the Matterhorn.
1901	Annie Taylor is the first person to go over Niagara Falls in a barrel.
1926	Gertrude Ederle is the first woman to swim the English Channel.
1947	Barbara Washburn becomes the first woman to climb Mount McKinley.
1963	Valentine Tereshkova becomes the first woman in space.
1975	Junko Tabei of Japan is the first woman to climb Mount Everest.
1976	Krystyna Choynowski-Liskiewicz of Poland is the first woman to sail around the world solo.
1984	Cosmonaut Svetlana Savitskaya becomes the first woman to walk in space.
1985	Tania Aebi, at nineteen, becomes the youngest person ever to sail alone around the world.
1985	Libby Riddles is the first woman to win the Iditarod Dog-Sled Race in Alaska.
1986	American Ann Bancroft becomes the first woman in the world to ski to the North Pole.
2001	Ann Bancroft and Norwegian Liv Arnesen are the first women to cross Antarctica on skis.
2005	Ellen MacArthur breaks the world record for sailing solo around the world.
2007	Eighteen-year-old Samantha Larson becomes the youngest person to climb the Seven Summits. (She and her father, Dr David Larson, are the first father-daughter team to complete the Seven Summits.)

She travelled to Turkey, the Middle East, Greece and Italy, but her passion was the Middle East. When she was thirty-five, she explored the forbidden territory of the Syrian Druze, travelling through 'The Valley of the Assassins' before being thrown into a military prison. In the 1930s, she went to the outback of southern Arabia, where few Westerners had explored, and discovered the hidden routes of the ancient incense trade. During World War II, she joined the Ministry of Information and helped create propaganda to encourage Arabic support of the Allies. Even in her sixties, she continued her travels, retracing Alexander the Great's journeys into Asia and writing three more books based on those trips. By the time of her death, at the age of 100, she had written two dozen books on her adventures.

Florence Baker

Lady Florence Baker (1841–1916) was born Barbara Maria Szász. She was orphaned at seven and at the age of seventeen she was due to be sold at an Ottoman slave market in Hungary when a thirty-eight-year-old English widower, Sam Baker, paid for her and rescued her from her captors. She was renamed Florence and years later she became Samuel Baker's wife. They were a perfect match: Sam was an established explorer and Florence a natural-born adventurer and so the two of them travelled to Africa, searching for the source of the Nile and shooting big game. They managed to reach the secondary source of the Nile, which they called Lake Albert in

Florence Baker

honour of Queen Victoria's recently deceased husband, and then in 1865 they made the journey to Britain, where they married (and where she met her stepchildren, Sam's children by his first wife) and where Sam received a knighthood. They returned to Africa in 1870 to report on the slave trade along the Nile. Later they journeyed to India and Japan before returning to Britain. Florence outlived Sam by twenty-three years and was cared for in her old age by her stepchildren.

HIDEOUTS AND DENS

— ◆ —

EVERY GIRL SHOULD HAVE a hideout or den of her own, and here are some ideas for making one. Several weekends may be spent sweating over the plans for a long-lasting outdoor Wendy house of wood beams and nails and real roofing tiles. But there are ways to make quicker work of this endeavour.

QUICK WENDY HOUSE

With 2-metre metal garden stakes, you can construct an outdoor Wendy house almost immediately. Garden stakes haven't the stability of wood beams, but the swiftness with which the walls go up easily makes up for that. Five stakes will do the trick.

The stakes come with footholds. Stand on them and they should push into the ground rather effortlessly. If there's a problem, a rubber mallet or a taller person can help; if it proves intractable, that may mean that there's a rock in the ground and you need to move the stake. Use one stake for each of the four corners. Set the fifth stake along one of the sides to create a space for the door.

Wrap the whole structure, except the doorway, with chicken wire or lighter-weight bird netting. Garden stakes have notches in them and you can attach the materials to the notches to form the basic wall. (Trim the bottom of the netting neatly at ground level, lest cats, birds or other small animals inadvertently get tangled inside; this happened to us.)

To add privacy, use large (disused) sheets or cloth as a second layer, or cardboard (you'll work out a way to attach these to the stakes). If you want a ceiling, the sheets or cloth will help, although they won't be waterproof, and rainwater will collect on top. You can use a tarpaulin, but the plastic can make the inside very hot. You'll work it out. A sixth stake, taller than the rest, can be added to the centre to create a sloped ceiling. From here, use string, rope, gaffer tape, wire, scissors, sticks, cardboard, plywood, and any other wood scraps you can find to build walls, create windows, ceilings and floors, and otherwise make it your own. There are no rules; it's your Wendy house.

LEAN-TO

A lean-to is a very primitive form of shelter that's little more than a wall or two and a roof. It's meant to keep you safe from the worst of the rain and wind, and often leans into existing walls or fences, hence the name. Find any tucked-in spot or corner, rig a tarpaulin roof with some ropes knotted to trees and lean a side of plywood against the house. Build up the front with branches, odd pieces of old fence your neighbours left out on bin day or even a picnic table turned on its side.

INDOOR HIDEOUT

The classic formula of sofa cushions, blankets, and the backs of settees and chairs is a good start for an indoor hideout, as is throwing blankets over the top of the dining room table (stacks of books on top help keep them in position).

You can improve upon these traditional dens. To make a hanging wall, screw a line of hooks or eyebolts into the ceiling. Run picture-hanging wire or clothesline rope through them. Attach clips or clothes pegs, and from these, dangle all sorts of sheets, light blankets, large swathes of cloth or oversized scarves to create a different kind of den.

LAMP, LANTERN, TORCH

◆

TAKE APART A TORCH and you'll see it's simply a battery-holding tube with an on-off switch at the side. You can build one with a quick trip to the DIY shop.

What you need

- ∗ Some AA batteries
- ∗ Copper wire (long strands of aluminium foil may be substituted)
- ∗ Electrical tape
- ∗ Torch bulb
- ∗ An empty glass jar
- ∗ Possibly tape, aluminium foil, paper, empty toilet-paper tube, scissors, or wire cutters

Start with an AA battery and a piece of copper wire about 30 centimetres long or so. With electrical tape, connect one end of the wire firmly to the bottom terminal of the battery. Wrap the other end of the wire tightly around the metal casing of a small torch light bulb. Position the light bulb so it touches the top of the battery. It should light up.

You've created a simple circuit that works when energy flows from the battery to the wire to the light bulb and back to the battery. If the bulb doesn't light, fiddle with the wires and connections until it does.

Once it lights, wrap the wire around the battery so the bulb stays put on top. That's the lamp. If the bottom wobbles, look for a holder. The electrical tape roll usually does a good job. If you spy an empty jar on the shelf, turn it upside down and place over the lamp and you have yourself a lantern.

You'll notice that the light bulb isn't that bright, and that regular torches use two AA bat-teries. Stack a second battery on top of the first. Use as much electrical tape as necessary to bind the two batteries together. Place the bulb on the top battery and you'll see the difference. The bulb will become slightly hot; don't touch it and burn yourself.

To adapt into a torch, fashion a holder, whether it be cardboard cut and taped to fit, a toilet-paper tube (lead the wire outside the tube), or lots more electrical wire wrapped around the two batteries (its bright colours provide decorative possibility).

Now for the on-off switch. For simplicity's sake, this can be accomplished by pulling the wire, forcing the bulb to move away from the battery and turn off. You can also cut the wire in half. To make the light go on, connect the wires and attach a sprig of electrical tape to hold them together. Remove the tape to detach the wires, break the circuit and turn the torch off.

ITALIAN TERMS OF ENDEARMENT, EXPRESSIONS AND OTHER ITEMS OF NOTE

TERMS OF ENDEARMENT

Tesoro
(My) treasure

Bella mia!
(*when addressing girls*)
My beauty! Hey, good-looking!

Bello mio!
(*when addressing boys*)
My beauty! Hey, good-looking!

Amore
(My) love

Caro/Cara
Darling

FUN WORDS TO SAY

L'ombelico
Bellybutton

Una zampa
Paw

Una lupetta
Baby she-wolf

Il carprifoglio
Honeysuckle

Una chiacchierata
A chat, chin-wag

Una fregiatura
A rip-off

Una farfalla
A butterfly

Un capro emissario
A scapegoat

Imbambolato/a
Discombobulated/sleepy/dopey
The word's derivative stem is **bambola**, *doll*, and is used to describe someone with a vacant, fixed expression, usually through lack of sleep, or confusion.

EXPRESSIONS

Quando il gatto non c'è, i topi ballano
While the cat's away, the mice can play. (While the cat's away, the mice dance.)

Anno nuovo, vita nuova
(New Year salutation)
Out with the old, in with the new. (New Year, new life.)

Chi dorme non piglia pesce
The early bird catches the worm. (He who sleeps doesn't catch fish.)

In bocca al lupo!
Good luck!
Literally translated, this means *To the mouth of the wolf.* When someone greets you with this, the correct response is **Crepi!**, which means *Let's hope he jumps!* It is seen as very bad luck to either greet someone with **Buona fortuna!**, the literal translation of *Good luck!*

Fare due passi
To go for a stroll.

Fare quattro chiacchiere
To have a chat.

Books with an Italian setting

The Name of the Rose
by Umberto Eco

A Room with a View
by E.M. Forster

The Divine Comedy
by Dante Alighieri

Six Characters in Search of an Author
by Luigi Pirandello

Pinocchio
by Carlo Collodi

New words (neologisms) borrowed from Italian into English

Paparazzo
This word came into existence after the seminal 1960s' Italian film *La Dolce Vita*, starring Marcello Mastroianni and Anita Ekberg. Paparazzo, a friend of the protagonist, is one of several cameramen who stalk the solipsistic lives of the beautiful glitterati in Rome. The enormous success of this film gave birth to this international word that refers to the now popular sport of celebrity-spotting by camera crews the world over.

Panino
This word is often used mistakenly in the plural, **panini**. The insertion of this word into everyday parlance demonstrates the influence of Mediterranean cuisine on British culture.

Italian food and drink

Tiramisu
This rich and highly caffeinated chocolate dessert has a title that describes it perfectly: the compound noun comprising three words **tirare** (to pick), **mi** (me) and **su** (up) is a fairly apt description of the treat's end result!

Cappuccino
To avoid derisory gazes, remember not to order this traditional Italian beverage after 11 a.m., and don't be surprised if it is served lukewarm. Its name derives from the traditional brown and white tunics of Capuchin monks.

WRITING LETTERS

Writing Good old-fashioned letters has somewhat fallen out of style with the advent of technology and the tempting immediacy of email, instant messaging and texting. But there are still circumstances where a typed or handwritten formal letter is required that calls for something more personal and professional than CU L8R, KTHXBYE!

The Thank You Letter

When you receive a present or other form of hospitality, it is polite to send a thank-you note or letter in response – and it is most polite that the letter is handwritten. Begin by greeting the person and then start the letter right away by saying 'Thank you'. You don't have to get fancy with an introduction; the whole point of the letter is to say thanks. So start with that: A simple 'thank you for your gift' will do. Then, mention how the gift will come in handy for you (or, if writing in response to a favour or gesture of hospitality, how useful their actions were to you: 'I really appreciated being able to stay with you when I visited Edinburgh last week.'). If you can, it's always nice to mention looking forward to seeing them at some future event. Then say thanks again and wrap up the letter by signing off with 'love', 'with gratitude', 'yours truly' or your preferred way of closing. A brief example:

Dear Aunt Jessie,

Thanks so much for the fantastic roller skates! I can't wait to use them at the skating party next month. When you visit over the summer, maybe we can go skating together. Thanks again!

Love,
Emi

Letter Writing Tips

From *Eight or Nine Wise Words About Letter Writing*, published in 1890 by Charles Dodgson (the pseudonym of *Alice in Wonderland* author Lewis Carroll)

Here is a golden Rule to begin with. Write legibly. The average temper of the human race would be perceptibly sweetened, if everybody obeyed this Rule! A great deal of the bad writing in the world comes simply from writing too quickly.

. . . My second Rule is, don't fill more than a page and a half with apologies for not having written sooner! The best subject, to begin with, is your friend's last letter. Write with the letter open before you. Answer his questions, and make any remarks his letter suggests. Then go on to what you want to say yourself. This arrangement is more courteous and pleasanter for the reader, than to fill the letter with your own invaluable remarks, and then hastily answer your friend's questions in a postscript. Your friend is much more likely to enjoy your wit, after his own anxiety for information has been satisfied.

A few more Rules may fitly be given here, for correspondence that has unfortunately become controversial. One is, don't repeat yourself. When once you have said your say, fully and clearly, on a certain point and have failed to convince your friend, drop that subject: to repeat your arguments, all over again, will simply lead to his doing the same; and so you will go on, like a Circulating Decimal. Did you ever know a Circulating Decimal come to an end?

Another Rule is, when you have written a letter that you feel may possibly irritate your friend, however necessary you may
have felt it to so express yourself, put it aside till the next day. Then read it over again and fancy it addressed to yourself. This will often lead to your writing it all over again, taking out a lot of the vinegar and pepper, and putting in honey instead and thus making a much more palatable dish of it! . . .

My fifth Rule is, if your friend makes a severe remark, either leave it unnoticed, or make your reply distinctly less severe: and if he makes a friendly remark, tending towards 'making up' the little difference that has arisen between you, let your reply be distinctly more friendly . . .

My sixth Rule (and my last remark about controversial correspondence) is, don't try to have the last word! How many a controversy would be nipped in the bud, if each was anxious to let the other have the last word! . . .

My seventh Rule is, if it should ever occur to you to write, jestingly, in dispraise of your friend, be sure you exaggerate enough to make the jesting obvious: a word spoken in jest, but taken as earnest, may lead to very serious consequences. I have known it to lead to the breaking-off of a friendship . . .

My eighth Rule. When you say, in your letter, 'I enclose cheque for £5,' or 'I enclose John's letter for you to see,' leave off writing for a moment – go and get the document referred to – and put it into the envelope. Otherwise, you are pretty certain to find it lying about, after the Post has gone!

Personal Letters

Longer than a thank-you note, a personal letter (or social note) has five parts and again should be handwritten.

The Heading: This consists of your address and the date, each on its own line, indented to the right of the page. After the heading, jump a line. If you are writing on preaddressed stationery, just write the date.

The Greeting: This can be formal or informal – beginning with 'Dear', or just writing the person's name (or even, simply, 'Hi'). Either way, the greeting ends with a comma, and you jump a line afterwards.

The Body: The main text of your letter. In this kind of letter, the beginning of each paragraph is indented, and no lines are missed between paragraphs.

The Closing: After the body, miss a line and write your closing line, which is usually just a few words like 'All best', 'Sincerely', 'Looking forward to seeing you', 'With love', etc. Whatever you write, this line should end in a comma and should be indented the same amount as your heading.

The Signature Line: This is where you sign your name. If your letter contains a postscript, skip a line after the signature line, begin the postscript by writing 'PS' and end it with your initials.

An additional postscript should be noted as PPS rather than PSS, as it is a post (after) postscript and not a postscript script.

FUN AT THE SEASIDE

◆

THERE'S ALWAYS PLENTY TO DO by the seaside – caves to explore, sandcastles to build, waves to ride. Here are a few ideas:

Eat a Knickerbocker Glory

Ice-cream is a great treat and always has been. Reportedly the first ice-cream was eaten by none other than King Charles II at a lavish banquet in 1671. It was a dessert that impressed the court as ice was a luxury, and at the time there was no way of keeping ice-cream frozen. It really was a dessert fit for a king. Since the eighteenth century ice-cream has become available to all, with the first recipe appearing in *Mrs Mary Eales' Receipts* in 1718. Mrs Eales was confectioner to Queen

Anne, and knew a thing or two about ice-cream. The craze for ice-cream really took off in the twentieth century as it became possible to keep it frozen and to produce it easily. Ice-cream parlours sprung up across the country, particularly in the 1950s,

when people were keen to leave post-war poverty well behind them.

The Knickerbocker Glory, so called after the ladies' stockings of the same name, is served in tall glasses with a long spoon. It is layered with fresh fruit, peach melba sauce, whipped cream and ice-cream. It tastes best on a hot day, in an ice-cream parlour overlooking the sea.

Mess around in Rock Pools

When the tide recedes from a rocky beach it reveals an exciting world that is normally hidden from view. In hollows in the ground, rock pools are formed, and in them you can find a wealth of sea life. Look out for periwinkle, crabs, brown and red seaweed, anemones and even prawns. Some small fish, such as suckers and gobies, also survive in this atmosphere. Get out your fishing net, get your feet wet and get looking for yourself!

Follow in the Footsteps of Famous Smugglers

The coasts of the United Kingdom have always attracted smugglers, thanks to the many caves that can be found in the cliffs by the sea. It was particularly popular in the late eighteenth century as high taxes meant that people were keen to find a way of getting their luxury goods at cut-price rates. You might think smuggling was purely a male occupation, but history tells of several female smugglers, and also the women who would act as look-outs, banging drums and pouring boiling water over the tax men as the smugglers brought the loot home.

To see for yourself the caves that smugglers used to store their goods, the cliff paths that they traversed in the dead of night and how towns were built around this profitable enterprise, try walking from Robin Hood's Bay to Ravenscar along the Cleveland Way in North Yorkshire. Robin Hood's Bay was ideal for smugglers due to its isolated location. Once loot was landed it was apparently possible to get it to the top of the town without having to leave any of the houses as they were all connected either by their cellars or by interconnecting cupboards. If you take the cliff path you'll come across Boggle Hole, an inlet where smugglers used to land with their goods. Keep on going and you'll find Stoup Beck where you can also reach the sea and explore the caves. The area is steeped in history and you can almost smell times gone by in the air.

Walk along Britain's Longest Pier

Southend Pier is officially Britain's longest pier at a length of 1.3 miles. Construction started in 1830 but it wasn't until 1848 that it was finished.

It was the longest wooden pier in Europe at the time. It has been ravaged by fire several times, and replaced in iron to save it from further damage. A train runs along its length, so you can always catch a lift back from the top of the pier!

Ride a Donkey

People have been riding donkeys at the seaside since around 1780. They became particularly popular in Victorian times as the seaside attracted more and more visitors. Believe it or not, donkeys were chosen over horses for seaside rides as, although they are often seen as stubborn, they are actually calmer and less easily startled than horses.

See the Blackpool Illuminations

The first ever illuminations in Blackpool appeared in 1879 when only eight arc lamps were turned on. Nowadays they are much bigger, of course! Over the years celebrities such as George Formby, Gracie Fields and Shirley Bassey have switched on the illuminations in grand ceremonies. While in Blackpool you must ride one of the trams that run along the seafront and of course have a go on the Big Dipper at the famous Blackpool Pleasure Beach.

Build a Sandcastle

Sandcastles are great fun to make, especially when you let your imagination run free. Don't forget two top tips: turrets are impressive, but only if they stay upright, so make sure that you pat the sand down into your bucket and add enough water to make it stick; and even better is a moat that can be filled up by the sea as it comes in, so try to work that into your castle. Pick up your bucket and spade and get digging.

Go on an Agatha Christie Tour

Agatha Christie, author of the Miss Marple and Poirot novels, was born beside the sea, in Torquay. You can find various landmarks associated with her and her books by going on an Agatha Christie walk around the town and harbour. Information about the walk is available from the tourist information centre on the harbour front.

Visit a Beach a Long Way from the Sea

If you don't live by the seaside, don't despair, there's something for you too. Beaches are popping up in the least likely of places: slap bang in the centre of some of our biggest towns and cities! These are temporary beaches put on in the summer so that our urban residents can get in the holiday spirit. Check out the beaches in Manchester, Shoreditch in East London, and Bristol. They've become so popular that more are bound to spring up in the summers to come.

MAKING A SEINE NET

---◆---

A SEINE NET IS JUST a long fishing net used for dipping into the ocean to collect and study marine life.

What you need

* Seine netting. Ours is 2 metres deep and 5 metres long, with a half-centimetre mesh, but these measurements are flexible, depending on how big or small you want your net to be, and what's available. It's nice when the net has a bit of Styrofoam at the top edge to keep it afloat, and some metal weights on the bottom to help it sink. Some seine netting comes this way. It can be bought at fishing shops.
* Two 2-metre poles or lengths of wood, to control the net, and to wind it up when you're finished.
* A large bucket, to keep your catch in water and to store the net.

Attach the shorter sides of the net to the poles. Do this by drilling a hole at each end of the pole (they might do this for you at a fishing shop, if you ask). Or, use a Swiss Army knife to whittle a channel at each end of the pole and wrap the rope there. Or forget the whittling and just wrap the rope very tight. If there's not already a thin rope at each corner of your net, find a small length of light rope or string and use that.

One person stands at the shoreline and holds a pole. The other person holds the second pole and wades into the water until the net is fully extended. Keep the top at water level and let the rest of the net sink. This is where the metal weights come in handy.

After a time, walk back to shore in a sweeping motion, keeping the net fully extended so that when you get to shore, you'll be a net-length away from your friend holding the other end of the net. As you get closer to shore, slowly change the net direction from vertical – where it is catching fish and other creatures – to horizontal, where you can scoop them up and lay out the net on the wet sand to see what you've got.

If you're not catching much of anything, change your position, or your location, or trawl a bit, walking around with the net stretched, giving more fish more time to end up in your hands. Both of you can walk further into the river or surf.

Throw back everything within a few minutes so that your catch can continue their lives at sea. Many towns have laws that tell you to throw the sea animals back where they belong, or else you will suffer a stiff penalty. (Some beaches ban large-scale commercial seine netting, but these small ones are usually okay.)

If you're going fishing, though, little minnows are good bait.

How to clean a shell

When your beachcombing and seine netting land you choice shells, here are two ways to clean them and turn them into long-lasting treasures.

1 Bury the shells 30 centimetres underground in your back garden and let the earthworms and all those soil bacteria do their work. This can take several months.

2 Boil for five minutes in a large pot, in a solution that is half water and half bleach. You'll see when the shells are clean. Take them out carefully with tongs, because the water will be scalding. Rinse with cool water.

WOMEN SPIES

Hedy Lamarr

Hedwig Eva Maria Kiesler is best known as Hedy Lamarr, film star of the 1930s and '40s. But she was also an inventor who patented an idea that was to become the key to modern wireless communication. During World War II, Hedy, along with George Antheil, invented a way to make military communications secure through frequency-hopping, an early form of a technology called spread spectrum. Hedy's status as a beautiful and successful actress provided her with the perfect cover: she was able to visit a variety of venues on tour and interact with many people, none of whom suspected that the stunning starlet might be listening closely and thinking of ways to help the US cause.

Princess Noor-un-nisa Inayat Khan

Princess Noor-un-nisa Inayat Khan was an author and a heroine of the French Resistance.

Hedy Lamarr

The Princess trained as a wireless operator in Britain and was sent into occupied France as a spy with the code name 'Madeleine'. She became the sole communications link between her unit of the French Resistance and home base before she was captured by the Gestapo and executed.

The Girl Guides

During the First World War, the Girl Guides were used as couriers for secret messages by MI5, Britain's counterintelligence agency. Messengers were needed to work in the War Office at the time, and at first Boy Scouts were used. But they proved to be difficult to manage, so Girl Guides were asked to serve instead. The girls, most of whom were between fourteen and eighteen years old, ran

Two famous and controversial World War I women spies, both of whom were executed, were Mata Hari (born Margaretha Geertruida Zelle McLeod) and Edith Cavell. Mata Hari was a dancer who used her vocation as a cover for her spy work for the Germans. She was shot by the French as a spy in 1917. Edith Cavell was a British nurse who worked in Belgium during the war. She secretly helped British, French and Belgian soldiers escape from behind the German lines, and she hid refugees in the nursing school she ran. By 1915 she had helped more than 200 soldiers, but the Germans grew suspicious and arrested her. She was executed by firing squad.

messages and patrolled on the roof; for their efforts they were paid ten shillings a week, plus food. Like all employees of MI5, they took a pledge of secrecy. But unlike many employees of MI5, they were among the least likely spies to arouse suspicion.

Virginia Hall

Virginia Hall, originally from the USA, spied for the French during World War II. She was chased by the Nazis over the Pyrenees into Spain and eluded them, even though she had a wooden leg. After escaping, she trained as a radio operator and transferred to the OSS, America's secret spy agency. In 1943 she returned to France as an undercover agent, gathering intelligence, helping to coordinate air drops in support of D-Day, and working with the French underground to disrupt German communications. After the war, Virginia was awarded America's Distinguished Service Cross, the only American civilian woman to receive such an honour. She continued to work for the OSS, and later the CIA, until her retirement in 1966.

Violette Szabo

Violette Bushell Szabo was recruited and trained by the British Special Operations Executive after her husband, a member of the French Foreign Legion, was killed in North Africa. She was sent to France, where she was captured during a shoot-out. She refused to give up her information and was sent to the Ravensbruck concentration camp, where she was eventually killed. She was awarded the George Cross and the Croix de Guerre posthumously in 1946.

Josephine Baker

Josephine Baker was another World War II-era entertainer whose celebrity status helped distract from her mission as a spy. Josephine was a dancer and singer from the US. She moved to Paris when she was nineteen and became an international star. When World War II began, she started working as an undercover operative for the French Resistance, transporting orders and maps from the Resistance into countries occupied by Germany. Her fame and renown made it easy for her to pass unsuspected, as foreign officials were thrilled to meet such a famous performer, but she wrote the secret information in disappearing ink on her sheet music just in case.

Josephine Baker

Amy Elizabeth Thorpe

Amy Elizabeth Thorpe, also known as Betty Pack and 'Code Name Cynthia', was an American spy first recruited by the British secret service and later by the American OSS. She is probably best remembered for her procurement of French naval codes, necessary for the Allies' invasion of North Africa, which she accomplished by tricking a man connected to the Vichy French Embassy into giving them to her. Not only did she steal French naval code books from the safe in his locked room, she also stole his heart: after the war they were married, and they spent the rest of their lives together.

Margery Urquhart

Margery Urquhart was the first woman ever to work for Special Branch. Born to Scottish parents in Chile, she was recruited into espionage work in 1935 and then became a spy for Britain during the Second World War. She was integral to the counter-espionage activity against the Germans. When the war ended she continued her work, and during her long career she worked on cases of terrorism in the UK. She later became a police officer with Surrey police and received the OBE in 1977 for service to her country.

HOW TO BE A SPY

◆

THE WORD 'SPY' comes to us from ancient words meaning 'to look at' or 'to watch'. And indeed, despite the modern movie emphasis on technology and machines as integral to a spy's bag of tricks, in essence what makes an excellent spy is her ability to watch, pay attention, look and learn.

TOP-SECRET COMMUNICATION

Girl Guide whistles and hand signals
These secret signals have been used by the Girl Guides since before World War I. You can use them to alert or direct your spy team when you are out in the field.

Whistle signals

* One long blast means 'silence / alert / listen for next signal'
* A succession of long slow blasts means 'go out / get further away' or 'advance / extend / scatter'
* A succession of quick short blasts means 'rally / close in / come together/ fall in'
* Alternate short and long blasts mean 'alarm / look out / be ready / man your alarm posts'

Hand signals

* Advance / forward: Swing the arm from rear to front, below the shoulder
* Retreat: Circle the arm above the head
* Halt: Raise the arm to full extension above the head

Secret codes

A code is a way to send a message while keeping it a secret from someone who isn't supposed to know about it. Codes can be easy or complicated – the trick is to make sure the person on the receiving end of your secret message has the key to decode it without making it too easy for anyone else to crack. Here are a few simple codes you can use.

* Write each word backwards
* Read every second letter
* Use numbers for letters (A=1, B=2, C=3, etc.)
* Reverse the alphabet (A=Z, B=Y, C=X, etc.)
* Sliding scale alphabet (move the alphabet by one letter: A=B, B=C, C=D, etc.)
* Use invisible ink (write with lemon or lime juice; after it dries hold the paper up to a light source to read the message)
* Pigpen code: Each letter is represented by the part of the 'pigpen' that surrounds it in the key. If it's the second letter in the box, then it has a dot in the middle.

Key

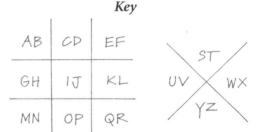

Code

TOP SECRET!

TOOLS

In films, spies often use high-tech equipment to accomplish covert tasks, but all spies are grounded in the basics: good, old-fashioned, low-tech observation that can be performed without the aid of any fancy technology. In World War II, women spies used something called an 'escape and evasion' scarf – these were scarves with maps printed on one side, so that any agent who needed to find an escape route or nearby town or road had a map that was easy to get to but not so easily detectable by someone else. You can make your own with an old scarf or other fabric and a permanent marker (providing you get permission to mark up the scarf first).

A few other tools that would be good for a spy to have handy are things like binoculars; a small notepad and pen; walkie-talkie; magnifying glass; Swiss Army knife; hat or wig for quick disguising; plimsolls or other quiet shoes for stealth walking; clothes in dark or subdued colours. The best tools of all, though, are your eyes, your ears and your ingenuity. Pay attention to everything that's going on around you, blend into your surroundings so you can observe without being noticed, look for subtle clues to tell you more about what's happening and write everything down. With any luck, you'll not only become a great spy, you'll be on your way to becoming a great writer. You know, just in case the espionage career doesn't work out.

YOUR SPY TEAM

The life of a spy can be a lonely one, with so much secrecy and subterfuge and no one to share it with at the risk of blowing your cover. It's much more fun to operate within a spy ring and work as a team to accomplish your undercover goals. On a team, spies can have specific tasks or areas of expertise, and of course code names.

The Agent-in-Charge: This is the head spy. She is responsible for directing, planning and organizing the mission. All team members report to her.

The Scout: This is the person who scopes out the physical landscape to see if it's safe for the rest of the team to move in. She goes ahead of the team when they are out in the field and no one moves in without a signal from her. She should have excellent eyesight and hearing and should be an expert on geography and the outdoors.

The Tracker: This person acts as the 'trigger', the spy whose job it is to monitor the target of investigation. She tracks and observes the suspect's actions and alerts the rest of the team when the suspect is in range.

The Techie: This is the group's technology maven. She knows about computers, tools and gadgets, from using them to fixing them to creating new ones. She is the one who draws up any maps, plans or charts, and also keeps notes about the mission.

The Wheel Artist: This is the person who organizes the getaway, or who can use her wheels to accomplish any stealth manoeuvre. If she can drive, that's great, but she doesn't have to be commandeering a car. The wheels can be anything that gets your spy team out of the field in a timely manner. She can oversee a fleet of scooters, ride another spy to safety on her bike or even accomplish a sensitive mission lightning quick on her skateboard or roller skates.

The Stealth Master: This is a small, quiet person who can sneak into tight places and generally move around unnoticed. It helps if she is also a master of disguise and an illusionist, able to use card and magic tricks for purposes of distraction.

The Social Engineer: This person is brave, chatty, outgoing and able to interact with suspects and others to extract information. She can be the public face of the team while other team members gather evidence or perform surveillance, using her considerable social skills to both distract and engage.

Of course, no matter what her speciality, a spy should be able to: appraise a situation, balance, bluff, climb, be diplomatic, escape when necessary, gather information, hide, intuit, be insightful, jump, listen, move silently, read lips and body language, respond quickly, tumble, transform and, above all, be level-headed.

After each mission, all members of the spy team should rendezvous at an agreed-upon meeting place or secret hideout, where they will report to the agent-in-charge and exchange information. No matter what her role on the team is, a spy should always note suspicious activity, try not to be seen or heard, cover her tracks and never reveal her true identity to outsiders.

Spy Lingo

Acorn
Someone who is performing an intelligence function.

Agent
A person officially employed by an intelligence service. (Also undercover agent: *a secret agent;* deep-cover agent: *an agent under permanent cover;* double agent: *an agent simultaneously working for two enemies;* agent-in-charge: *the head agent.)*

Babysitter
Bodyguard.

Blowback
Unexpected negative consequences of spying.

Blown
Detected, as in 'your cover is blown.'

Bona Fides
Proof of a person's claimed identity.

Brush Contact or Brush Pass
Brief contact between two agents who are passing information, documents or equipment.

Burn Notice
An official statement from an intelligence agency saying that an individual or group is an unreliable source.

Chicken Feed
Low-grade information given by a double agent to an adversary to build the credibility of the double agent.

Cobbler
Spy who creates false passports, visas, certificates and other documents.

Comm
Small note or other written communication.

Cover
A secret identity.

Dead Drop
A secret hiding place somewhere in public where communications, documents or equipment are placed for another agent to collect.

Doppelganger
A decoy or lookalike.

E&E
Escape and evasion.

Ears Only
Material too secret to commit to writing.

Eyes Only
Documents too secret to be talked about.

Floater
A person used occasionally or even unknowingly for an intelligence operation.

Friend
An agent or informant providing information.

Front
A legitimate-appearing business created to provide cover for spies and their operations.

Ghoul
Agent who searches obituaries and graveyards for names to be used by agents.

Honey Pot/Honey Trap
Slang for use of men or women to trap a person using affection or romance.

Informant
A person who provides intelligence to the surveillance team.

Joe
A deep-cover agent.

Legend
Background story or documents to support your cover.

Letterbox
A person who acts as a go-between.

Mole
An agent who penetrates enemy organizations.

Naked
A spy operating without cover or backup.

Paroles
Passwords agents use to identify each other.

Peep
Photographer.

Pocket Litter
Items in a spy's pocket (receipts, coins, etc.) that add authenticity to her identity.

Ring
A network of spies or agents.

Safe House
A secret hideout.

Sanitize
To 'clean up' a report or other document to hide sensitive information.

Sleeper Agents
Spies who are placed in a target country or organization, not to undertake an immediate mission, but to be activated later.

Spook
Another word for spy.

Target
The person being spied on. (Also hard target: A target who actively maintains secrecy and doesn't let on that she is aware of the surveillance team.)

The Take
Information gathered by spying.

Trigger
An agent who watches for the target and alerts the rest of the surveillance team when the target is spotted.

Unsub
An unknown subject in a surveillance operation.

Undercover
Disguising your identity, or using an assumed identity, in order to learn secret information.

Window Dressing
Like pocket litter, this is extra information included in a cover story to help make it seem more real.

CLIMBING

———— ◆ ————

JO MARCH, the heroine of *Little Women,* declares that no girl can be her friend who refuses to climb trees and leap fences. Louisa May Alcott wrote that book in 1868. Another author, Charlotte Yonge, wrote in the late 1800s that girls showed 'a wholesome delight in rushing about at full speed, playing at active games, climbing trees, rowing boats, making dirt-pies and the like'. Award-winning actress Beah Richards penned a poem in 1951 called 'Keep Climbing, Girls', in which she urged girls to 'climb right up to the toppermost bough of the very tallest tree'. To keep you in tune with your adventuresome foremothers, here are some tree-climbing tips that Jo March might have suggested to new friends, along with some ideas for shimmying up ropes.

TREES

The key to successful tree climbing is understanding that you are not pulling yourself up vertically; tree climbing is hard enough without trying to entirely defy gravity. You are sturdily pushing the plane of your body into the tree diagonally while your arms reach around the trunk and shimmying up, bit by bit. Tree climbing doesn't necessarily cause injury, but falling out of one certainly does. Climb with caution.

ROPES

Read these directions and trust that when you're standing in front of a rope in gym class, they will make good sense. Here's how to tackle the miraculous feat that is rope climbing:

* Grab the rope with your hands and pull the rope down as you jump up.
* This sounds odd, but it works: Just after you grab and jump, grapple the rope with your legs so that one ankle wraps around the rope, then end in a position where your two feet hold tightly against the rope. You are up.
* To climb: Hold tight with your legs and stretch your arms, one after the other, as high up as possible on the rope. Now comes the secret trick. Use your stomach muscles, or abdominals, to crunch your legs up towards your arms. You may not move far, but keep shimmying, bit by bit. Reach your arms, crunch with your stomach and grab the rope with your feet. As your torso gets stronger, and your arms and legs, too, rope climbing will become much easier and all the more gratifying.

Climbing walls at gyms are a great place to practise. Keep climbing, but remember once you go up, you still have to figure out how to get down safely!

QUEENS OF THE ANCIENT WORLD III

Cleopatra of Egypt: Queen of Kings

CLEOPATRA VII was the last of a long line of ancient Egyptian queens. She ruled Egypt for twenty-one years, from 51 to 30 BC, and was famously linked with the Roman generals Julius Caesar and Mark Antony. It was the Greek historian Plutarch (46–122 AD), however, who turned Cleopatra into a legend. Plutarch reports that although she was not conventionally beautiful, Cleopatra's persona was bewitching and irresistible. The sound of her voice brought pleasure, like an instrument of many strings, and she was intelligent, charming, witty and outrageous.

Cleopatra's City: Alexandria

Cleopatra was born in 70 BC, one of King Ptolemy XII's six children. She came of age in Alexandria, Egypt's capital city and a bustling port on the Mediterranean Sea. The Pharos Lighthouse, one of the Seven Wonders of the Ancient World, gleamed over Alexandria's harbour and welcomed ships and people to this vibrant and cosmopolitan city. The celebrated mathematician Euclid had lived there and published his thirteen-volume *Elements*, filled with all the known principles of geometry and algebra. Alexandria's marble library was the largest in the world and philosophers in the Greek tradition of Aristotle and Plato roamed Alexandria's streets.

Egypt was wealthy, besides. Craftspeople produced glass, metal, papyrus writing sheets, and cloth. The fertile countryside produced grain that was shipped all over the Mediterranean region to make bread.

Queen of a Threatened Nation

Despite this grand history, in the 50s BC, Egypt was struggling. Rome's armies had already conquered most of the nearby nations. Egypt remained independent, but no one knew how long it would be able to survive Rome's expansion. Cleopatra's father, Ptolemy XII, had made an unequal alliance with Rome. He had lost several territories, like the island of Cyprus, and faced political rebellions from his own children.

When her father died in 51 BC, Cleopatra was only eighteen years old. Still, she was named his successor, along with her twelve-year-old brother, Ptolemy XIII. Throughout her long reign, she vowed to protect Egypt's independence. She did so until the bitter end with the help of a strong navy and her romantic alliances with the most powerful men of Rome.

Cleopatra and Julius Caesar

When Cleopatra became queen, Rome was embroiled in its own civil drama. Rome had long been a republic that prided itself on democracy and on measured rule by its Senate. Now, ambitious men were taking over. Three of these power-hungry men – Julius Caesar, Pompey and Crassus – secretly joined forces as The First Triumvirate in 60 BC to gain more control. Soon though, they began to fight each other.

In 48 BC, Julius Caesar conquered Gaul, just north of Italy. Flushed with the thrill of victory, he led his soldiers back to Rome. There was a tradition that no general's soldiers were to cross the Rubicon River into the city, but Caesar ignored that and brought his army across. He waged armed civil war against his now-enemy Pompey and the Senate, on land and at sea. Pompey fled to Alexandria, with Caesar in pursuit.

Alexandria had fallen into violence. Cleopatra and her brother were quarrelling, as each tried to steal power from the other, and there was no law and order. The sibling rulers looked to Roman rivals Pompey and Julius Caesar, knowing they needed to make an alliance but not knowing which of them they should trust.

As the fighting in Alexandria worsened, Cleopatra fled the city with her younger sister. At the same time, one of her brother's fighters, feeling emboldened, assassinated Pompey. He hoped the act would endear him to Julius Caesar, who would then take the brother's side and install him as sole Pharaoh of Egypt. However, when Caesar saw the remains of Pompey, including his signet ring with an emblem of a lion holding a sword in his paws, he was furious. Roman generals had their own sense of honour and this was no way for the life of a famed Roman leader to end. Julius Caesar was angry with the brother and banished him from Egypt.

And so in 47 BC, Cleopatra became the sole Queen of Egypt. Julius Caesar named her Pharaoh and Queen of Kings and Cleopatra styled herself as the incarnation of the Egyptian mother goddess Isis. She and Julius Caesar also fell in love. The Roman conqueror and the Egyptian queen had a child together. They named him Ptolemy Caesar, thus joining the traditional names of Egypt and Rome. His nickname was Caesarion.

Soon after Caesarion's birth, a cabal of Roman senators who feared Caesar's growing power assassinated him on the infamous Ides of March (15 March, 44 BC). Cleopatra and her son had been with Caesar in Rome and, after his death, they returned by ship to Alexandria. Having seen Roman politics up close, Cleopatra knew that Rome would play an important role in her future, but she knew not how.

Cleopatra and Mark Antony

After Caesar's death, Rome was ruled by a Second Triumvirate: Octavian, Lepidus and Mark Antony. Antony was in charge of Rome's eastern provinces and had his eye set on Egypt. In 42 BC, he summoned Cleopatra to a meeting. Cleopatra finally agreed to meet Mark Antony in the city of Tarsus. She arrived in grandeur, on a golden ship with brilliant purple sails and demanded that he come aboard and talk with her there. They too fell in love and, nine months later, she gave birth to their twins, named Alexander Helios and Cleopatra Selene II.

Mark Antony was worn out by the political life of Rome. Despite his great popularity with the Roman people, he was losing political ground to his nemesis, the brilliant Octavian. Antony moved to Alexandria to live with Cleopatra and they had another child.

ANTONIUS et CLEOPATRA.

Cleopatra's fate would now be inseparable from that of Mark Antony and his foe Octavian. Octavian wanted Egypt's wealth and he wanted Mark Antony's power. Julius Caesar had named Octavian his legal heir before he died, but Octavian still feared that Caesarion (Caesar's son with Cleopatra) would one day challenge him for the leadership of Rome.

Octavian and the Roman Senate declared war against Antony and Cleopatra. Octavian's general Agrippa captured one of Antony's Greek cities, Methone. On a September morning in 31 BC, Antony and Cleopatra commanded a flotilla of ships to arrive at the Gulf of Actium, on the western coast of Greece, to win the city back.

Egypt's Last Queen

The battle would be a disaster for Cleopatra. Before day's end she would turn her ships back to Alexandria, followed by Mark Antony, who had lost many ships and many men. Their day was over. Soon, Octavian's forces threatened Alexandria. With Antony already dead by his own hand, Cleopatra chose to kill herself rather than be taken prisoner and displayed in Octavian's triumphal march through the streets of Rome.

Still considering Caesarion a threat, Octavian had the twelve-year-old put to death. He brought Cleopatra's three children with Mark Antony to Rome, where they were raised by Octavian's sister Octavia, who had also been Antony's Roman wife and was now his widow.

One era ended and another began. Cleopatra was independent Egypt's last Queen and reigning Pharaoh. Having defeated Cleopatra, Octavian declared Egypt a Roman province. He commandeered Egypt's immense treasure to pay his soldiers. Having vanquished Mark Antony, Octavian ushered in the Pax Romana, or Roman Peace, and became the first Emperor of Rome.

MAKING YOUR OWN JEWELLERY

$\diamond$

MAKING YOUR OWN JEWELLERY is great fun and not as difficult as you might think. The first thing is to pay a visit to a craft shop or a specialist bead shop to stock up on beads, catches and wire. Bead shops are great places to spend time rooting through bowls of pretty beads, imagining what you could make from them. Even better, prices start at only a few pence. If you don't live near a shop that sells beads, it's likely that someone you know has a basket full of odds and ends: buttons, fabrics, old beads – a treasure trove of things you can use again.

NECKLACES

Necklaces can be as simple or as complicated as you like. Whatever your design, you'll need a clasp, some wire and some beads. Simply thread the beads onto the wire, securing either end onto the clasp, and there you have it.

A slightly more complicated necklace, which will look really impressive, is the floating bead necklace. You'll need several 'crimp' beads, which are beads which hold the main beads in place. Start in the middle of your necklace, feeding on one crimp bead and pressing it into place with some needle-nose pliers. It should be secure on the wire and not move. Then feed on your main bead – a single bead looks nice, or you can try several – and add another crimp bead afterwards, securing it into place again. Repeat as many times as you like to create a necklace where the beads look as though they are floating around your neck.

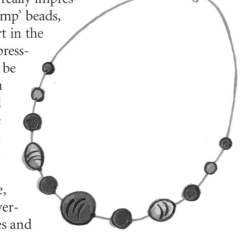

Once you've got the hang of the necklaces above, experiment. You can add more than one wire strand, layering several wires at different heights. Or try different sizes and feels of beads to create completely different looks.

BRACELETS

To make a bracelet, you can repeat the same steps as for the necklace, just on a smaller scale. Alternatively, try a bracelet on an elasticated cord simply by stringing beads onto a piece of elastic and securing with a knot.

Earrings may seem a little more complicated but are worth the extra effort. You'll need two head pins (straight, non-bendable wire with a flat pin head on the bottom). String your beads onto the head pins, remembering to keep them the same on each pin: you wouldn't want uneven earrings! Then bend the top of the wire of the head pin into a hook using needle-nose pliers. Loop this onto an earring clasp, and you have a finished pair of earrings. This works for both pierced ears and non-pierced ears; just make sure you buy the right fittings.

You can turn your new-found skills into a way of making a bit of money, too. Why not set up a jewellery stall and sell your creations to friends, family and neighbours?

Calculating your profit

If you are setting up your jewellery stall to save up money for a Swiss Army knife or a special book, you must understand how to work out how much you earned – that is, your profit. Let's say you make two necklaces, five bracelets and a pair of earrings. From the sale of one of those necklaces, three bracelets and the pair of earrings you made £11.50.

First work out the profit, using this standard equation:

Revenue (money taken in) minus **Expenses** (materials) equals **Profit**

Revenue: You sold one necklace at £3, three bracelets at £2 each and a pair of earrings at £2.50, so you earned £11.50.

Expenses:	£
50 beads at 5p each	2.50
Wire	1.00
Clasps and fittings	0.75
Total expenses	4.25

Now plug the numbers into the equation: £11.50 − £4.25 = £7.25. You cleared £7.25 in profit.

HOW TO PADDLE A CANOE

THERE ARE LARGER, faster and more complex boats than a canoe, kayak or raft, but in none of those fancier boats can you feel the water so closely or slip into creeks and shallow wetlands to drift silently alongside cormorants, ospreys and swans.

Paddling a boat is an art that, like most pursuits, just needs practice to master. Huck Finn may have floated the Mississippi on a raft, and white-water kayaking is a thrill, but short of those, nothing beats a canoe for a water adventure.

Sometimes you need to be alone and your canoe is there for you. Other times you want to adventure with a friend and canoeing together is an exhilarating lesson in teamwork.

To learn to canoe, you should know these basic boat words, strokes and concepts.

The ordinary canoe stroke is the *forward stroke*. To paddle on the right, grab the grip (or top knob of the paddle) with your left hand and the shaft with your right. Put the paddle into the water, perpendicular to the boat, and pull it back and then out of the water. Keep your arms straight and twist your torso as you paddle. To paddle on the left, hold the grip with your right hand, the shaft with your left, and repeat.

To change course and return from whence you came, turn the boat and then paddle forward in the new direction. The *back stroke*, then, merely causes the boat to slow, or even stop. Put the paddle in the water slightly back, near the line of your hips and push towards the front, and then out.

It's important to remember that a canoe is not a bicycle. If you turn bicycle handlebars to the right, the bike will turn rightward. Not so in a canoe. When you paddle to the right, the boat will shift left. The opposite is true, too:

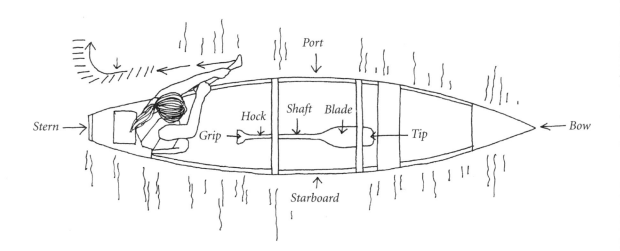

left paddling pushes the boat to the right. Rotate your body as you paddle, since the power comes not from your arms exactly, but from your torso. With practice, you will learn to do this instinctively, using your hips and body weight to control the boat's direction.

Two-person canoeing is a delicate dance whereby the person at stern steers and gives directions while the person at bow paddles, changing sides at will to keep the boat in its line.

When you paddle alone it is essential to know the *J-stroke*, which, by means of a small flip at the end, keeps the boat in a straight line. The J-stroke is just that. As you paddle on the left side, draw the letter J (see the canoe illustration). On the right side, it will look like a mirror-image J, or a fishhook. In other words, put the paddle in the water close to the canoe and before your forward stroke ends, turn the paddle out and away from the boat; that's the J. Then lift the paddle out of the water and ready it to start again.

Some beginning canoers constantly move the paddle from right to left sides, but that's a quick way to tire your arms. Using a *C-stroke* to steer will allow you to paddle to one side more of the time. Start as with a forward stroke, but trace a C (on the left, or its mirror image on the right) in the water. When you do this, turn the blade so it's nearly parallel to the water.

This next stroke has many names, *crossback* being one of them. It's a stop. Drag the blade into the water and hold it still. Really, really hold the paddle tight against the water's rush. This stops the boat. It also turns it to that side, but this is not a suggested way to turn, since it slows the boat down too much.

One final stroke is perfect for when you find yourself in a cove with no company other than a family of mallards and two swans nestling on the nearby rock. The *quietest possible stroke* will break no water and make no sound. Put the paddle in the water and keep it there, making a figure eight, over and again.

Now, in the big scheme of life, all you need is a boat and a paddle. In real life, some additional gear is essential, the first being a lifejacket. It's itchy and annoying and you'll be tempted to leave it on shore. Don't. Please. It can save your life in bad weather. In a less dire circumstance, if you tip, it will give you a leg up as you grab your paddle and pull yourself into your boat.

Drinking water is necessary and, last but not least, bring a rope. Ropes are key to canoe adventures. You might find a stray canoe that needs to be towed to shore, or need to tie the canoe to a tree while you explore a riverbank. Perhaps the tide has gone out in a creek and you need to hop out of the boat and pull your canoe back to deeper waters. Lifejacket, water, rope and you're set.

Last tips: In general, the closer to the boat you paddle, the straighter it will go. To turn, paddle further from the boat. Crouch low in the boat when getting in and out. Read the tide charts so you know where the water is.

Breathe deep, paddle smart and enjoy your voyage.

GREAT FILMS FOR GIRLS

◆

W'RE NOT SAYING that you have to be a girl to enjoy these films. Or even that as a girl you'll definitely like all of these films. What we do know is that these are films that will make you laugh and cry, and that will stay with you long after you have first watched them.

Gone with the Wind

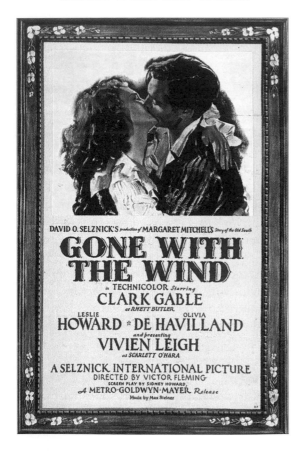

A sweeping, epic romance set against the backdrop of the American Civil War and Reconstruction, *Gone with the Wind*, adapted from the novel of the same name by Margaret Mitchell, is the story of wilful, indomitable Scarlett O'Hara. It's a story of survival, of love both requited and unrequited, and a startling portrait of its times.

★ Stars: Vivien Leigh and Clark Gable
? Did you know that this was the only novel that Margaret Mitchell ever wrote?

Rebecca

Based on the novel by Daphne du Maurier, *Rebecca* is an intense and hypnotic film directed by Alfred Hitchcock. A young bride, the second Mrs de Winter, is taken to Mandalay, the home of her new husband, Maxim de Winter, and also the home he shared with his first wife, the enigmatic and beautiful Rebecca, who died in mysterious circumstances. Rebecca haunts the story; her presence is everywhere in the house, and her faithful servant Mrs Danvers is determined not to allow the new Mrs de Winter to erase her memory.

★ Stars: Laurence Olivier, Joan Fontaine
? Did you know that in order to make Joan Fontaine feel nervous and paranoid, just like her character, Alfred Hitchcock apparently told her that everyone on set disliked her? Guaranteed to make anyone feel out of place! The only person on set who did really dislike her was Olivier, who was annoyed that his then girlfriend, Vivien Leigh, didn't get the role.

The Wizard of Oz

A classic film, *The Wizard of Oz* is a firm favourite with every generation. The songs have become part of popular culture in their own right, and this is the film that made Judy Garland a legend.

★ Stars: Judy Garland, Margaret Hamilton
❓ Did you know that Terry, the dog who played Toto, was accidentally stepped on during filming and a double had to be brought in for two weeks while she recovered?

Amélie

Amélie is a whimsical girl living in Paris whose overactive imagination gives this film its charm. Amélie is determined to give people happiness through secret and random acts of kindness, but will she ever find her own true happiness?

★ Stars: Audrey Tautou
❓ Did you know that director Jean-Pierre Jeunet had all the graffiti and rubbish cleared from the locations before he filmed there so as to make his Paris appear more magical?

Casablanca

Set in Casablanca, Morocco, just as the Second World War has broken out, this is the story of Rick Blaine, an American expat and owner of an illicit gambling den. When Ilsa, the love of his life, arrives in town with her husband, Victor, Rick finds he has a power over them; in his hands lies their chance of escape to America.

★ Stars: Ingrid Bergman, Humphrey Bogart
❓ Did you know that the actors weren't aware how the film was going to end until the very last minute?

Elizabeth

The early reign of the Virgin Queen is brought to life in this dramatic period drama. Fantastic costumes, stunning settings and history brought to life make this a film all girls should watch.

★ Stars: Cate Blanchett, Joseph Fiennes
❓ Did you know that the film was shot in a variety of locations, including York Minster, Durham Cathedral and Alnwick Castle?

Bonnie and Clyde

Based on the real story of gangsters Bonnie and Clyde and their passionate love affair, this was a huge hit when it first came out. It was also controversial in the way it was said to glamorize murder and romanticize the affair between two notorious criminals. Nevertheless, us girls like a handsome rogue – as long as he is safely ensconced on a screen!

★ Stars: Faye Dunaway, Warren Beatty
? Did you know that a non-actor, school-teacher Mabel Cavitt, was chosen to play Bonnie's mother after she was spotted off-set on location?

The African Queen

Set in East Africa during the Second World War, this is a film full of adventure. Katharine Hepburn plays Rose Sayer, a missionary in Africa who has guts and daring and is not afraid of a bit of danger.

★ Stars: Katharine Hepburn, Humphrey Bogart
? Did you know that, during a scene where Bogart's character is covered in leeches, Bogart refused to have real leeches put on him so the leeches you see are actually made of rubber?

The English Patient

As a young nurse cares for soldiers injured in battle, she determines never to get too attached to any of them, unable to bear it when they die. But one patient, a man who does not give his name, catches her attention, and draws her closer to him than she had ever intended.

★ Stars: Kristin Scott Thomas, Ralph Fiennes
? Did you know that there is a very quick reference in the film to the great explorer and archaeologist Gertrude Bell, a woman who spent many years in the Middle East, where *The English Patient* is set?

BIRD WATCHING

B IRD WATCHING might seem difficult (or even boring), but we can assure you it is not. Birds are everywhere – easy to spot and fun to observe. Most birders keep a life-list journal, a kind of bird diary, writing down the birds they see. As you begin to bird, you can use a small spiral notebook to make a life-list journal for yourself, writing down the names of the birds you find, or sketching their distinguishing features so you can look them up in a bird identification book once you're back home. All you need to go bird watching is a pair of binoculars, a good bird guidebook, comfortable clothes, your life-list journal – and some patience. Bird watching demands a certain kind of presence on the part of the birder. You must become a part of nature rather than stand outside it. Here are eight common birds to start you off on a lifetime pursuit of bird watching.

Robin

The robin is a popular bird and a regular visitor to gardens and allotments. It can be seen throughout Europe and is recognizable by its grey-green head and orange underbelly (usually brighter in the male). During the breeding season female robins build cup-shaped nests, mostly in shrubs and bushes but sometimes in odd places like toilet cisterns or barrels! The robin's song sounds like a whistled musical phrase and can be heard all year round, including at night.

Cool fact:
In the children's story *Babes in the Wood* robins come across the bodies of two children abandoned in the forest and cover them up with leaves to protect them.

Blue Tit

The blue tit is a pretty little bird resident in the UK which is yellow on the underside with blue wings, tail and cap. They are cheeky birds, not particularly timid, and were among the first birds in the UK to start feeding from domestic bird tables in people's gardens. Their population is on the increase, maybe partly due to their ability to find food all year round, crucial as they don't migrate to warmer countries during winter.

Birding Tips from Peter Cashwell

(author of *The Verb 'To Bird'*)

1 Get up early. It's good to get outside before sunrise if you want to see and hear birds with the fewest possible distractions (traffic, factory noise, etc.). You can keep birding all day, of course, but the early morning is the best time.

2 Learn a few common birds' appearances well. They give you something to compare to the bird you saw. If you know the robin, you can tell whether this bird was smaller than a robin, or had a whiter belly, or had a thicker bill.

3 Set up a feeder or a birdbath. This brings birds into your garden where you can watch them up close and over a long time. You'll probably also attract several different kinds of birds, which will help you with no.2.

4 Bird with others. More experienced birders can show you all kinds of things you'd probably miss on your own, and most birders like to show less experienced birders the ropes. Even if it's just you and a friend who doesn't know much about birds, two sets of eyes will see more than one (and two sets of field marks will help you figure out what you saw).

5 Bird everywhere. You don't have to be in a national park to see unusual or interesting birds. Some will be at the beach, others in the city park, still others in your garden, and some in that empty plot across the road. Keep looking and you'll see things everywhere.

Cool facts:

Baby blue tits are not actually blue; they start life a more yellow colour and become more blue as they grow older. Blue tits are also responsible for pecking into the foil milk bottle caps and drinking the cream from the top of the pint. As less milk is delivered to the door nowadays, they are having to find alternative sources of food.

Common Kingfisher

The common kingfisher is found by water in the UK. It is the only type of kingfisher found here, and it can be identified by its bright, almost metallic blue upper body and orange lower body and its quick, almost whirring way of flying. It catches its food from the water by perching on sticks protruding from the surface, and its main diet consists of small fish and insects.

Cool fact:

When feeding, the common kingfisher plunges and dives into the water, sometimes submerging entirely to catch its prey.

Kestrel

Kestrels are the commonest bird of prey in the UK. They are large birds with a wing span of around 70–80 centimetres. They tend to hover around 20 metres off the ground, on the lookout for prey. They are not choosy about what they eat and are capable of catching and killing small mammals such as voles and other smaller birds. Their strong eyesight enables them to spot prey from a distance before swooping in for the kill.

Cool fact:

Kestrels sometimes catch their prey and save it for later, to ensure that they don't find themselves without food later in the day. They need to eat around six to eight voles a day to keep them in good condition.

Mallard

The mallard is the most common duck in the UK, and it is said that all other ducks are descended from it. The male has a distinctive green head and grey body, and the female is a drabber brown colour. You'll find them everywhere from local duck ponds to rivers and lakes, and you have almost certainly fed them bread at least once. Mallard ducklings are yellow and brown and can often be seen following the mother mallard in a line.

Cool fact:
When mallards dip their heads into the water, leaving their tails sticking up, they are looking for food under the surface of the water. This movement is called 'dabbling'; drop that into your conversation to impress your friends!

Mute Swan

This is the official name for the birds we usually just refer to as swans. Mute swans are large white birds that live on rivers and lakes. Many people believe that they pair for life, but this is not always the case. They are incredibly loyal to their mate and can be aggressive when defending them. Britain's heaviest birds, they can weigh up to 15 kilos.

Cool fact:
It is a widely known fact that the Queen owns all the swans in England. This is not actually true: she owns all except those owned by the Dyers and Vintners – two livery companies of the City of London.

Tawny Owl

The tawny owl is the commonest owl in the UK. It is a nocturnal bird, which means that you will have to get out and about at night if you are ever to catch a glimpse of it. You have most likely heard its distinctive 'twit twoo' call, but did you know that the 'twit' is the male and the 'twoo' is the female? We didn't make that up, honestly!

Cool fact:
The tawny owl may look sweet, but don't get too close to it as it can be fierce in defending its nest and young. Humans have been injured and even killed by tawny owls.

And now, a birding poem to inspire you:

A Bird Came Down the Walk
by Emily Dickinson

A Bird came down the Walk –
He did not know I saw –
He bit an angle-worm in halves
And ate the fellow, raw.

And then he drank a Dew
From a convenient Grass
And then hopped sidewise to the Wall
To let a Beetle pass –

He glanced with rapid eyes
That hurried all abroad –
They looked like frightened Beads,
    I thought –
He stirred his velvet head

Like one in danger, Cautious,
I offered him a Crumb,
And he unrolled his feathers
And rowed him softer home –

Than Oars divide the Ocean
Too silver for a seam –
Or Butterflies, off Banks of Noon,
Leap, plashless as they swim.

RULES OF THE GAME: LACROSSE

---◆---

WE OFTEN THINK OF LACROSSE as a sport played and originated in British public schools, but in fact it was first played by native North Americans as far back as the fifteenth century. It came to the UK in the nineteenth century, and has been played here ever since.

EQUIPMENT

Lacrosse is played with a crosse: a wooden stick with a net at the end which is used to catch and throw the ball between players.

TEAM

A lacrosse team is made up of twelve players: normally five attackers, six defenders and a goalkeeper.

HOW TO PLAY

The game is played in two halves of thirty minutes each way on a pitch made up of a goal at either end with two restraining lines and a centre section. The aim of the game is to score goals by throwing the balls into your opponents' goal.

Play starts at the centre point as a member from each team crosses sticks and a ball is thrown into the air. The first girl to catch it gets possession of the ball. If you catch the ball, you may run with it in your crosse or pass it to another player in your team. Your opponents will try to take control of the ball either by intercepting it during a throw or by trying to dislodge it from your crosse. This is called a 'check' and the player performing the check must be in front of the player with the ball and must not lean across her to try to tap the ball out of her crosse.

If the ball is thrown out of the boundary of the pitch, the player closest to it when it went out is given possession.

The restraining line at each end of the pitch marks off the area where only seven attackers and eight defenders are allowed at any one time. Within this area is a semicircle in front of the goal where players must keep at least one stick-length away from each other.

FOULS

There are two types of foul: major and minor.

Major fouls include blocking another player, slashing at another player with your crosse, charging into or at another player, throwing a ball in a dangerous or uncontrolled way, and obstructing another player.

Minor fouls include using your body to hit the ball for your own advantage, using your hand to ward off another player, checking a player who doesn't have the ball in her crosse, and fouling in the goal area.

The penalty for fouls is a free position for the player fouled against. Major fouls result in the offending player having to stand four metres behind the girl with the free position while she is allowed to take the ball. Minor fouls result in the offender having to stand four metres off from the girl with the free position, in the direction that she came from when she committed the foul.

MATHS TRICKS

———— ◆ ————

EARLY IN THE LAST CENTURY, sometime between 1911 and 1918, a Hindu scholar and mathematician discovered ancient Indian scriptures outlining a series of mathematical formulas. This hitherto unexplored section of the ancient Indian Vedas, the sacred text written around 1500–900 BC, had been dismissed by scholars who had been unable to decipher any of the mathematics. But Sri Bharati Krishna Tirthaji dedicated himself to translating and examining the texts and, after years of study, he was able to reconstruct what turned out to be a unique system of aphorisms, or easily remembered rules, used to solve a range of mathematical problems from simple arithmetic to trigonometry and calculus. He called this 'Vedic Mathematics', playing on both meanings of the word *veda*, which essentially means 'knowledge' but also refers to the ancient sacred literature of Hinduism, which dates back over 4,000 years. There are sixteen total *sutras*, or sayings, in Vedic maths. The three discussed below will help in many of your everyday maths problems: 'By one more than the one before' (*Ekadhikina Purvena*); 'All from 9 and the last from 10' (*Nikhilam Navatashcaramam Dashatah*); and 'vertically and crosswise' (*Urdhva-Tiryagbyham*).

'By one more than the one before'

Remembering this sutra when squaring numbers ending in 5 can help you come up with the answer quickly, and without having to write anything down.

For instance: let's take the number 35^2. To find the answer the usual way, we'd multiply 35 by 35 by writing down the numbers, doing the multiplication and addition, and finally arriving at 1225. Using this first sutra, 'By one more than the one before', we can do this problem in our heads. The answer has two parts to it: since the number we're squaring ends in 5, the last two numbers will always be 25, because 5×5 is 25. To arrive at the first two numbers, we use the sutra multiplying 'by one more than the one before'. In '35', the number 'before' the last number is 3. 'One more' than 3 is 4. So we multiply 3 by 4 to get 12. We know the last two digits of our answer will be 25. So 1225 is our answer.

Let's try another example: 15^2
We know the last part of our answer will be 25. Following the 'by one more than the one before' rule, we need to multiply the first numeral in '15' by one more than itself. So that's 1 (our first numeral) multiplied by 2 (one more than our first numeral, 1), which equals 2. So our answer is 225.

Another example: 105^2
We know the last part of our answer will be 25. Following the 'by one more than the one before' rule, we need to multiply 10 by 11 (one more than 10), which equals 110. So our answer is 11025.

'All from 9 and the last from 10'

This is an easy rule for subtracting numbers from 100, 1000, 10,000, etc.

In the equation '10,000 – 6347', you can figure the answer by using 'all from the 9 and the last from 10': subtracting each of the digits in 6347 from 9, except the last digit, which you subtract from 10. So that's 9 minus 6 (which is 3), 9 minus 3 (which is 6), 9 minus 4 (which is 5), and 10 minus 7 (which is 3), which gives you the answer 3653. This rule works when you have one zero for each digit you're subtracting – no more, no less. Here are some examples in action:

$$100 - 47 = 53 \qquad 1000 - 345 = 655 \qquad 10,000 - 4,572 = 5,428$$

'Vertically and crosswise'

This can be used for multiplying numbers and also adding and subtracting fractions. Let's tackle fractions first, adding $^6/_7$ and $^5/_3$. The way we have traditionally been taught to compute this can get a bit complicated. But using 'vertically and crosswise', we can do this in our heads.

$$\frac{6}{7} \times \frac{5}{3} = \frac{18 + 35}{21} = \frac{53}{21}$$

To get the 'top' part of our answer, we multiply 6 by 3 and 7 by 5. That gives us 18 and 35. Add those together to get our final top number, 53. For the bottom number we multiply the two bottom numbers of our equation, 7 and 3. That gives 21, and so our answer is $^{53}/_{21}$.

Let's try another example: $^{3}/_{2} + ^{5}/_{6}$

$$\frac{3}{2} \times \frac{5}{6} = \frac{18 + 10}{12} = \frac{28}{12}$$

To get the top number of our answer, multiply 3 × 6 (that gives us 18) and 2 × 5 (that gives us 10), then add those together (28). To get the bottom number, multiply the two bottom numbers of the equation, 2 and 6. That gives us 12. So our answer is $^{28}/_{12}$.

This works the same with subtracting fractions. Let's use our second example, subtracting instead of adding this time: $^{3}/_{2} - ^{5}/_{6}$

$$\frac{3}{2} \times \frac{5}{6} = \frac{18 - 10}{12} = \frac{8}{12}$$

To get the top number of our answer, multiply 3 × 6 (that makes 18) and 2 × 5 (that's 10), then subtract instead of add: 18 − 10 = 8. That's our top number. Multiply the bottom two numbers of the equation, 2 and 6, and that gives us our bottom number, 12. Our answer is $^{8}/_{12}$ (which can be further reduced to $^{2}/_{3}$).

'Vertically and crosswise' also works with multiplying numbers. If you've memorized your times-tables, you might know some basic multiplication by rote. But Vedic maths offers a creative way to arrive at answers to long multiplication problems that makes multiplying even more fun.

Multiplying 21 × 23 the usual way will get us an answer of 483, but using Vedic maths will help us get there faster. Imagine 23 sitting just below 21 and multiply vertically and crosswise, using the following three steps, to arrive at the answer:

$$\begin{array}{r} 2 \quad 1 \\ \times \ 2 \quad 3 \\ \hline 4 \ 8 \ 3 \end{array}$$

1. Multiply vertically on the right to get the final digit of the answer. In this case, that's 1 × 3, which equals 3.
2. Multiply crosswise and then add to get the middle digit of the answer. In this case, that's 2 × 3 added to 1 × 2, which gives us 8. (If multiplying crosswise and adding gives you 10 or over, you'll have to carry over the first digit of the number and add that to the answer in step 3.)

3. Multiply vertically on the left (and then add any carried-over number, if necessary) to get the first digit of the answer. In this case, that's 2 × 2, which equals 4.

Here's another example: 61 × 31

Multiply vertically on the right (1 × 1) to get the final digit of the answer (1); multiply crosswise (6 × 1 and 1 × 3) and then add to get the middle digit (9); and multiply vertically on the left (6 × 3) to get the first digit of your answer (18). The result is 1891.

With two-digit numbers that are close to 100, you can use 'vertically and crosswise' as follows. Let's try 88 × 97. Write out the equation and then subtract both 88 and 97 from 100, writing the results to the right, as shown below. (100 − 88 is 12, and 100 − 97 is 3, so write 12 to the right of 88 and 3 to the right of 97.)

Now use 'vertically and crosswise': Multiply the two numbers on the right to get the last two digits of your answer – in this case 36 (12 × 3 = 36). Subtract crosswise, either 88 − 3 or 97 − 12 (it doesn't matter which one you use, as they will both result in the same answer!), to arrive at the first two digits of your answer: 85. So your final answer is 8536.

In some instances, you may have to carry over. For example, let's try 90 × 76. Write this out as before, with 90 above 76. You can use the 'all from 9 and the last from 10' rule to subtract both 90 and 76 from 100: write the corresponding answers to the right, as shown below.

Multiply the numbers on the right to get the last two digits of the answer. But in this case, 10 × 24 gives us 240 – a three-digit number. The 2 in 240 is our extra digit, and it must be carried over. Write down 40 beneath the 10 and 24, and carry the 2 over, writing it on top of the 90 so you don't forget to add it later. Now subtract crosswise, 76 − 10 or 90 − 24. Either way will give you the answer of 66. To that, add the 2 you carried over. That gives you 68, the first two digits of your answer. Your final answer is 6840.

RULES OF THE GAME: DARTS

◆

DARTS IS ANOTHER GAME with a long history. The game is thought to have been invented by soldiers throwing arrows at the bottom of tree trunks or wooden casks. Modern dartboards are most commonly made of boar bristles or sisal fibres (or, in the case of Velcro dart games, felt). Playing darts takes some practice and some maths skills, but mostly it's just fun to throw something across the room. Make sure you give annoying siblings and small animals a wide berth.

Setting up the board

A regulation board has a diameter of 45 centimetres and is divided by thin metal wire into 22 sections. Make sure to mount your dartboard so that the centre of the double bull (the bull's-eye) is 173 centimetres from the floor. Mark the toeline, called the oche (pronounced to rhyme with 'hockey'), 237 centimetres from the face of the board.

Basic rules

To determine shooting order, each player shoots for the bull's-eye. The one who comes closest gets to go first. Each turn consists of three darts, which must be thrown from behind the oche. For a throw to count, the point of the dart must touch the board. If a dart bounces off the board or misses it completely, it does not get a score (and also can't be rethrown).

Scoring

The dartboard is divided into wedges, with point values marked along the outer edge of the circle. Two rings overlap the playing area; landing outside these rings scores a player face-value points for that area of the board. Landing between the first inner ring and the second inner ring scores a player double the points for that section. Landing between the second inner ring and the bull's-eye earns triple points. Hitting outside the outer wire scores nothing.

How to throw

First, aim. Look at the target you want to hit. Lift your arm up, bent at the elbow so that the sharp end of the dart faces the dartboard. The dart should be tipped slightly up. Check your aim and line up the dart with your sight line. Move the hand holding the dart back towards your body, then pitch the dart forward, releasing the dart and making sure to follow through with your arm. The optimal follow-through will end with your hand pointing at the target (not having your hand fall to your side). When throwing, try not to move your body – the throwing action should come from your shoulder.

PLAYING THE GAME: THE 301

The object of this game, which is most commonly played by two people, is to start with a score of 301 and count down to exactly zero. Each player has a three-throw turn, and the point value of their hits is subtracted from 301. A player can only start subtracting once they 'double' – that is, hit one of the doubles on the board. Once that is accomplished, the scores will begin to count. If the total score of the three throws exceeds the remaining score for that player, the score returns to what it was at the start of the turn. A double must be hit to end the game.

PLAYING THE GAME: ROUND THE CLOCK

In this game, players take turns trying to hit each number, from 1 to 20. Each player has a three-throw turn; players advance to the next number on the board by hitting each number in order. The first person to get to 20 wins.

PLAYING THE GAME: CRICKET

This strategy game is typically played with two players, or two teams of two players each. To win at Cricket, a player must 'close' the numbers 15 to 20 and the bull's-eye before any other player, and must also have the highest point count. 'Closing' a number means hitting it three times in one or more turns (hitting a single closes a number in three throws; hitting a double and then a single closes a number in two throws; and hitting a triple closes a number in a single throw). You don't have to close numbers in any particular order – but you do want to close them before the other players.

To keep track of the score, you'll need a scoreboard (a blackboard on the wall or a pen and pad of paper will work). Write out the numbers vertically for each player, from 20 down to 15, then 'B' for bull's-eye. Each player's turn consists of three throws and only darts that land in the numbers 15–20 or in the bull's-eye count. (You don't get points for hitting numbers 1–14.) Points start to accumulate once a number is closed and are tallied as follows: the centre of the bull's-eye is worth 50 points and the outer ring of the bull's-eye gets 25; numbers 15–20 are worth their face value, but landing in the doubles ring doubles the number's value and landing in the triple ring (the inner ring between the doubles ring and the bull's-eye) triples it.

When a player hits a number once, you put a slash (/) by the number. When that number is hit a second time by a player, you turn the slash into an X. When that number is 'closed', or hit a third time, you draw a circle around the X. Once a number has been closed, if any player hits it, the points for that number go to the player who originally closed it. Once a number has been closed by all the players, no points are awarded for that number for the rest of the game. Total up the points after one player closes all her numbers plus the bull's-eye, and the person or team with the highest number of points is the winner.

Darts Lingo

Arrows: Darts

Bust: Hitting a number higher than you need to go out

Chucker: Indifferent thrower

Clock: Dartboard

Double In: Starting a game with a double

Double Out: Winning a game on a double

Hat Trick: Three bull's-eyes

Leg: One game of a match

Slop: Hitting a number other than the one intended

Trombones: A total turn score of 76 points

Wet Feet: Standing with your feet over the line

WORDS TO IMPRESS

◆

STRUNK AND WHITE, in *The Elements of Style,* tell us about sesquipedalian words: 'Do not be tempted by a twenty-dollar word when there is a ten-center handy, ready and able.' But daring girls are never afraid to drop a spectacular multisyllabic bombshell when necessary. Here are some you can use when quotidian vocabulary fails.

aleatoric
(EY-lee-uh-tohr-ik)
dependent on luck or a random outcome, like a roll of the dice
Aurora just laughed when doubters attributed her triumph over the pirate rogues to aleatoric influences.

brobdingnagian
(brob-ding-NAG-ee-uhn)
gigantic, enormous, tremendous
Lisa made constant use of her brobdingnagian vocabulary.

callipygian
(kal-uh-PIJ-ee-uhn)
having shapely buttocks
Jen's callipygian beauty was matched only by her strong right hook.

crepuscular
(kri-PUHS-kyuh-ler)
dim; resembling or having to do with twilight
Janet's habit of planning all her best pranks to occur immediately after dinner led her mother to declare her utterly crepuscular in nature.

diaphanous
(dahy-AF-uh-nuhs)
almost entirely transparent or translucent
Halloween had been a success, thought Belinda, even though little children kept bumping into her costume's diaphanous fairy wings.

echolalia
(ek-oh-LEY-lee-uh)
repeating or echoing a person's speech, often in a pathological way
The baby's curious echolalia almost sounded like real conversation.

frangible
(FRAN-juh-bull)
fragile; easily broken; brittle
After seeing what happened to his brothers, the third little pig resolved to build his house from a less frangible material.

frustraneous
(fruhs-TREY-nee-uhs)
vain; useless; frustrating
After several frustraneous attempts, Katie gave up on trying to get her sister's attention.

gustatory
(GUHS-tuh-tohr-ee)
of or pertaining to taste or tasting
Rachel dug into her dinner with gustatory glee.

hagiology
(hag-ee-OL-uh-jee)
literature dealing with the lives of saints; a list of saints
Julie's notebook was practically a hagiology of current boy bands.

ineluctable
(in-ih-LUCK-tuh-bull)
inevitable, inescapable
(From the Latin word *luctari,* 'to wrestle'.)
Sarah was unable to escape the ineluctable gaze of her mother.

jejune
(ji-JOON)
immature, uninteresting, dull; lacking nutrition
Molly resolved to use an interesting vocabulary, the better to avoid appearing jejune.

knurl

(nurl)

a knob, knot, or other small protuberance; one of a series of small ridges or grooves on the surface or edge of a metal object, such as a thumbscrew, to aid in gripping
Felicity learned to rock climb by grabbing on to the knurls all the way up the wall.

languorous

(LANG-ger-uhs)

lacking spirit or liveliness; dreamy; lazy
Amelia spent a languorous day by the pool.

luculent

(LOO-kyoo-luhnt)

easily understood; clear or lucid
Sometimes Rebecca's homework needed to be a little more luculent.

mellifluous

(muh-LIF-loo-uhs)

flowing with sweetness or honey; smooth and sweet
Anna always enjoyed chorus; she knew her voice was mellifluous.

miasma

(mahy-AZ-muh)

foul vapours emitted from rotting matter; unwholesome air or atmosphere
Jemima held her nose as she passed the miasma of what her little brother referred to as 'the stinky parking garage'.

natalitious

(nay-tuh-LIH-shis)

pertaining to one's birthday
Mary designed elaborate invitations to announce her natalitious festivities.

nemesis

(NEM-uh-sis)

a source of harm; an opponent that cannot be beaten; mythological Greek goddess of vengeance
On a good day, Christina's brother was her ally; on a bad day, he was her nemesis.

obsequious

(uhb-SEE-kwee-uhs)

fawning; attentive in an ingratiating manner
Eager to win her parents' approval, Vanessa was polite to the point of being obsequious.

persiflage

(PURR-suh-flahzh)

light banter; frivolous discussion
'We must be careful to keep our persiflage to a minimum,' Harriet whispered to Margot during class.

quiescence

(kwee-ES-uhns)

stillness, quietness, inactivity
Hannah revelled in the extraordinary quiescence of early morning when she awoke before anyone else.

quotidian

(kwoh-TIHD-ee-uhn)

everyday, commonplace, ordinary; recurring daily
Dorothy sighed, bored by the quotidian sameness of it all.

rapprochement

(rap-rohsh-MAHN)

reconciliation; the reestablishing of cordial relations
After holding a grudge against him for so long, Eleanor felt it was almost a relief to have reached a rapprochement with her brother.

risible

(RIZ-uh-buhl)

laughable, causing laughter
The girls knew they could always count on Polly for a risible remark.

sesquipedalian

(SESS-kwih-puh-DAY-lee-un)

characteristic of a long word; given to using long words
Daring girls are not shy about their sesquipedalian abilities.

sprezzatura

(SPRETTS-ah-TOO-ruh)

nonchalance, effortlessness
After reading The Daring Book for Girls, *Emily was able to cartwheel with sprezzatura and verve.*

Truculent
(TRUCK-yuh-lunt)
pugnacious, belligerent,
scathing
*When Nancy was pushed too
far, she became truculent.*

ultracrepidarian
(ull-truh-krep-ih-DAIR-
ee-uhn)
giving opinions or criticizing
beyond one's own range of
expertise
*'I'd tell you what I think about
your outfit, but I don't want to
be all ultracrepidarian,' said
Karen.*

vitiate
(VISH-ee-ayt)
to weaken, impair, or render
invalid
*Penelope's debate in class
vitiated Rob's argument.*

winsome
(WIN-suhm)
sweetly or innocently
charming
*Holly was too busy building
her treehouse to act winsome.*

xenophobe
(ZEE-nuh-fohb)
a person who fears or hates
foreigners
*It was a nerve-racking
moment at the picnic, when
the neighbourhood xenophobe
showed up with potato salad.*

yawl
(yawl)
a ship's small boat; a yowl or
howl
*Helen let out a loud yawl as
the boat tipped over.*

zaftig
(ZAHF-tik)
having a shapely figure (From
the Yiddish word *zaftik*,
'juicy'.)
*Bridget was proud of her
strong, zaftig figure.*

zeitgeist
(TSIYT-giyst)
the spirit of the time; the
outlook of a particular
generation
*Catherine was convinced the
latest pop star embodied the
zeitgeist of her contemporaries.*

TREE SWING

◆

What you need

* Wood, 60 centimetres × 20 centimetres long
* Rope
* Two eyebolts, 20 centimetres long, with a
  1-centimetre thread, two nuts and four washers
* A tennis ball, a sock, and some string
* Drill with 1-centimetre bit

THE HARDEST PART of building a tree swing is
finding a well-suited branch. We can tell you that a tree-
swing branch should be at least 20 centimetres in diameter,

but on a tree tall enough for a swing, that can be difficult to measure precisely. You'll also need a strong rope long enough to get around the branch and down to the ground and back up again.

Your swing should not be on a birch tree, because those rubbery branches readily bend. Look for a hardy oak or maple. The spot on the branch where you hang your swing should be far enough from the trunk so no one is hurt when they swing, but close enough so the branch is still strong.

The second hardest part is getting the rope up and over the branch. To forestall several hours of standing with a rope and squinting into the sun, we have a strategy to suggest:

* Put a tennis ball in an old sock. Wrap string around the sock and make a knot so the tennis ball stays put, and make sure you have enough string on the skein so it can unfurl the length up to the tree branch, and back down again.

* Stand under the tree and aim the tennis ball in the sock over the branch. It may take a few tries, but it is much easier than just flinging the rope up to the branch.

* Once up and over, the tennis-ball sock will land near your feet, trailed by a long strand of string. Knot the string to the rope to be used in the tree swing. (Try a sheetbend knot, it's designed to join different sized-ropes.) Pull the string until the rope is over the branch. You might want to toss the ball/rope combo over again, to double-loop the rope over the branch. When all is in place, detach the string. The rope is set.

The easiest part is making the seat and procuring a long length of knot. Find or cut a 60-centimetre-long piece of 20 centimetre-wide wood. Draw a line down the centre, lengthwise, and measure 5 centimetres in from either side. That's where to drill the two holes. Put an eyebolt through each hole, with a washer above the wood and a washer and nut below it. Knot the two ends of the rope to the eyes of the eyebolt (a tautline hitch is handy here).

If you don't want to use the bolts, you can push the ropes themselves through the holes and tie with strong stopper knots.

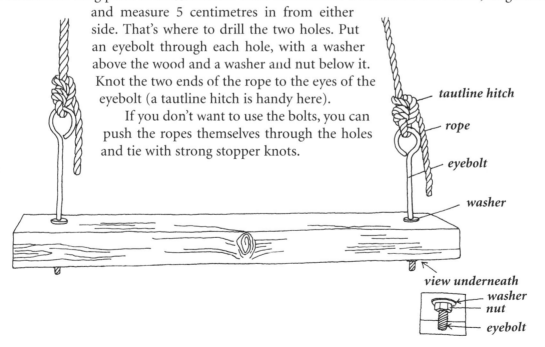

tautline hitch

rope

eyebolt

washer

view underneath
washer
nut
eyebolt

TREE SWING

YOGA: SUN SALUTATION
(surya namaskara)

◆

THE WORD *yoga* comes from the Sanskrit root *yuj*, 'to yoke' or 'to unite', and dates from roughly 5000 BC according to Vedic texts. In the sun salutation, as with all flowing or dynamic yoga postures, what is joined is your movement and your breathing. The sun salutation – *surya namaskara* in Sanskrit – is done differently depending on which style of yoga you choose to follow, but in its most basic form, it is a series of 12 or so postures (*asanas*) linking movement with inhalation and exhalation. Here is the Ashtanga yoga version of the most basic sun salutation.

The most important thing to keep in mind when doing any kind of yoga is your breathing: inhaling with each extension or stretch and exhaling as you fold or contract. The best way to breathe during this exercise is to first suck in your stomach so that it feels like your belly button is pulled back towards your spine. Now keep it there and breathe – through your nose, with your mouth closed – deeply into your chest. Your chest should rise and fall with your breath as your stomach stays tight, and you should breathe this way through the entire series.

Traditionally, the sun salutation is performed at sunrise – if you're really hard-core, it's done just before dawn, facing the east, with mantras and libations in honour of the sun god, but you don't have to go that far. First thing in the morning, on an empty stomach, is good enough. In fact, the sun salutation can be done any time you feel like taking a moment to

1
tadasana
(mountain)

2
hasta uttanasana
(raised arm pose)
inhale

3
uttanasana A
(standing
forward bend)
exhale

4
uttanasana B
(forward bend with
flat back)
inhale

5
chaturanga dandasana
(four limb staff pose)
exhale

6
urdhva muhka svanasana
(upward-facing dog)
inhale

breathe, move and become energized. It can be a foundation for your yoga practise, or it can be a practice in and of itself. Either way, the sun salutation is something you can do for the rest of your life.

What you need

If you have a yoga mat or yoga rug, use that – otherwise, take a large beach towel and lay it on the ground outside, or on the floor inside. (If you're doing the sun salutation inside and are using a towel, make sure to do it on a non-slippery surface.)

1 Stand in *tadasana*, 'mountain pose'. Your feet and toes should be firmly on the ground, your arms at your sides, your shoulders back and your neck long. Take a few breaths to prepare yourself (remember to breathe through your nose, with your bellybutton pulled in towards your spine).

2 Inhale and raise your arms out to the side, palms up, bringing them up overhead until your palms touch. This is *hasta uttanasana*, raised arm pose. Raise your gaze so that you look up at your thumbs. Try not to

tilt your head back or scrunch up your eyebrows when you look up and also try to keep your shoulders from creeping up around your ears.

3 Exhale as you bring your arms down in front of you and move into a forward bend (*uttanasana*). If you can place your hands on the ground next to your feet, great. If not, place your hands on your ankles or knees. Try to keep your back extended rather than rounded; if it feels like too much on your lower back, you can bend your knees slightly.

7
adho muhka svanasana
(downward-facing dog)
exhale,
hold for five breaths

8
jump forward to

9
uttanasana B
inhale

10
uttanasana A
(standing forward
bend)
exhale

11
hasta uttanasana
(raised arm pose)
inhale

12
tadasana
exhale

4 Inhale as you look up, your shoulders back and your fingertips still touching the ground (or your ankles/knees). Your back should be flat and you should feel like a diver just about to dive into the pool.

5 Place your palms on the mat, fingers spread, and exhale as you jump or walk back into *chaturanga dandasana,* a low push-up position. Unlike a regular push-up, in this posture your elbows need to stay very close to your body and your upper arms should be squeezing against your ribcage. The weight of your body is on your hands and your toes. Take care not to sag your hips down; your body should be a straight line. If this is too much, keep your hands and toes where they are and lower the knees to the ground to help support yourself.

6 From here, inhale as you push yourself forward into *urdhva muhka svanasana* (upward-facing dog). Push from your toes as you roll through from a flexed foot position to a pointed-toe position. Your hands and the tops of your toes should be the only parts of your body touching the ground. Look up as you arch your back, and try to keep those shoulders down (and those eyebrows from rising).

7 Exhale as you lift yourself back into *adho muhka svanasana* (downward-facing dog), rolling back over your toes to the soles of your feet and keeping your palms on the floor. Stay here for five deep breaths. When you look at your feet as you breathe in this posture, you should not be able to see your heels. Move your heels so they are in line with your ankles and try to think about the soles of your feet moving towards the floor. Looking up towards your stomach will help keep you from hyperextending around your back and ribcage. Think about moving your chest towards your feet and your head towards the floor.

8 Look towards your hands as you bend your knees and either jump or walk your feet to your hands.

9 Inhale as you look up with a flat back, your fingertips on the floor (*uttanasana* B).

10 Exhale as you bend forward into a full forward bend (*uttanasana* A). Think about having your stomach and chest on your thighs rather than curving over with a rounded back.

11 Inhale as you lift all the way up into *hasta uttanasana,* looking up towards your thumbs as your palms touch.

12 Exhale as you return to *tadasana,* mountain pose.

WOMEN WHO CHANGED
THE WORLD

❖

The Suffrage Movement

T HE RIGHT TO VOTE is something we tend to take for granted today, but it was hard won by women only a few generations ago. It is a part of history that is vital for every girl to know. You should never take for granted something so important.

The **1832 Reform Act** was instrumental in bringing into life the Women's Suffrage movement. It was passed with the intention of updating the voting system, which was agreed to be outdated and archaic, but it only gave suffrage (the right to vote) to men who owned property producing an annual income of over £10. This provoked debate about women's entitlement to suffrage, but it wasn't until forty years later that organized women's suffrage movements were first formed by women determined to get what they saw as their democratic rights.

SUFFRAGISTS V. SUFFRAGETTES

You may have heard both these names when people refer to the Women's Suffrage movement. They sound very similar, but they actually refer to two distinct groups of women who pursued two very different ways of achieving the same end.

Suffragists were on the whole a peaceful group whose aim was to achieve the vote for women through non-violent protest. In 1897 the National Union of Women's Suffrage Societies (NUWSS) was formed, with the intention of achieving the vote for women through education and democratic reform. Led by Millicent Fawcett, the group argued that women paid taxes, as men did, and ought to be afforded the same rights in choosing their government as men.

Suffragettes distinguished themselves from the Suffragists in that they were prepared to

take violent and direct action to achieve their aims. They reasoned that the Suffragists were failing in their non-confrontational approach

and that a more direct style was needed. So in 1903 Emmeline Pankhurst formed the Women's Social and Political Union (WSPU), a group that would take militant action. Its members, who included Pankhurst's daughters Christabel and Sylvia, chained themselves to railings, disrupted meetings, damaged property, and even firebombed and destroyed part of the house belonging to the prominent politician David Lloyd George, who was soon to become Prime Minister. And it was the Suffragettes who had their first martyr: Emily Davison who was killed when she threw herself under the King's horse at the Derby.

THE FIRST WORLD WAR

The activities of both groups were disrupted by the outbreak of the First World War as women set aside their protests in favour of patriotic activities in a time of war. But it was actually the war that allowed women to prove themselves. As the men went to fight, women were left to take over traditionally male roles in order to keep the economy running. Women worked as farm labourers, in munition factories, in aircraft manufacture. They also took on paid work just in order to survive financially and physically. Nursing was also a hugely important role, and women found themselves in the thick of war in a way they hadn't before.

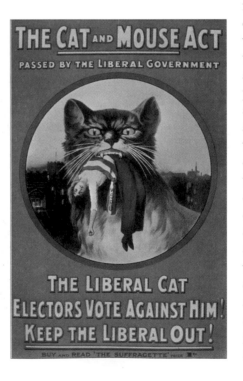

VICTORY!

As the war drew to a close, the strength the women of Britain had demonstrated was rewarded as they were given the right to vote in 1918. It was a victory and a step towards equality, but it didn't go all the way. The right to vote was only extended to women over the age of 30 who were either householders or the wives of householders. It wasn't until 1928 that women were given the same rights as men, and women over the age of 21 were allowed to vote. In 1969 the voting age was lowered to 18, where it remains today.

IMPORTANT TERMS

The Cat and Mouse Act This was a law passed by Parliament in 1913 which allowed prisons to release inmates who were ill and also allowed for their re-imprisonment on their recovery. This Act was passed in response to the Suffragette hunger strikers who, once in prison, would refuse food as a continued political stand. Under the Act these women would be released once they became too weak to remain in prison, and in effect they were too weak to continue their struggle once they were free. If they committed another act of violence once they were out they could be re-arrested, where it was assumed that they would go back on hunger strike and the whole process would start again. It was an aggressive attempt by the government to try to control the Suffragette movement, but in reality it had very little effect.

Enfranchise To give someone the vote, literally to liberate

NUWSS National Union of Women's Suffrage Societies, often called the Suffragists

Suffrage The civil right to vote

WSPU Women's Social and Political Union, often called the Suffragettes

KEY FIGURES

Emmeline Pankhurst is seen by many as the pre-eminent Suffragette. She was born Emmeline Gouldon in 1858 and in 1879 married Richard Pankhurst, himself a prominent supporter of women's rights. When Richard died suddenly in 1898, Emmeline threw herself into political activism on a greater scale. In 1903 she formed the Women's Social and Political Union

(WSPU) and was instrumental in the militant action taken by the group. She was arrested several times and went on hunger strike while in prison. Undeterred, she continued her political activism. Once the First World War broke out she transferred her energies into making sure that women were allowed to take over the traditionally male jobs, organizing a mass rally of over 30,000 women in Hyde Park in 1914. Emmeline was still leading the WSPU in 1918 when women were enfranchised. She died at the age of 68, having achieved her goal.

Emily Davison was a passionate Suffragette. She was committed to the WSPU from its creation and voiced her call for women's suffrage through a series of direct actions which included breaking the windows of the House of Commons, arson attacks and, once in prison, hunger strikes. She strongly believed that it would take only one act of martyrdom to make the Establishment see sense and give women the vote. So in 1913 she made the ultimate sacrifice for her cause and threw herself under King George V's horse at the Derby. Little did she realize that this act would actually create more controversy, with men arguing that if this was the way women behaved they couldn't be trusted with the vote. She was buried with their slogan 'Deeds Not Words' on her headstone.

Millicent Fawcett founded the moderate National Union of Women's Suffrage Societies (NUWSS) in 1897 and was a leading Suffragist. Born Millicent Garrett in 1847, she saw the need for equality for women from a young age and, with her sisters Elizabeth and

Emily, planned to study the male-dominated subjects of Politics, Medicine and Education (respectively). In the 1860s and early 1870s she was involved in a series of lectures for women that led to the foundation of Newnham College, Cambridge, the second college in the UK to admit women (the first being Girton College, Cambridge). As a Suffragist she distanced herself from the militant actions of the Suffragettes, which she saw as damaging to the cause and only alienating the Establishment. She died in 1929, just a year after women were given equal suffrage to men.

Josephine Butler was a passionate campaigner not only for women's rights but for the rights of all vulnerable people. She supported the fight for women's suffrage as she saw the role of women as one of caring and supporting the weak of the country and she hoped that enabling women to vote would result in a more equal and socially responsible society as a whole. Born in 1828, she was somewhat older than many other leading women in the women's suffrage movement. She campaigned against the Contagious Diseases Act of the 1860s, which she saw as degrading to women; it was finally repealed in 1886. Josephine continued to support the Suffragists, and campaigned in particular against trafficking and the prostitution of women and children. She died in 1906 before women were enfranchised.

Rebecca West was a committed Suffragist. She began her writing life on the Suffragist magazine, the *Freewoman*, in 1911. She was born Cicily Fairfield but changed her name as she argued that her given name didn't inspire authority. She admired Emily Davison and Emmeline Pankhurst and wrote essays on each of them: 'The Sterner Sex' and 'The Reed of Steel'. She went on to become a well-respected novelist most famous perhaps for *The Return of the Soldier* and *The Fountain Overflows*. She was given a CBE in 1949 and became a Dame of the British Empire in 1959.

Women and voting around the world	
Country	**Year of women's enfranchisement**
USA	1869–1920 (individual states)
New Zealand	1893
Australia	1902
Finland	1906
Norway	1913
Denmark	1915
Canada	1917
Germany	1918
Poland	1918
Sweden	1921
Turkey	1926
South Africa	1930
India	1935
France	1945
Italy	1946
Morocco	1963
Switzerland	1971
Liechtenstein	1984
Bahrain	2002
Oman	2003
Kuwait	2005

CAT'S CRADLE

◆

CAT'S CRADLE IS A FUN GAME played with two people and a length of string. It's been around for centuries and, perhaps because it is so simple, it remains popular today. There are lots of shapes you can make; here are a few to begin with.

You will need

* a long piece of string, perhaps a metre in length, tied at the ends so it forms a circle
* a friend to play with

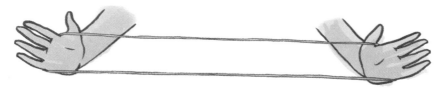

First put your hands inside the circle of string, with your thumbs sticking out of the circle.

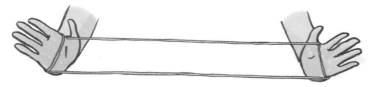

Then loop the string around your hands so it crosses your palms.

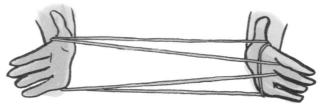

With your middle finger, pull the loop that crosses the opposite palm.

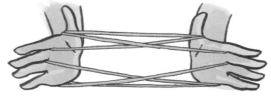

Repeat with the other hand.

This is the 'Cat's Cradle'. But this is just the beginning. Keep going!

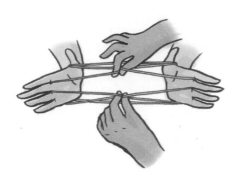

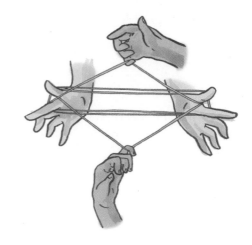

Your friend should take hold of the crosses – one on each side of the cat's cradle – with her forefingers.

Then she pulls them out and pushes them under and up through the middle of the cradle. You should then let go of the string so it ends up on your friend's hands.

Then she turns her hands downwards, into the triangles this has formed, and goes under, remembering to keep hold with her little fingers.

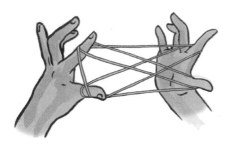

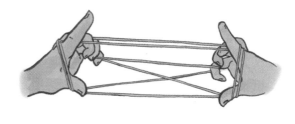

Now you take hold of the crosses from the top and pull them out, under and up through the middle, taking the string back from your friend.

This is the 'Manger'. Now you take over, grabbing the crosses from the side and pulling them out, over and this time down into the middle, so you end up with the string formation on your hands with your hands pointing downwards.

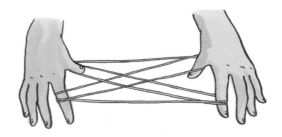

Now you have the 'Candles'. Here it gets a little complicated. Your friend needs to take one of the long middle strings with her little finger and pull it across to the other side. Then she does the same with the other long piece of string.

You can keep going and get ever more complicated. Have fun practising!

PEACH STONE RINGS

◆

FUNNY THE THINGS girls used to do. This piece of girl lore, rubbing a peach stone into a ring, is really a pretext for hanging out with your friends on a late summer afternoon. Here's how to do it.

1. Eat a peach.
2. Scrape the peach stone on the pavement back and forth on one side, then back and forth on the other. You will think nothing is happening, but in fact, microscopic peach stone fibres are being rubbed off.
3. Eventually the sides will begin to flatten and the inner pith will peek through.
4. Once the sides are flat the ring is close at hand. Just smooth the top and bottom, and rub the inside smooth with a stick.

If you don't want to make the stone into a ring, you can plant it. Clean the stone and place it in a plastic bag in the back of the fridge. In late September, plant it 12 centimetres down in healthy soil. In spring, if you are very lucky – and in the right temperate zone – the peach tree will grow, slowly. Water and fertilize, and in two or three years, the tree might bear fruit.

WOMEN WHO CHANGED THE WORLD

◆

Florence Nightingale, Clara Barton and Mary Seacole

Florence Nightingale (1820–1910)

Born in 1820 to a well-off family, Florence Nightingale was not expected to work in the not-then respectable profession of nursing. She grew up studying Greek, Latin, French, German, Italian, history, grammar, philosophy, and – over parental objection – mathematics. But in 1837, Florence heard what she called the voice of God telling her that she had a mission in life. Four years later, she discovered that mission – nursing – and abandoned the life of a socialite and mother that was expected of her.

Florence Nightingale

She trained in Germany and Paris and by 1853 was the superintendent of London's Institution for the Care of Sick Gentlewomen. After the Crimean War broke out and she heard about the awful conditions for wounded soldiers, she volunteered to go to the war front in Turkey and took thirty-eight women with her as nurses. During her time in the English military hospitals in Turkey, she established new standards for sanitary conditions and supplies; six months after her arrival, the mortality rate had fallen from sixty per cent to two per cent. Her status as the only woman in the wards at night led to her being called 'The Lady with the Lamp'.

She eventually became general superintendent of the Female Nursing Establishment of the Military Hospitals of the Army, helped establish the Royal Commission on the Health of the Army and in 1860 founded the Nightingale School and Home for Nurses.

But in addition to being a nursing pioneer and health care reformer, Florence Nightingale was also a remarkable mathematician. Her innovations in statistical analysis led to her invention of the 'polar-area diagram' – better known to us as the pie chart – and revolutionized the use of statistics to analyse disease and mortality.

In 1858 she was elected the first female member of the Royal Statistical Society. In 1907 she became the first woman to be awarded the Order of Merit. Although bedridden for years before her death, she continued her work in the field of hospital planning. She died in 1910.

Clara Barton (1821–1912)

Clara Barton was the first president of the American Red Cross. She grew up the youngest of five children and began teaching school at the age of fifteen; she later clerked in the US Patent

Office. After the Civil War broke out and she learned the wounded were suffering from a lack of medical care, she established a service of supplies for soldiers and worked in army camps and on the front lines, earning her the nickname 'Angel of the Battlefield'. For three years she cared for casualties of war in Virginia and South Carolina and in 1865 President Lincoln appointed her to organize a programme to locate men missing in action. She travelled to Europe in 1870 at the outbreak of the Franco-Prussian War and worked behind the German lines for the International Red Cross. After returning to the United States, she organized the American National Red Cross, which she headed until 1904.

Clara Barton

Mary Seacole (1805–1881)

Born in 1805 to a Scottish soldier and a Jamaican mother, Mary Seacole grew up in Jamaica and trained as a nurse. She visited London once in the 1820s to stay with relatives but returned to Jamaica after a year. She married for love and had a comfortable life and good position in Jamaica. At the outbreak of the Crimean War in 1854, Seacole heeded the call for nurses and travelled to England in search of someone who would take her to the front. But, most probably because of her colour, she was unable to find a position and was forced to borrow the money she needed for the journey to the Crimea. Once there, she worked tirelessly on the front, often under enemy fire and for little reward. Her deeds were overshadowed by those of Florence Nightingale for many years but she now receives the place in history that she deserves.

Mary Seacole

GARDENS, ALLOTMENTS AND WINDOW BOXES

G ROWING YOUR OWN fruit and vegetables is a lot of fun and very satisfying. You don't need a lot of space – you can even grow things in window boxes if you don't have access to a garden. What you do need is a little time, a little effort, some sunshine, some rain and a lot of patience.

ALLOTMENTS AND VEGETABLE GARDENS

These can be as large or small as the space you have available. Make sure you ask before digging up someone's prized lawn, though! Mark out the area with pegs and string and start by preparing the ground. You'll need to cut down any tall plants and brambles and dig out all the weeds too. Then turn over the soil with a spade, loosening it and making it easier to work with.

plants watered. Friends are always happy to help out if you go away. Make sure you label your seeds clearly using a waterproof pen so you know what you have planted and where!

A SHORT HISTORY OF ALLOTMENTS

Growing your own vegetables has long been popular, but allotments have their own history born more of necessity than you might realize. Allotments are usually found in built-up areas and are large plots of land divided into smaller sections which are allotted (therein the reason for the name) to individuals. Allotments have been popular since the eighteenth and nineteenth centuries when

Now your area is prepared, the most important thing you can do is get your plans in order. The more organized you are, the better your produce will be. First of all, work out which way is north so you can plant your seeds in the spots that work best for them. Then note which areas get a lot of sun and which are more shady.

Now all you need to decide is which vegetables you like! There's no point in growing vegetables that will go uneaten because in a good year your harvest is likely to be plentiful. Growing from seed is the most satisfying way to go, and you'll need to follow the instructions on the packets about when to sow and when to harvest as each vegetable varies. Some will need growing indoors first and then transplanting outside.

Once you have sown your seeds, make sure you tend your garden carefully, removing weeds and pests regularly, and keeping the

most towns were surrounded by land set aside for allotments. The popularity of allotments increased as part of a campaign by Britain's wartime government in the 1940s. At the time Britain imported a large proportion of its food, but the seas around our islands were full of enemy ships and it was impossible to bring in enough food for everyone. So the government encouraged people to 'Dig for Victory' by producing their own food. If the people could feed themselves, they would be strong enough to defend their borders and defeat the enemy! It was seen as your patriotic duty to grow your own fruit and vegetables but it was also much more productive than queuing at the local shops for the sparse supplies that were available to buy with ration coupons.

After the end of the war, as rationing drew to an end, it was housing that Britain needed most urgently, so many allotments were covered over by new housing to replace the old that had been destroyed by German bombs.

Today allotments are still available, but as there are fewer of them there can sometimes be a waiting list. Allotments are run by local councils, so get in touch with your council who can tell you how to go about getting an allotment in your area.

WINDOW BOXES

If you don't have access to a garden or allotment, don't worry: there is plenty that you can grow in a simple window box.

First make sure that your window box is securely fastened – you don't want it becoming loose and falling off the sill. A chain and two hooks fastened to the wall should do the trick.

Your box needs to be well drained, so fill the bottom with bits of broken crockery.

There are certain plants that will work better in window boxes than others, so stick to these. Here are a few ideas to get you started:

* Herbs: Mint, rosemary, chives, thyme, basil, oregano and sage all work well in window boxes.
* Cherry tomatoes.
* Lettuces: Rocket, lamb's lettuce and bijou all work well. Try sowing in sections so you can harvest one section as the others are growing.
* Radishes: Very easy and quick to grow.

GROW BAGS

If you have a small amount of outside space but no earth, grow bags are a great way of growing things. Cucumbers, sweet peppers, courgettes and aubergines all grow well in grow bags. Make sure you keep them well watered, though.

Whatever the size or shape of your plot, you should be able to grow some delicious fruit and vegetables. And remember, food you grow yourself always tastes better than any you can buy from the shops.

Fruit and Vegetables You Can Grow

What to Grow	When to Plant	When to Harvest	Top Tips
Potatoes	March	June–September	Start with a seed potato and allow it to sprout tubers. Start this in January/February by standing your potatoes on a windowsill, out of direct sunlight. Then plant outside in March.
Courgettes	March–May	August	You need to propagate the seeds indoors and then transfer to your outdoor plot in May. Courgettes provide beautiful yellow flowers that are also edible.
Tomatoes	January–May	July–September	There are lots of varieties of tomatoes, including cherry tomatoes which can be grown in hanging baskets. They all need to be propagated indoors to start with.
Salads	April–September	April–September	Salads are very easy and quick to grow, so you can keep resowing and regrowing them around every four weeks. Plant them right into the ground, or alternatively you can grow them in window boxes.
Rhubarb	October–December	May–June	It is best to grow rhubarb from young plants rather than from seed. Make sure you don't eat the leaves, though, as they are poisonous!
Strawberries	June–September	June–September	Again it is better to start with young plants than to grow from seed. Plant outside in June and check the plants every day for signs of slugs as these can destroy your strawberries.

QUEENS OF THE
ANCIENT WORLD IV

◆

Boudicca's Rebellion against Rome

BOUDICCA WAS A WARRIOR QUEEN, with a fierce way about her and brilliant red hair that flowed to her waist. As Queen of the Celtic tribe of the Iceni in the first century AD, Boudicca organized a revolt against the Romans, hoping to regain and protect her people's independence.

In the year 43 AD, Roman soldiers marched to the French edge of the European continent, crossed the Channel and began their invasion of Britain. The Emperor Claudius, whose reign had begun in 41 AD and would last until 54 AD, dreamed of conquering the mysterious British island. Rome was at the height of its power. Its huge army helped expand the boundaries of Rome in all directions. Britain was a special challenge. It sat beyond a choppy channel of water and was the furthest spot to the northwest that the Romans could imagine, with a cold, unfathomable and terrifyingly large sea beyond.

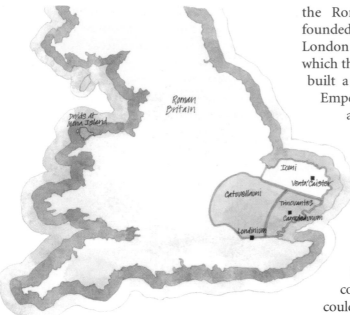

Britain was the home of Celtic tribes and Druids, with their mystical traditions and religious groves of trees. In Rome, the lives of women and girls were as controlled as the tightly wound hair braids and coils that were the fashion of the day. There, men dominated public life and women, especially those in wealthy and powerful families, lived more private lives. By contrast, Celtic women had many more rights. They could govern and make laws, marry more freely, own property and, alongside men, they could work and take part in their community's marketplace. Their hair, too, showed their freedom: the fashion was to grow it long and leave it down, ready to fly with the wind.

Boudicca was of the Iceni tribe, which inhabited the eastern part of Britain, and she had married Prasutagus, the tribe's King. As Roman legions invaded and took over the land of the Celts, Boudicca watched, unbelievingly. The Romans declared much of Britain to be the Roman province of Britannia. They founded the cities of Londinium – now called London – and Camulodunum (Colchester), which they made into their capital. There they built a massive Roman-style temple to the Emperor Claudius and a towering statue of a woman representing Victory.

Facing troops with greater weapons, the Iceni and nearby Celtic tribes followed the path of many local tribes. They feared that active resistance would mean death for many and slavery for the rest and so they submitted. When the Romans came to the Iceni kingdom, they decided that Prasutagus should continue to rule his people. The Iceni could remain semi-independent so long as they stayed loyal to Rome. The Romans often made arrangements like this, charging local rulers to keep the peace and to collect taxes for the Empire. Prasutagus' small kingdom lasted this way for nearly twenty years, until he died in the year 60 AD, leaving behind Boudicca and their two daughters.

Most of what we know about Boudicca's life comes to us from the Roman historian Tacitus, who in 109 AD wrote the *Annals,* detailing Rome's first-century exploits. Tacitus reports that under Roman rule, Prasutagus and Boudicca remained prosperous. After Prasutagus' death, however, it was learned that he had been wheeling and dealing with the Romans and this included borrowing a great deal of money from the Roman governor. Prasutagus' will directed that half the kingdom be turned over to the Romans to pay his debt. The other half he gave to his two daughters, for them to rule as queens.

Prasutagus had hoped his deathbed directions would protect his family, but this didn't happen. The Roman governor Suetonius had already decided that when Prasutagus died, he would disarm the Iceni people, confiscate their arrows and spears and darts and annex their land fully into the Roman province of Britannia.

Roman soldiers soon arrived at Boudicca's palace to plunder Prasutagus' wealth and claim his entire kingdom as their own. They captured Boudicca and made a show of torturing her and her two daughters in front of the Iceni tribesmen and women. Their cousins, aunts and uncles were made into slaves.

Later that year, the Roman governor Suetonius decided to conquer Wales. As the soldiers of his fearsome legion marched westward, they left the cities of Camulodunum and Londinium largely undefended.

Boudicca sensed her chance. She claimed the mantle of leadership and stirred her people to reclaim their freedom and liberty. She reminded them of the horror and cruelty of Roman rule and rallied them to win back their lands.

Boudicca outlined her plan. Suetonius was in Wales, routing Druids on the Isle of Mona. Leading the way in her horse-drawn chariot, with 100,000 British fighters behind her, she would attack Camulodunum first. All around, miraculous omens pointed to Boudicca's success; ancient reports tell us that the city's Victory statue fell from its tall base to the ground below with no cause, as if Rome were already yielding.

Boudicca's troops stormed the city's gates. By day's end the city was in flames. A small group of Roman soldiers and leaders locked themselves inside the Temple of Claudius, holding out for two days until Boudicca burned the temple to the ground.

After hearing of Boudicca's victory at Camulodunum, the Roman governor Suetonius left Wales and headed straight back to London to protect it from Boudicca's rampaging soldiers.

Seeing Boudicca's willingness to burn cities to the ground, he decided, however, to abandon London to her fires. Boudicca's soldiers left 25,000 people dead in London before advancing to Verulamium (St Albans), Britain's third-largest city, where they killed everyone who had cooperated with the Romans and then destroyed the city.

Boudicca's army began to falter. As Suetonius' men approached, they burned the crops in the fields, sending ripened corn and beans into smoke and leaving nothing to feed Boudicca's troops and keep them strong. Boudicca had successfully destroyed unarmed cities, but Suetonius and his professional legions were too strong for the relatively untrained British Celts, whose luck now turned. Boudicca fought one final battle, the place of which is unknown. Her troops had to start from the bottom of a tall hill and face off against the Romans, who were strategically encamped at the top. Roman arrows and pikes rained down on the Celts. Boudicca's fighters were overpowered and many were lost to battle.

The rebellion was over. As night fell, Boudicca abandoned the glorious bronze chariot that had served her well. She grabbed her two teenage daughters by the hand and together the three of them ran through the darkness, returning home to their palace along hidden paths and back roads. Once home, they knew they would be captured and brought to Rome to be displayed in chains to the jeering crowds at the Colosseum. Instead, Boudicca decided to end her own life by drinking a cup of poison and her princess daughters took the same route. It is said that when her closest relatives entered the palace, they found Boudicca wearing her legendary tunic of brilliant colours, covered with a deep auburn cloak, her flaming red hair still untamed.

ROLLER SKATING

◆

THE FIRST ROLLER SKATES, created in the 1700s, resembled today's in-line skates: a single line of metal wheels. Even in the next century, the first patented roller skate design followed the alignment of three wheels in a row. It wasn't until 1863 that a man named James Plimpton revolutionized the design by inventing a skate with two pairs of wheels set side by side, also known as a quad skate. The new skate quickly became the standard, due to its greater control and ease in turning, and even more refinements were made: ball and cone bearings helped improve the skate's manoeuvrability and the toe stop was patented in 1876. Roller skating increased in popularity and reached its heyday during the 1970s and 1980s; in the 1990s a modern in-line skate design, the Rollerblade, took the lead as roller rinks gave way to outdoor skating. But roller skates are still made, and the fun to be had on skates is everything it used to be.

If you've never skated before – and even if you have – it's a good idea to get used to your new skates. Find yourself a smooth, flat, safe, traffic-free place to skate, and before you do anything else, practise the skills of starting, turning and stopping. And even if you're not a beginner, wear protective gear, including knee pads, wrist guards, elbow pads and a helmet.

STARTING OUT

Before you skate, find your balance and get comfortable in your skates by walking on a flat, grassy or carpeted surface. First, just stand, feeling the sensation of your weight distributed evenly over the middle of your skates rather than in your toes or heels. Do not lock your knees. Then, stand with your feet in a 'V' position, your heels together and your toes apart. Bend your knees slightly, put your arms out at your sides, and then march slowly, right, left, right, left, to get a feel for your skates. When you feel comfortable with this, move to a paved surface and try to balance on your skates. Bend only at the knees, never at the waist.

FALLING

It sounds funny, because a fall should seem like something to avoid, but falling is one of the most important things to practise. When you fall forward on skates, your skate stops but your upper body keeps going. Practising falling forward on your bed or another cushioned surface can prepare you for how it feels to fall, so that if a fall occurs your reaction can be reflexive and you can minimize injury. When falling forward, drop to your knees (which should always be protected with knee pads) and sit on your bottom and thighs – avoid putting your arms down or falling forward onto your hands. When falling backwards, try to regain your balance by leaning forward and resist the urge to flail your arms or put your arms out to break your fall.

SKATING FORWARD

Begin with your feet in a 'V' position, your heels together and your toes apart. With slightly bent knees and your arms held out to steady you, lean onto your right foot and coast forward, pushing off lightly with your left. Bring your left foot to meet your right foot, again in a 'V' with your heels together, and as you place your left foot down, lean to the left, gliding on your left foot and pushing off lightly with your right. Repeat, alternating feet. Remember to relax, keep your knees bent and lean your body in the direction of the foot carrying your weight.

STOPPING

It's possible to use the toe-stop to stop yourself by pointing your toe and dragging the rubber stop on the ground, but that can be a little tricky. A surer way is the four-wheel 'T' stop. Gliding on your forward skate, lift your back skate and bring it behind your front skate at a 45-degree angle, creating a 'T'. Gradually let the rear skate touch the ground and create a drag to slow you to a stop. Another method of stopping is to simply lean into a turn. If you keep leaning in the same direction, you will gradually spin to a stop.

STROKING

Begin with your feet close together, shift your weight to the right foot and push off to the side with your left. Glide forward on your right foot with your left foot off the floor. Be careful not to bend at the waist, turn or twist your shoulders, or swing your arms. Bring your left skate alongside your right one and place it on the floor. Now shift your weight to

your left foot and glide forward the same way. Keep repeating these glides, swaying right and then left and remember to look ahead of you in the distance, not down at your feet. Gradually make each glide or stroke longer as you build up speed.

STEERING/TURNING

To steer yourself into a curve, lean in the direction of the curve. For a left turn, lean left; for a right turn, lean right.

CROSS-FRONT

After you are comfortable with stroking, you can practise the cross-front. Glide forward, your weight on your left foot, with knees bent and close together. Swinging from the hip, cross your right leg over your left and step your right foot as close to your left as you can. Continually crossing over in front is one way to navigate a turn.

SKATING BACKWARDS

Start with your feet in an inverted 'V', with your toes together and your heels apart. Press down on the inside of the left foot while lifting your right foot off the floor. Point your right toe down and shift your weight to the right. Lean slightly forward, bend your knees and look back over your shoulder while you push off with your right foot and glide backwards on your left. Bring your right foot back down and alongside the left. Push off your left foot and glide backwards on your right. Your balance foot is in front of you. Bring your left foot alongside the right and start over. Another

technique for skating backwards is to move your skates in an hourglass shape without lifting your feet off the ground. Start with a wide stance, your skates far apart, and then apply pressure on the inside edges of your skates to roll them close together. Once they're close, apply pressure to the outside edges, making your skates roll away from each other. Try this going forward, too!

SKATING A FIGURE OF EIGHT

Build up speed by stroking, then skate on your right foot only and lean in to the circle; when you complete the circle, switch from your right foot to your left foot and lean in to finish.

BOYS

———◆———

WITHOUT A DOUBT you have already received many confusing messages about what, if anything, you should be doing with boys. Some girls are led to believe that being liked by boys is important above all else. Some girls are told that boys are different and that girls should adapt themselves to be like the boys they like or take care not to be too threatening – learn about sports if a boy likes sports, or pretend to be stupid about subjects a boy likes to excel in. Some girls are encouraged to think of boys as protectors, or, alternatively, as creatures that need protecting. It may seem to some girls that suddenly boys matter a whole lot more than they should; still others wonder what all the fuss is about.

Many things are said of boys: Boys like sports, boys are messy, boys don't have any feelings, boys like trucks, boys don't like girly things, boys like to run around and eat horrible food. Whatever the specific generalization, the point of these notions about boys is to set them apart from girls as being entirely different.

Similar statements are made about girls: Girls like pink, girls like flowers, girls are neat and clean, girls are frivolous, girls are emotional. Are any of these things true about all girls? Of course not. But it's easier to think about boys and girls as being entirely different than it is to think about boys and girls as having lots of common ground.

As concerns boys themselves, you have several options. The first, of course, is to ignore them until you (and they) are nineteen. Or twenty-one. Or twenty-five.

Alternatively, you could make a boy your best friend. Boys can be excellent friends. In general, they like to do things and that makes them rather fun.

Of course a third option is romance. Some girls might be interested in this kind of thing (you will recognize them by their doodles of their name and a boy's name in a heart on their science homework); other girls might think that would be too icky to even imagine. If you are in the latter group, don't worry, you have plenty of company.

If you are in the former group, there are two main things to keep in mind. One, if a boy doesn't like you the way you are, the problem is him, not you. And two, don't try to make a boy change for you – it's important to appreciate people for who they are.

Wherever you fall on the spectrum of how you feel about boys, do treat all your friends, boys and girls, with kindness. This has gone out of fashion and that's a sad mistake.

Overall, the truth is that there's no great big mystery about boys. Boys are people and, like all people, they are complicated. And that's what makes being friends with other people interesting: you get to learn about how other people think and act and, in the process, learn a little bit more about yourself.

RUNNING A MEETING, GROUP OR CLUB

———— ◆ ————

LEADING A GROUP or meeting can be a daunting task and one that might be slightly overwhelming. But don't worry, you are not alone in feeling this way! The best way to approach any meeting is to be prepared; the more prepared you are, the more confident you will feel. Henry Robert, an engineer of the nineteenth century, found out for himself the difficulties of running a meeting. So he resolved to learn the best way to go about it and produced his *Pocket Manual of Rules of Order for Deliberative Assemblies*, first published in 1876 and known today as *Robert's Rules of Order*. You and your friends can use these rules to run your own clubs and meetings.

The basic rules of parliamentary procedure:

* The rights of the organization supersede the rights of individual members
* All members are equal and their rights (to attend meetings, make motions, speak in debate, nominate, vote, hold office) are equal
* A quorum must be present to do business
* The majority rules
* Silence is consent
* One question at a time and one speaker at a time
* Debatable motions must receive full debate
* Once a question is decided, it is not in order to bring up the same motion or one essentially like it at the same meeting
* Slurs, comments and personal remarks in debate are always out of order

Running a Meeting

BEING THE CHAIR

The chair is in charge of the meeting and has a gavel, like a judge. She should prepare an agenda, an outline of a meeting that lists the items to be discussed or acted upon. Here is a typical example, with a basic script to follow:

1 **Roll call of members present.** This is done to determine a quorum – making sure there are enough members present to run the meeting. The secretary reads members' names from a list and members respond.

2 **Call to order.** 'Welcome. A quorum being present, the meeting will come to order.' (Bang your gavel once, for good effect.)

3 **Read the minutes of the last meeting.** 'The first business in order is the approval of the minutes of the previous meeting. Will [the secretary who keeps the minutes] please read the minutes of the last meeting? Are there any corrections to the minutes? There being no corrections, the minutes are approved as read.' (If there are corrections, they should be noted and recorded by the secretary.)

4 **Officers' reports.** 'The next business in order will be the reports of the officers.' (Call on those officers you know to have reports.)

5 **Treasurer's report.** 'The treasurer [call by name] will give her report.' After the report is read: 'Are there any questions? There being no questions, the report will be filed for audit.'

6 **Committee reports.** 'The next business in order will be the reports of committees.'

After reports have been made: 'Thank you. The report will be filed with the minutes of this meeting.'

7 **Special orders.** This is any business previously designated for consideration at this meeting.

8 **Unfinished business.** Only announce this if there is business that has been postponed from the last meeting to the current meeting. 'The next business in order will be the [whatever the unfinished business is] that was postponed to this meeting.'

9 **New business.** 'The next business in order will be new business. Is there any new business to come before the group?'

10 **Announcements or programme.** If there are announcements to be made but no programme at the meeting: 'If there is no further new business to come before the group, the secretary will read the announcements.'

If there is a programme at the meeting: 'If there is no further business to come before the group, [the programme chair] will introduce today's speaker.'

11 **Adjournment.** 'If there is no further business and there is no objection, the meeting will be adjourned. There being no objection, the meeting is adjourned.'

BEING THE SECRETARY

The secretary of your group is responsible for several things: sending out notices of upcoming meetings; maintaining the organization's records, including the membership list, lists of all committees and their members and an up-to-date version of the group's bylaws; and, most importantly, writing the minutes of the organization. The minutes should be written as concisely and precisely as possible, as they constitute the official record of everything that takes place within your group.

Vocabulary

Agenda: *A list of items to be discussed at a meeting*

Appeal: *A motion to object to a ruling*

Ballot Vote: *A secret vote, written on a piece of paper*

Bylaws: *Written rules for governing an organization*

Carried: *To adopt a motion*

Debate: *The formal discussion of a motion*

Dilatory Tactic: *The misuse of a parliamentary procedure (such as repeatedly using division or appealing previous decisions)*

Division: *To call for a recount of a vote*

Floor: *To be given permission to speak at a meeting (as in 'to have the floor')*

Minutes: *The official written record of a meeting*

Motion: *A proposal that some action be taken or an opinion expressed by the group*

New Business: *New matters brought for consideration*

Nominate: *Formally name a person as a candidate for election or office*

Order of Business: *The schedule of business to be considered*

Out of Order: *Not correct from a parliamentary standpoint*

Pending: *Questions that are under consideration*

Point of Order: *An objection made for improper procedure*

Preamble: *The introduction to a resolution that begins with 'whereas'*

Putting the Question: *Placing the motion before the group for a vote*

Quorum: *The number of members that must be present for business to take place*

Recess: *To take a short break during a meeting*

Resolution: *A formal written motion*

Unfinished Business: *Matters from a previous meeting that were postponed or brought over to the next meeting*

Yield: *To give way when you have been assigned the floor*

The format for writing the minutes is as follows:

* **First paragraph**
   Include the kind of meeting (whether it's regular or a special meeting), the name of your organization, date and place of meeting, presence of the president and secretary or the names of substitutes, presence of a quorum, time the meeting was called to order and whether the minutes of the previous meeting were approved or corrected.

* **Body**
   List the reports given, including the name of the reporter and any action taken; all motions; all points of order or appeal; important announcements; if there is a programme, the name of the speaker and the topic of the programme.

* **Final paragraph**
   Record the adjournment and the time of adjournment and sign and date the document.

When writing minutes, be sure to record all adopted and defeated motions, the name of the person who makes any motion, names of all members who report, names of anyone elected or appointed and the number of votes on each side in a ballot or counted vote. Do not write down your personal opinion of any discussion, motions that are withdrawn or entire reports that are given at a meeting. (Instead of transcribing the report, write: '[Person's name and title] reported on [topic]. The report is attached to the original of these minutes.')

After writing the minutes (which you should do as promptly as possible), sign and date them and send a copy to the president of your organization, making sure to alert her to any items of unfinished business. When making corrections, do not erase or obliterate the original. Instead, make any corrections in red ink and note the date of the correction.

BEING THE TREASURER

The treasurer is the person responsible for the money of an organization. Her job is to receive and disburse monies according to the organization's rules and to bill for and collect any annual dues. She maintains a permanent record of all money received and paid out; any corrections made are clearly indicated in red, just as in the secretary's minutes. The treasurer gives a brief report at each meeting summarizing any collections or expenditures and bringing up any unusual items. Once a year, the treasurer's books are audited, meaning that they are verified and all the numbers checked and an audit report is dated and signed by the auditing committee.

A treasurer's report should list:

* The date of meeting
* Balance on hand at the date of last meeting
* Receipts (money received)
* Disbursements (money paid out)
* Reserve funds (if any)
* Balance on hand at the date of report (the original balance on hand, plus receipts, minus disbursements, plus reserve fund)

The treasurer should sign the report at the bottom.

BEING A MEMBER

The point of parliamentary procedure is that everyone has a chance for her voice to be heard – even members who aren't officers or chairpeople. A member makes herself and her ideas known through something called a motion. A motion is a method of introducing business in a meeting and there are two kinds of motions: main motions and secondary motions.

A main motion is a proposal that action be taken (or an opinion expressed) by the group. This kind of motion cannot be made when any other motion is on the floor (that is, being discussed), and always yields to secondary motions. Main motions require a 'second' (a second person who supports the motion) unless they are made by a committee. Main motions can be debated and amended and they always require a majority vote.

A secondary motion is one that can be made while a main motion is on the floor, even before it has been decided. There are three kinds of secondary motions: subsidiary motions, privileged motions and incidental motions. Subsidiary motions pertain to the main motion on the floor and their purpose is to change or affect how a main motion is handled. They are voted on before a main motion. Privileged motions are urgent motions, such as recess or adjournment, that do not relate to pending business. Incidental motions deal with process and procedure – correcting errors, verifying votes – and must be considered before the other motion.

Making a Motion

First, request the floor by standing and addressing the chairperson: 'Madam President'. Once you are recognized by the chairperson, introduce your motion by saying, 'I move that . . .' and then stating your proposal. Another member (who does not need to stand or be recognized by the chairperson) supports your motion by saying, 'I second the motion.' If your motion is not seconded, the chairperson can dismiss it, saying, 'Since there is no second, the motion is not before this meeting.' If your motion is seconded, the chairperson announces and restates your motion, saying, 'It has been moved and seconded that [your proposal here].' Now the motion is 'pending', that is, awaiting debate before it can be voted on and finalized. The chairperson asks, 'Is there any discussion?' The chairperson recognizes members who wish to debate the motion. After the discussion is over, she puts the question to a vote, saying, 'The question is on the motion that [your proposal here]. All in favour of the motion say "aye"; all opposed say "no".' The chair then announces the results of the vote.

You can modify or withdraw your motion before it has been stated by the chairperson. After it has been stated by the chairperson, if you wish to change the motion, you may offer an amendment; if you wish to withdraw it, you must ask permission of the group to do so. Keep in mind that your motion may be ruled 'out of order' (inappropriate or incorrect) if it: goes against your group's bylaws, repeats a question asked or motion made on the same day, conflicts with another already adopted motion, or is frivolous or rude.

Voting on a Motion

How your group votes depends on the policy of your organization, but in general there are five voting methods most often used: voting by voice, by roll call, by general consent, by division, and by ballot voting. The chairperson counts the vote.

In a voice vote, the chairperson asks those in favour to say 'aye', those opposed to say 'no'. In a roll call, each member answers 'yes' or 'no' as her name is called. In a vote by general consent, when a motion is likely to be agreeable, the chairperson says, 'If there is no objection . . .' and the members demonstrate agreement by remaining silent (but if even one member says, 'I object,' the item must be put to a vote). In a vote by division, a voice vote is clarified by members raising their hands or standing to indicate their vote. And in a vote by ballot, members write their vote on a piece of paper.

Your group can also make a motion instead of voting: you can make a motion to 'table', which means to set aside the motion under consideration until a later date. (A 'tabled' motion can always be put back on the table.) Or you can make a motion to 'postpone indefinitely'.

WRITING THE BYLAWS

Bylaws are the fundamental principles and rules governing an organization. They should be clear and concise, as their goal is to help a group by defining and protecting its purpose. A group doesn't officially exist until its bylaws are written. Here is a typical format for constructing your group's bylaws.

ARTICLE I: Your group's name

ARTICLE II: Purpose of your group

ARTICLE III: Members
  1. Classes of membership (active, honorary, etc.)

  2. Eligibility or qualifications for membership
  3. Membership fees or dues
  4. Rights of membership
  5. Resignations and disciplinary action

ARTICLE IV: Officers
1. List in order of rank (president, vice president, etc.)
2. Duties (what each officer does)
3. Term of office (how long they get to be an officer)
4. Nominations and elections (how new officers are nominated and elected)

ARTICLE V: Meetings
1. Regular meetings
2. Annual meetings
3. Special meetings
4. Quorum (how many members need to be present for a meeting to take place)

ARTICLE VI: Board of Directors
1. Composition (who is on the board)
2. Powers (what can the board do)
3. Meetings (how often does it meet)
4. Quorum

ARTICLE VII: Executive Committee
A board within the board of directors

ARTICLE VIII: Committees
List all committees, including the committee name, number of members, manner of selection and duties. Then list 'special committees', permitting the establishment 'of such special committees as necessary to carry on the work of the organization'.

ARTICLE IX: Parliamentary Authority

ARTICLE X: Amendment of the Bylaws
Outlines the procedure for amending the bylaws (usually a two-thirds vote is required)

ARTICLE XI: Dissolution
States what will happen to the assets if the organization should be dissolved

WATERCOLOUR PAINTING ON THE GO

ONE OF THE MOST ENJOYABLE ways to begin watercolour painting is to work outdoors, when the weather is nice and the light is good. Working outdoors is also great because nature is a fabulous subject for beginners to paint. Unlike trying to paint, say, a family portrait, or a picture of your friend, a landscape is a forgiving subject: even if you aren't able to capture the rolling hills and colourful flowers perfectly, your painting can still resemble an outdoors scene. (And you can always call it 'impressionistic' if it doesn't!) Here is what you'll need in your travelling watercolour kit.

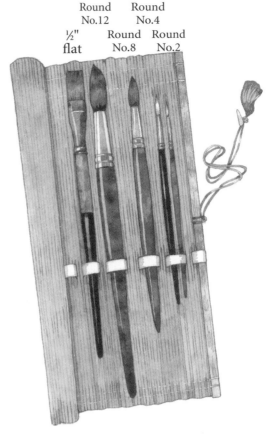

Round No.12 Round No.4
½" flat Round No.8 Round No.2

* **Brushes**
Bring an assortment of round and flat watercolour brushes in a variety of sizes (0, 2, 4, 8, 12). Synthetic sable is an economical, long-lasting alternative to the more expensive pure sable bristles.

* **Brush holder**
A flat bamboo mat that can be rolled up and tied with a ribbon or string. Weave a piece of white elastic band through the lower third of the mat and insert brushes. Roll up and tie!

* **Travel-sized palette**
Make sure the mixing area is large enough and that there's a good range of colours (red, orange, yellow, green, blue, violet, yellow ochre, burnt sienna).

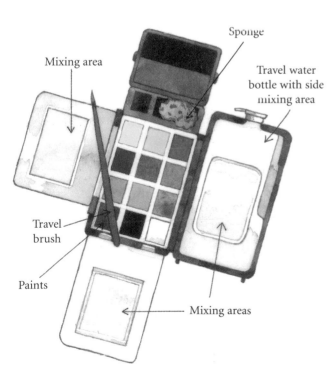

Sponge

Mixing area

Travel water bottle with side mixing area

Travel brush

Paints

Mixing areas

* **Water containers**
Two plastic collapsible water containers (they look like Chinese lanterns), or plastic jars – one for clean water and one for dirty.

* **Bottled water**
If you're not near a water fountain or a bathroom with a sink, bring your own bottled water.

* **Paper, or a watercolour block, A3**

* **A sharp tool to remove sheets of paper from the block**

* **A No. 2 pencil and a kneaded rubber**

* **A towel to sit on, or a small beach chair**

Never leave your watercolour brush standing in water – it will ruin the bristles. Instead, keep the brushes on your bamboo mat. Let them dry in the air.

Clean your brushes before adding a new colour (especially when changing from dark to light hues).

If you wish to work on a separate sheet of paper rather than a block, use watercolour masking tape to secure all sides and edges of the paper to a board. Not doing so will allow air to get underneath and buckle the paper.

Do not overwork your painting! Wait for an area to dry completely before adding more water or pigment. Too much water can break down the fibres in the paper and make it look too 'scrubbed'. As with so many things in life, less is more.

Less water will give you a more opaque, darker colour. More water will yield a more transparent, lighter colour.

Lightly sketch your landscape or seascape in pencil before starting – you can always erase pencils marks, once the paper is completely dry, with a kneaded eraser. Darker, heavier lines are more difficult to remove.

GREAT WATERCOLOUR ARTISTS TO CHECK OUT

Beatrix Potter (nineteenth-century British watercolourist)

Sara Midda (contemporary British watercolourist and designer)

John Singer Sargent (American, nineteenth-early twentieth century)

Charles Demuth (American, early twentieth century)

Carl Larsson (Swedish illustrator, late nineteenth-early twentieth centuries)

Charles Reid (contemporary American watercolourist)

JMW Turner (British, nineteenth century)

Albrecht Dürer (German, Northern Renaissance)

Phansakdi Chakkaphak (contemporary Thai botanical watercolourist)

Charles Rennie Mackintosh (Scottish, late nineteenth century)

MAKING A PEG BOARD GAME

◆

PERFECT FOR CAR JOURNEYS or rainy days, this ancient logic game is surprisingly easy to make but difficult to master. Traditionally, it is a triangular board with fourteen pegs and fifteen holes. The goal is to jump one peg over another until only one remains.

What you need

* 1 flat board of wood, 15 centimetres × 15 centimetres (at least one 2 centimetres thick is a good size). Any shape is fine; it doesn't have to be triangular.
* 14 fluted dowel pins, ³/₄ centimetre × 2 centimetres. Available at any DIY shop.
* Ruler
* Power drill, with a ³/₄ centimetre bit.

Make a dot at the top of the board for your starting point. Lightly draw one diagonal line and then another, marking your triangle on the wood. In addition to the top dot, mark four dots down one side of the triangle, four along the other side and three dots along the bottom. Draw dots for the middle holes, too. Use your ruler so everything lines up.

You will need help with the next power drilling step.

Drill a 1-centimetre hole right where you have drawn each dot. Some people measure 1 centimetre up the drill bit and put some masking tape on that spot so they can easily gauge the hole, although once you do enough of these, you'll get the feel of it. Test each hole with a dowel, making sure the dowel easily moves in and out. When all fifteen holes are done, shake out the sawdust and you're ready to play.

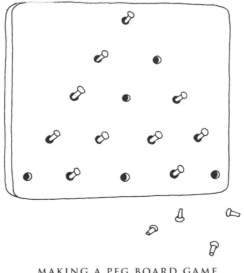

HANDCLAP GAMES

◆

HANDCLAP GAMES, or pavement songs, are not only fun to play, they are a fantastic oral storytelling tradition. Many of the rhyming, clapping games flirt with grown-up ideas like 'bad words', courtship and power and they do so with inventive language, simple songs and entertaining, sometimes tricky, choreography.

The lyrics and movements to handclap games can vary depending on where a girl lives. Different regions often have different clap sequences or alternate lyrics that become popular with the girls who practise them. Below we've included the most standardized lyrics and verses for the most popular handclap songs, but you and your friends may know other variations.

BASIC

The basic handclapping pattern involves two people standing facing one another. The clapping begins with each person bringing up her right hand, palm facing out, and clapping hands with the other person, then clapping her own hands together, then bringing up the left hand and clapping the other person's left hand, then clapping her own hands together. Repeat this pattern until the rhyme is done. (You can also begin with clapping your own hands, then clapping right hands together, etc.)

CROSS-ARMS

Begin with arms crossed against the chest, uncross your arms and clap your hands on your upper thighs, clap your hands together, clap right hands with your partner, clap your hands together, clap left hands with your partner, clap your hands together, clap right hands with your partner – then back to arms crossed and repeat from the beginning. Repeat until the rhyme is done.

UP-DOWN

Begin facing each other, both players with right hands up, palms facing down, and left hands down, palms facing up. Bring your right hands down and left hands up, clapping together; then switch so your left hands are up, palms facing down, and your right hands are down, palms facing up. Bring your left hands down and right hands up, clapping together. Then clap palms together straight on, then clap your own hands together. Repeat from the beginning until the rhyme is done. (Another variation is to clap as instructed, then after clapping your own hands, clap right hands together, clap your own hands, clap left hands together, clap your own hands, then start from the very beginning.)

BACK-FRONT DOUBLE CLAP

Begin by clapping right hands with your partner, clap your hands together, clap left hands together, clap your hands together TWICE, clap backs of hands with your partner, then palms of hands with your partner, then clap your hands together – then back to the beginning. Repeat until the rhyme is done.

Here are five favourites.

Down by the Banks

(This rhyme uses the 'Basic' handclap pattern, beginning with partners clapping right hands together. This game can also be played as an elimination-style game in a group. Everyone stands in a circle with each girl's right hand on top of the left hand of the girl on her right. Going clockwise, each girl slaps the hand of the girl to her left. At the end of the rhyme, if it is your turn and you manage to hit the next girl's hand before she pulls it away, she is out – but if you miss, you are out. When there are only two people left, the game reverts to the two-person basic pattern.)

*Down by the banks of hanky panky
where the bullfrogs jump from bank
    to banky
with a hip hop, shimmy-shimmy pop
the bank was too far and they went
    ker-plop!*

Three Sailors

(This rhyme uses the 'Basic' handclap pattern, beginning with a clap, then partners clapping right hands together.)

*Three sailors went to sea, sea, sea
[Salute like a sailor for each 'sea']
To see what they could see, see, see,
[Point to your eye for each 'see']
But all that they could see, see, see,
Was the bottom of the deep blue sea,
    sea, sea*

The 'I love you' version:

1. *Three sailors went to I, I, I, to see what they could I, I, I . . . etc.*
[point to yourself for each 'I, I, I']

2. *Three sailors went to love, love, love to see what they could love, love, love . . . etc.*
[cross your arms against your chest for each 'love, love, love']

3. *Three sailors went to you, you, you to see what they could you, you, you . . . etc.*
[point to your partner for each 'you, you, you']

4. *Three sailors went to I LOVE YOU
To see what they could I LOVE YOU
But all that they could I LOVE YOU
Was the bottom of the deep blue I LOVE YOU*
[perform all three signs for each 'I LOVE YOU']

Miss Susie Had a Steamboat

(This rhyme uses the 'Up-Down' pattern.)

> Miss Susie had a steamboat,
> the steamboat had a bell
> Miss Susie went to heaven,
> the steamboat went to —
> HELLO, operator,
> please give me number nine
> and if you disconnect me,
> I'll kick you from —
> BEHIND the 'frigerator
> there was a piece of glass,
> Miss Susie fell upon it
> and broke her little —
> ASK me no more questions,
> I'll tell you no more lies,
> Miss Susie's in the kitchen,
> Making her mud pies.

Say, Say, Oh Playmate

(This rhyme uses the 'Back-Front Double Clap', with a small 'intro' and a small 'ending'. Intro: on the words 'say, say, oh' you grab hands and swing them towards each other for the first 'say', back out for the next 'say', and then clap your hands together on 'oh', then begin the Back-Front pattern. Ending: at the words 'forever more', on the first and second 'more's you clap hands with your partner then clap hands yourself, then on the words 'shut the door!' you clap hands with your partner three times.)

> Say, say, oh playmate,
> Come out and play with me
> And bring your dollies three,
> Climb up my apple tree.
> Slide down my rainbow,
> Into my cellar door,
> And we'll be jolly friends
> Forever more, more, shut the door!

(Sometimes this verse is followed with:

> I'm sorry playmate,
> I can not play with you.
> My dolly has the flu,
> Boo-hoo hoo hoo hoo hoo.
> Ain't got no rainbow,
> Ain't got no cellar door,
> But we'll still be jolly friends
> Forever more more, ever more!)

FINANCE: INTEREST, STOCKS AND BONDS

◆

WE'VE ALL HEARD THE SAYINGS: 'Time is money' and 'Put your money where your mouth is.' Despite its reputation as being 'the root of all evil', money is, most basically, anything that is used as a means of payment. Today we use paper, coins and plastic cards; in the past, people used rocks, tobacco leaves, cigarettes, and gold and silver. Money buys us everything from food to fun and it's important to think about money now because pretty soon you'll be in charge of your own money, and the more you understand about it, the more you will be able to make good use of it. Part of learning about money includes knowing where to put your savings, which is the money you keep instead of spending. The value of your savings increases differently, depending on what you do with it.

INTEREST

When you put money in a bank account, you are actually lending your money to the bank. For the privilege of doing this, the bank pays you a tiny bit each year to 'rent' your money. This is called interest. You can take your money out of the bank if you need to, but while it's in there, the bank pays you interest – usually a set percentage of every pound that you keep in your account, called an interest rate. So if the annual interest rate is 5% and you put £100 in your bank account, at the end of one year you'll have £105.

COMPOUNDING

Thanks to something called compounding, your money can turn into even more money. If you keep that £105 in the bank for another year, now you're earning 5% interest on £105. So in other words, after two years, the £100 you started with will turn into £110.25. And all you had to do was not spend it. If you saved that £100 for twenty years, with the interest compounding every year you'd end up with £265.33. Without compounding interest, that £100 would only turn into £200 after twenty years.

Compounding interest is why saving even little bits of money can add up to much more later. However, compounding works against you when you are the one borrowing the money – which is what you are doing when you use a credit card. (It might feel like free money, but it's not!) When you buy things with a credit card, you're charged interest – interest that compounds. So if you spend money using a credit card and you don't pay off your debt every month when the bill comes due, the £100 you spent turns out to cost you much more.

INVESTING: STOCKS, BONDS AND MUTUAL FUNDS

Putting your money in a savings account is just one way to invest it, or make your money earn money. There are other ways to invest money, but they are riskier, which means while you might earn more, you can also lose some (or all) of your money. Dealing with money means working out how much risk you want to take for different kinds of possible rewards.

Stocks

Stock is ownership of a company. When you buy stock (one piece of which is called a share) in a company, that makes you a stockholder (also called a shareholder) and the more stock you own, the bigger your stake in the company. Owning stock means that you own a small piece of the company – so when a company does well and makes money, you make money too. And if it does badly, well, you can lose money instead.

The price of stock can vary from pennies to thousands of pounds, depending on the company. You get to decide when to buy a stock and when to sell a stock. You do this through a stockbroker or directly through the company. The idea is to buy low and sell high to make a profit: buying shares of a stock when it's priced low and then selling that stock at a higher price is one way you make money on your investment with stocks. Stocks are bought and sold – traded – in stock markets, like the London Stock Exchange. You can follow the progress of your stock in the newspaper, on television or on the Internet.

The other way to make money with stocks is when companies pay out dividends – money paid to all the stockholders every year, the amount of which varies depending on how much a company earns.

Bonds

A bond is basically an 'IOU'. When you buy a bond, you are lending your money to a company or government, which they will pay you back later. Bonds give you an interest rate that is generally higher than what you're going to get in a savings account. The interest is worked into the bond price and you get both the interest and your money back on the 'maturity date'.

Mutual Funds

Mutual funds are another way to invest your money. With mutual funds, a money manager – a person whose job it is to know about investments – decides what stocks and bonds to buy and sell. When you buy into a mutual fund, you buy shares in the fund the same way you buy a share of a single company, but instead you're putting your money into a big collection (a 'fund') that the money manager uses to buy and sell investments to make money for you. Of course, she keeps a little piece for herself in the end.

Mutual funds are one way to balance out risk, as they involve diversification. When you diversify your investments, you make an effort not to put all your money in one risky thing, or all your money in one safe thing. Instead, you put a little into something more risky, a little into something safe, and a little into something in between.

MARCO POLO AND WATER POLO

◆

ACCESS TO A POOL, lake, pond, creek, river, stream, ocean or garden hose is critical on a hot summer day. Contests are always fun: swimming stroke races (on your mark, get set, go!), diving and seeing who can make up the funniest jumps. Cannonballs are great fun, as you run off the diving board, hurl into the air, grab onto your legs and make a huge splash. Underwater tricks like handstands and multiple back flips are also a nice way to cool off, as are attempts to mimic the intricacies of synchronized swimming. On a rainy day, you can watch old movies by water-ballet star Esther Williams for inspiration.

With water games, the main challenge is usually not the game itself, at least once you're on your way to mastering swimming – it's your nose, and how to keep water from rushing into it. You have three choices:

1. Breathe out sharply through your nose as you jump or duck underwater. The air coming out of your nose will keep water out.

2. Use one hand to hold your nose.

3. Find yourself an old-fashioned nose plug, the kind attached to the front of a rubber necklace. Clip your nose shut.

Thus prepared, below are a couple of aquatic games for those who can get to a pool or other slow-moving body of water.

MARCO POLO

The famed explorer Marco Polo was seventeen when he left Venice, Italy, to join his dad and uncle on a horseback journey to China. He did not return home for twenty-four years. While travelling, he befriended the Emperor Kublai Khan and was one of the first Western travellers of the Silk Road. He was fascinated by China's use of paper money and its intricate postal delivery system, innovations that far outstripped Europe's development at the time.

How Marco Polo's name got attached to the internationally known pool game, no one knows, but here are the rules.

You need at least three friends and everyone starts in the water. One person is It and her goal is to tag the other people. She closes her eyes, thus blinded (or you can use your handy bandana for a blindfold). Then she counts to five, or whatever number you all agree on. To try to find the other kids without seeing them, It must listen and sense where they are. Whenever she wants, she yells 'Marco'. Everyone in the game must immediately respond 'Polo'. The girl who is It uses the sounds of the other people's movements and voices to find and tag someone. Whoever she tags becomes the new It.

VARIATIONS

Now, there are some alterations you can employ to make Marco Polo more amusing and challenging. If you choose to, you can allow 'fish out of water'. This means the non-It players can get out of the pool. However, at any time, It can yell 'fish out of water' and if someone is out of the pool, that person automatically becomes the new It. If no one is out of the water, the other players often yell 'no'. (Hint: This can help It reorient and find them, too.)

You can also allow 'mermaid on the rocks', which is similar to 'fish out of water'. If someone is a mermaid on the rocks, she is sitting on the ledge of the pool or the lakeshore with only her feet in the water. Again, if It yells 'mermaid on the rocks', any mermaid becomes the new It. For either of these out-of-the-water variations, if It calls for fish or mermaids and there are none, she must do the start-of-game countdown again.

Another fun addition is 'alligator eyes', which allows It to call out 'alligator eyes' (or 'submarine', if you prefer) and then swim underwater with eyes open for one breath. Usually It is allowed to use this only once. We've heard of some places where It is allowed to go underwater and look around any time, but cannot move until she is above water with eyes closed or blindfold on again. We haven't played this one, but you may want to try it.

WATER POLO

While Marco Polo can thank the real Marco Polo for its name, water polo's comes from the game's rubber ball, which came from India, where the word for ball is *pulu,* hence polo.

Water polo was invented in England in the 1870s, though a similar kind of game may have been played in rivers in Africa and in flooded rice paddies in China many centuries before. While water polo claimed to resemble rugby, in practice it was more akin to underwater wrestling, with players hitting and ducking each other underwater with great regularity. Players would protect the ball by sticking it in their swimsuit and swimming underwater towards the goal. A much loved but extremely dangerous water polo feat had one player jumping off the backs of teammates and flying through the air, ball in hand, towards the opposing goal.

Good thing the more civilized 'Scottish' rules replaced the former free-for-all. The new rules instituted fouls for pushing and hitting, declared that the ball had to stay above water (no more bathing-suit tricks!), and stated that only a player holding the ball could be tackled (thus lowering the number of players who ended the game in casualty).

HOW TO PLAY

A water polo team has six field swimmers and a goalie. Teammates pass the ball and keep it from the other side, until one of them can lob it into the goal and score. To move forward in water polo you swim with your head out of water, since you'll need to see where the ball is. To backstroke, you sit in the water, use your arms to make small short strokes and use the eggbeater kick to stay up and moving: as you sit in the water, bend your knees and circle each leg towards the other, like an eggbeater.

Rules

* You can touch the ball with your hands – though with only one hand at a time, which means you'll catch the ball and pass it quickly.

* Don't touch the bottom of the pool. This sport is about constant motion, no rest, and never touching the bottom.

* No pushing, pulling, hitting or holding on to the other players – that's a foul. Fouls are also called if you hold the ball underwater, touch it with two hands or hold on to it longer than thirty-five seconds; or if you touch the bottom, push off the side of the pool, or use bad language.

While Marco Polo will never be an Olympic sport, water polo is. Male Olympians have played water polo since 1900. Ever since the 2000 Olympics in Sydney, women's water polo has been on the roster, too and there's a terrific story behind its entry. After a decade or two of polite behind-the-scenes negotiation with the International Olympic Committee, the Australian women's national water polo team pushed the issue. The upcoming Olympics were on their turf, after all, and they wanted to compete. In 1998, members of the Olympic Committee were set to arrive at Sydney airport, in town for a planning visit. Led by their goalkeeper Liz Weekes – she's called the team's 'glamour girl' because she's also a model – the Aussie women water polo players put on their swimsuits and caps and strode through Sydney airport to meet them, and, very much in the public eye, they asked again to be included, and met with success.

Better yet, after fighting so hard to be included, the Australian women's team won the gold medal, with player Yvette Higgins scoring the winning goal during the last second of the championship game, to the applause of fans who filled the stadium.

WOMEN WHO CHANGED THE WORLD

Anne Frank (1929–45)

◆

ANNE FRANK certainly didn't mean to change the world, and you could say that her legacy has been one of *reminding* rather than changing the world. She was a normal girl who lived in extraordinary times and, as many girls do, she kept a record of her experiences. That diary became *The Diary of a Young Girl* (also known as *The Diary of Anne Frank*) and would be read by millions across the world.

Anne Frank was a young Jewish girl living in Amsterdam with her parents, her sister Margot and her cat Moortje. On her thirteenth birthday she received her first diary, a treasured gift in which she would commit her thoughts, her fears and her joys to paper. Shortly after Anne's birthday, Margot received a demand from the Nazis to leave for a work camp and their father, Otto, put into action the plan he had been working on for several months. The family was to go into hiding. Little did they realize that this hiding place would become their home for the next two years.

Dit is een foto, zoals
ik me zou wensen,
altijd zo te zijn.
Dan had ik nog wel
een kans om naar
Holywood te komen.

Anne Frank.
10 Oct. 1942

(translation)
"This is a photo as I would wish
myself to look all the time. Then
I would maybe have a chance to
come to Hollywood."
Anne Frank, 10 Oct. 1942

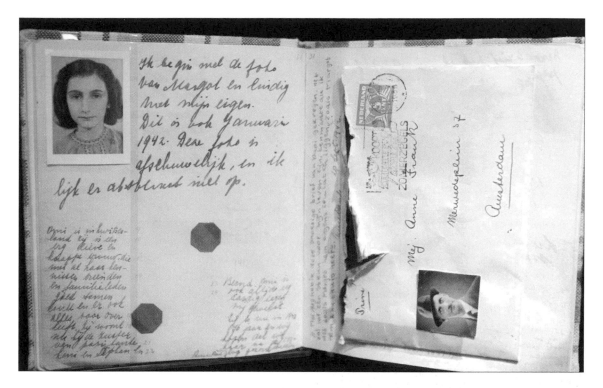

Hidden at the top of a tall office building in the western quarter of Amsterdam, the Secret Annexe (as Anne would call it in her diary) was concealed by a large bookcase. Behind that bookcase were the rooms that the Franks shared and that they would later share with four other Jews. The family was protected by friends who would bring them food and news of the war – no small feat in a country where harbouring a Jew would result in the death penalty.

Anne wrote of her life in the cramped and claustrophobic flat: her fear of discovery, her boredom at being shut away for so long, her frustration. But she also wrote of her feelings much as any other girl of her age would: how her mother irritated her, arguments with her sister, her budding feelings of tenderness towards Peter, the son of the other family living in the Annexe. Her walls were covered in pictures of film stars, she longed to go to Hollywood, she longed to become a writer, she wondered if she would ever be married.

The diaries were never meant for public consumption. In 1944 the family was discovered by the Nazis and all the inhabitants of the Secret Annexe were sent to work camps. The only member of the family to survive was Otto Frank, and it was he who released Anne's diaries to serve as a reminder of the crimes committed against the Jews during the Holocaust.

The legacy that Anne Frank left is one that must not be forgotten. She was just one of the 6 million Jews killed during the Holocaust, but her diaries allow us to see the humanity behind the suffering. She was a normal girl, and her words speak to girls today, even after sixty years.

WOMEN WHO CHANGED THE WORLD

Mary Wollstonecraft (1759–97)

MARY WOLLSTONECRAFT lived in volatile and uncertain times. The monarch, King George III, had lost his mind, causing what was known as the Regency Crisis. Over the Channel in France, revolution was stirring. The Bastille was stormed, the palace at Versailles was attacked and the French king, Louis XVI, and his queen, Marie Antoinette, along with most of their court, were executed by the people.

The sense of change and revolution led many people to question the ways in which they lived and opened up a vibrant debate among political thinkers and writers. Mary Wollstonecraft was key to this scene, and her writings would lead to a dramatic change in the lives of women and the way they were viewed in society.

Wollstonecraft is mostly known for her turbulent and unconventional life. She was a passionate woman who loved two men deeply in her lifetime. The first was George Imray, an American,

with whom she moved to France in the 1790s. They had a daughter together but their affair was blighted by Imray's infidelities and they parted company. Wollstonecraft, much affected by this split, attempted suicide twice but was unsuccessful. She then met William Godwin, an English writer, whom she married. Their daughter Mary would later marry the poet Shelley and would become well known in her own right for writing the gothic novel *Frankenstein*.

However, it was Wollstonecraft's writing that changed the world. She worked as a governess, and her experiences led her to question the education of women in society. The French philosopher Rousseau thought that women's education should be cultivated only for the entertainment of men, and his views were echoed by men across the country. But Wollstonecraft saw this as an attempt by men to control women and to keep them, through lack of education, as inferiors to men. Women, she argued in her seminal work, *A Vindication of the Rights of Woman*, were just as capable and intelligent as men, and if only they were given an equal education society would benefit. This seems sensible to us nowadays, but at the time it was a radical suggestion and one that many people, women and men, disagreed with strongly.

In Wollstonecraft's view, the education of women would lead to a more equal relationship between men and women and would also better equip women to act as companions to men, standing at their side intellectually rather than beneath them. She attacked the fashionable notion of 'sensibility', which meant an excess of emotion and a lack of rational thought, or 'sense'. You might recognize this debate from the title of one of Jane Austen's most popular novels: *Sense and Sensibility*.

Wollstonecraft's writings started an argument about the role of women in society, and many see her as a forerunner of the suffrage movement that would result in women winning the vote and gaining political equality. She wasn't particularly popular during her lifetime or in the years after she died – people looked down on what they saw as her dissolute life – but *A Vindication of the Rights of Woman* has become one of the most important books written at the time.

RULES OF THE GAME: HOCKEY

◆

HOCKEY IS A GAME we all remember from school. Played mostly in the rain, or so it seems, it's a fast-moving and energetic team sport. It's mainly played by girls at school and university level, but boys and men do play it too.

A SHORT HISTORY OF HOCKEY

Playing a game with a ball and a curved stick can be traced back to antiquity, but the game we know today dates from the nineteenth century. It was popular at English public schools and it is thought that the first rules in Britain were laid out at Eton. Different variations of the game are played throughout the world; what we play is known as Field Hockey, but other countries have adapted the game and play Ice Hockey, Roller Hockey and Road Hockey.

POSITIONS

Hockey is played by two teams made up of eleven players each.

Each team consists of the following positions, and, in a similar way to football, it is up to the players as to how many of each position they have:

* Defenders
* Midfielders
* Attackers
* Goalkeeper

EQUIPMENT

* A hockey stick – a long, curved wooden stick with a rounded section at its tip
* A small hard ball
* Shin pads. They don't look cool but they will save your legs from injury. If you don't have access to plastic shin pads, you can always compromise with pads of newspapers stuck into your long socks.

HOW TO PLAY

A game lasts for thirty-five minutes each way with a five-minute break at half-time. The aim of the game is to score as many goals as possible by hitting the ball past the other team's goalkeeper and into their goal. Players are permitted to tackle each other and may hit the ball with any part of the stick apart from the back, curved section.

Players may not:
* obstruct other players deliberately
* kick the ball
* make contact between their stick and another player
* raise their stick higher than shoulder height

If you hit the ball off the pitch over the sideline, play is given to the other team who can hit it from the point on the sideline where it left the pitch. If the ball is hit off the pitch over the backline, a fifteen-metre hit is awarded to the other team.

Free hits These are either five-metre hits or, as mentioned above, fifteen-metre hits. The players from the team not awarded the hit must move away from the ball by the specified distance while the other girl makes her play.

Long corner Awarded when the ball goes off the backline of the pitch, after being hit off by a defender. The attacking team may take a shot at the goal from five metres away from the corner of the pitch nearest where the ball went off.

Penalty corner Awarded against the defending team if they deliberately foul in the defending/goal area.

HOW TO CHANGE A TYRE

CHANGING A TYRE is one of those life skills that never seem essential until the moment you need it. This is a good thing to learn even if you don't yet have your driving licence.

1 The car should be parked on level ground, out of danger's way, with the engine off and the handbrake on. Ask everyone to hop out of the car to make it lighter.

2 Check to make sure you have all the necessary equipment: a functioning spare tyre, a tyre jack and a cross wrench. If you are missing any of these you will unfortunately have to wait for the breakdown vehicle.

3 If you have tyre blocks, put them under the other tyres to keep the car in place. Medium-sized rocks work too.

4 Start to loosen the wheel nuts; these are the nuts that keep the hubcap on. Not all cars have hubcaps, but look and you'll see what needs to be loosened. Put the lug wrench on each lug nut. Remember 'righty-tighty, lefty-loosey' to guide you which way to turn the socket wrench.

If your car's wheel nuts were last tightened with a hydraulic wheel nut tightener in a garage, they will be very tight. Jump on the cross wrench. Get everyone in your family to jump on the cross wrench and in any other way work the wheel nuts free. Some very organized people keep a length of hollow pipe in their car, which can be attached to the socket wrench for extra leverage. If you have it, WD-40 also helps. Some people swear that, if you are really stuck, pouring cola over the wheel nuts will do the trick. Caution: don't take the nuts all the way off, just loosen them.

5 The jack will keep the car up and off the ground while the tyre is changed. Each car has a slightly different way to do this, so consult the manual if it's nearby. In general, there's a solid metal plate on the car frame, in front of the back tyre frame and just behind the front tyre. Once you've found this, the cool part begins, in which you raise the car.

Put the jack right under the metal plate, and start pumping. The car will lift off the ground. From time to time make sure that the jack stays connected to the metal plate. Stop pumping when the car tyre is 15 to 20 centimetres off the ground.

6 Now you can remove the wheel nuts entirely. Stash them somewhere safe. Grab the tyre and pull it towards you. It will be dirty. You can wash your hands later.

7 Pick up the spare tyre and align its holes with the bolts. Push the spare onto the tyre bolts until it absolutely stops. Replace the lug nuts and tighten, but not all the way.

8 Carefully pump down the jack to lower the car, stopping when all four tyres are back on the ground.

9 Now tighten the wheel nuts. Don't tighten them around the circle; instead, tighten the first, then tighten the nut across from it, and continue on from there. You're finished.

HOW TO NEGOTIATE A SALARY
for Dog-Walking, Errand-Running, Babysitting – or Anything!

❖

'Let us never negotiate out of fear, but let us never fear to negotiate.'
JOHN F. KENNEDY, INAUGURAL ADDRESS, 1961.

THE WORD 'NEGOTIATE' comes from the Latin word *negotiari*, meaning 'to trade'. When you negotiate something, you are essentially asking for someone to trade you something and making a case for why that would be a good idea. There are several steps to a successful negotiation: preparation, presentation, contemplation and sealing the deal.

Preparation

Define your goals. Do you want a higher salary? Do you want more hours? Do you want to be paid extra for overtime? Narrowing down what it is you want will help you approach the task of asking for it.

Do your research. Find out what the going rate is in your neighbourhood for the work you do – how much do your friends get paid for the same work? Does the amount they get depend on the level of responsibility they have? Once you know the answers to these questions, you'll know the facts about what other people are paid and you'll be better prepared to ask for what you want.

Presentation

Plan what you're going to say and how you're going to say it.

Begin with lower-priority requests, if possible, and work your way up to the big ones. (When you get to the big request, you can trade off some of the lower-priority requests if necessary.)

Accentuate the positive. This is not the time for modesty – emphasize your accomplishments and abilities and point out why it is you deserve what you are asking for. Smile, be confident and be friendly.

Contemplation

Listen. Sometimes the most important part of a conversation is the part when you're not talking. When it's time for the other person to respond, listen carefully to what he or she has to say.

Think. You may be presented with a counteroffer – an offer made in response to your offer. You don't have to respond to a counteroffer right away. You can take your time and think about it, even if that means not giving your answer for a few days.

Sealing the deal

Sign on the dotted line. Once both parties have reached an agreement, it's a good idea to put that final offer in writing and for both of you to sign the document. This will prevent any future misunderstandings or miscommunications about what was actually agreed upon during your negotiation. Still, sometimes a good old-fashioned handshake will do.

Common mistakes

Not preparing. Make sure you have done your research and know what you are talking about. If you're not sure, postpone the negotiation until you've had time to get ready.

Trying to win at all costs. Arguing or using intimidating behaviour is going to hinder rather than help the negotiation process. Remember, the central process of negotiation is discussion with others to reach an agreement or compromise. It's a dialogue, not a monologue.

Talking too much. Listen carefully to what the other person has to say and when it's your turn to speak, be direct and to the point.

Trying to be someone you're not. The key in negotiation is to be comfortable. If you are trying to act 'tough' because you think it will make the discussion go your way, you may be sadly disappointed. Being the most confident version of yourself is better than trying to be the kind of person you think you should be in order to win.

Tips

Even though it might make you nervous to ask for something, whether it's a higher salary or more responsibility, it's important to try to maintain an open and confident attitude. You want to make the person you're negotiating with want to say yes to you – and it's very hard to say no to a smiling, friendly person. Some people call this technique to 'disarm with charm'. But whether or not you're good at being 'charming', try to smile, look people directly in the eye and concentrate on not speaking too fast. Remember, this is just a conversation! You have those all the time. (Also, the people you're negotiating with may expect you to be nervous or insecure about the negotiation process – so acting comfortable and confident may catch them off guard and make them even more likely to say yes to your request.)

PUBLIC SPEAKING

◆

IF YOU WOULD RATHER DIE than speak in public, you're in good company: glossophobia (fear of speaking in public, or 'stage fright') affects as much as seventy-five per cent of the population. But speaking in front of a group doesn't have to be nerve-racking, especially if you practise before you do it. Public speaking shares many of the principles of a good negotiation: Preparation, Practice and Presenting – with the confidence to 'seal the deal'.

Prepare

Know what you're going to say. Write out your speech, and practise saying it aloud. You don't necessarily need to memorize it, but you should know it well enough so that if you had to talk without your notes, you could pull it off.

Know who you're going to say it to. Knowing your audience is good advice no matter what you are performing. If you know you will be giving a speech in your history class, that's going to inform your material much differently than if you were giving a toast at your dad's fiftieth birthday party. You want to adapt your speech to fit the people you are speaking to. That way nobody gets bored, and what you say will be a good match for your audience.

Know where you're going to say it. It's a good idea to familiarize yourself with the place where you'll be speaking, if you can. Is it a big room or a small one? Will you have to speak loud and project, or will there be a micro-phone that you will have to adjust? Is there a lectern or a chair, or will you be able to move around while you talk? When you have some information about where you'll be, you'll know what to expect before you get there, and that will help cut down on your nerves once it's showtime.

Practise

Visualize. Most of the fear we have around public speaking isn't about talking in front of people, but about doing something potentially embarrassing in front of people. To combat this, practise imagining yourself giving your speech and doing a great job. Walk yourself through it in your head, from beginning to end, giving yourself a chance to visualize yourself doing well instead of living out your worst fears.

Realize. Make it real by practising your speech ahead of time – by yourself, in front of your family, in front of your friends, the family pets, whoever you can get to be an audience for you. It's a good idea to either write out your speech on notecards or print it out in a very big font so that you can quickly look down, see what you need to say and look back up to say it. Practising delivering your speech so that it becomes routine will stand you in good stead when you start to feel unnerved onstage or in front of the class. Practising with an audience is also a chance to realize that your audience wants you to succeed. People want to hear what you have to say, and they want you to do well.

Exercise. If you are waiting around while others speak before you, it is helpful to step outside the room just before you speak to calm yourself down with deep-breathing exercises, breathing in slowly through your nose and breathing out through your mouth. If you're too nervous to breathe, you might channel that energy into a quick set of jumping jacks, or shaking out your arms and legs. Then take some deep breaths to feel calm and centred. This is something you can do in practice and in performance.

Present

It's not about you. Remember as you begin your presentation, it's about your speech, not about you. It's helpful to concentrate on the message – not the medium. That way instead of thinking about all the different ways things could go wrong as you deliver your talk, you focus yourself on the content of your talk and about getting those points across.

It's all about you. Whether or not you crumble out of nervousness or do fantastically well thanks to sheer nerve is completely up to you – in other words, it is in your control. When you're incredibly nervous, you have the opportunity to harness that energy and transform it into vitality and enthusiasm. Take a deep breath and dive in!

It's all good. No matter how you do, it is always good in the sense that every time you speak in public, you gain experience. Use this to build your sense of self-confidence: if you've done well, you now have proof for the next time around that you can do well. And if nerves have got the better of you, you now have proof that the worst has happened and you've survived. Either way, you know that you've done it – you've spoken in public once, and you can do it again. This confidence-building is crucial, because having confidence is the key to speaking well.

Quick tips

Keep it short and sweet.

Slow down: Don't talk too fast.

Look up: If it's too scary to look at the audience in the front row, look at the people in the back of the room.

Smile: Look confident, even if you don't feel confident.

Pretend: Try imagining that everyone in the audience is sitting there in their underwear.

Find a friendly face in the audience and pretend you're only talking to that person.

Practise: Join the debate team, dare yourself to speak up in class, give a speech in front of a mirror. The more opportunities you have to speak in public, the easier it gets.

Biggest asset: Self-confidence. Act as though you have a right to be there – because you do.

TELLING GHOST STORIES

S O: YOU'VE PITCHED YOUR TENT, set up your campfire and toasted your marshmallows. Or maybe you've made a sleepover den at your best friend's house, played Truth or Dare and Bloody Mary, and taken out the torches and sleeping bags. What next? Two words: ghost stories.

Everybody loves a scary story, especially late at night around a flickering campfire, or in the dark of an unfamiliar living room with a small torch illuminating your face. And you may have noticed, if you've been on a few camp-outs or sleepovers, that many of these stories have similar themes: a ghost out for revenge or literally haunted by grief; a lonely road or abandoned house; an element of shock or surprise; and just enough true-life details to make it all seem believable in the dead of night.

Some stories involve real people and places – and supposedly real sightings – like the ghost of Queen Anne Boleyn, second wife of King Henry VIII, who is said to haunt both the Tower of London, where she was imprisoned and beheaded in 1536, and Hever Castle in Kent, her childhood home and the setting of her first encounter with the king who would later sentence her to death. Other stories are about more anonymous ghosts – regular people who lived in the not-too-distant past and had believably scary things happen to them. And don't discount the shock value of a good old urban legend – supposedly real stories of supposedly real people who had scary things happen to them: the woman who died of spider bites after a spider nested in her hair; the man who picked up a hitchhiker only to discover that she was a ghost haunting the highway where she had been killed in a car wreck forty years before; the girl who died when her shrink-to-fit jeans shrunk so much while she wore them that she was crushed by their constricting force.

Whichever kind of story you choose to tell, here are some tips for making up good ones and telling them right.

ELEMENTS OF A GHOST STORY

Mix and match these common elements to make your own ghost story.

Common characters

* A young girl
* An old woman
* A camper
* A person driving alone
* Two friends who think they're braver than they are
* A person from your city's past
* A distant relative
* A hitchhiker

Common ghost features

* Able to be sensed by animals and children
* Haunting the place where they died
* Appearing at night and vanishing by dawn
* Playful or prankish – playing music or moving things to scare people

Common ghost motivations

* Ghost needs to find an object or person they left behind
* Ghost needs to warn the main character about something
* Ghost needs to deliver a comforting message to the main character
* Ghost is out for revenge

Common settings

* Your house
* An abandoned mine
* A graveyard
* The woods
* Your local scary place (creepy neighbour's house, the old creek, etc.)
* A long, empty hallway
* A castle
* Any isolated, spooky place

Common situations

* Going out alone at night
* Being alone in a spooky place
* Getting trapped in a haunted house overnight
* Picking up a hitchhiker
* Disregarding a ghost's warning or a local legend
* Triggering events that summon a ghost

Don't forget to use spooky ghost story words, like graveyard, curse, legend, bone-chilling, creepy, ominous, deadly, mysterious, eerie, grisly, gruesome, blood-curdling... anything that adds to the scary mood.

Using realistic details can make your story even spookier – having the main character be a girl who used to go to your school years ago, or having the story take place in your town, or down the street from your house, lends the tale an air of believability that draws your listeners in. Sometimes it's helpful to have a friend in on the story – so that when you end your story with something like, 'The girl was never found' (said in a sombre, dramatic voice, of course), your friend can scream out, 'I'm here!!!!' and make everyone else shriek.

TELLING IT RIGHT

Make sure you prepare – practise ahead of time, and coordinate with a friend if you're going to be using a sidekick for maximum scaring. When you tell your story, speak slowly, in a serious voice and look at everyone you're speaking to. Make sure to take your audience into consideration: if there are little sisters or younger girls there, you might want to save the super-scary stuff for after they're asleep. And even if your crowd is a bit older, seriously scary stories can make for some sleepless nights. It's fun to make yourself a little scared, but if a listener finds your tale too frightening, it's also okay to turn on the light and remind everyone that it's just a story.

> **Some famous ghost stories in classic literature**
>
> Edgar Allan Poe's
> *The Tell Tale Heart* (1843)
> Washington Irving's
> *The Legend of Sleepy Hollow* (1820)
> W. W. Jacobs'
> *The Monkey's Paw* (1902)
> Charles Dickens'
> *A Christmas Carol* (1843)
> Oscar Wilde's
> *The Canterville Ghost* (1887)
> Shakespeare's
> *Hamlet* (1602)

OR IS IT??????

In this passage from Act I, Scene V, of the play *Hamlet*, we witness one of the spookiest scenes in all of Shakespeare: Hamlet is confronted by the ghost of his father, the former King of Denmark, who tries to tell Hamlet that he was murdered by his own brother.

GHOST
I am thy father's spirit,
Doom'd for a certain term to walk the night,
And for the day confined to fast in fires,
Till the foul crimes done in my days of nature
Are burnt and purged away. But that I am
*   forbid*
To tell the secrets of my prison-house,
I could a tale unfold whose lightest word
Would harrow up thy soul, freeze thy young
*   blood,*
Make thy two eyes, like stars, start from their
*   spheres,*
Thy knotted and combined locks to part
And each particular hair to stand on end,
Like quills upon the fretful porpentine:
But this eternal blazon must not be
To ears of flesh and blood. List, list, O, list!
If thou didst ever thy dear father love –

HAMLET
O God!

GHOST
Revenge his foul and most unnatural murder.

HAMLET
Murder!

GHOST
Murder most foul, as in the best it is;
But this most foul, strange and unnatural.

HAMLET
Haste me to know't, that I, with wings as swift
As meditation or the thoughts of love,
May sweep to my revenge.

GHOST

I find thee apt;
And duller shouldst thou be than the fat weed
That roots itself in ease on Lethe wharf,
Wouldst thou not stir in this. Now, Hamlet, hear:
'Tis given out that, sleeping in my orchard,
A serpent stung me; so the whole ear of
    Denmark
Is by a forged process of my death
Rankly abused: but know, thou noble youth,
The serpent that did sting thy father's life
Now wears his crown.

HAMLET

O my prophetic soul! My uncle!

GHOST

Ay, that incestuous, that adulterate beast,
With witchcraft of his wit, with traitorous
    gifts, –
O wicked wit and gifts, that have the power
So to seduce! – won to his shameful lust
The will of my most seeming-virtuous queen:
O Hamlet, what a falling-off was there!
From me, whose love was of that dignity
That it went hand in hand even with the vow
I made to her in marriage, and to decline

Upon a wretch whose natural gifts were poor
To those of mine!
But virtue, as it never will be moved,
Though lewdness court it in a shape of heaven,
So lust, though to a radiant angel link'd,
Will sate itself in a celestial bed,
And prey on garbage.
But, soft! methinks I scent the morning air;
Brief let me be. Sleeping within my orchard,
My custom always of the afternoon,
Upon my secure hour thy uncle stole,
With juice of cursed hebenon in a vial,
And in the porches of my ears did pour
The leperous distilment; whose effect
Holds such an enmity with blood of man
That swift as quicksilver it courses through
The natural gates and alleys of the body,
And with a sudden vigour doth posset
And curd, like eager droppings into milk,
The thin and wholesome blood: so did it mine;
And a most instant tetter bark'd about,
Most lazar-like, with vile and loathsome crust,
All my smooth body.
Thus was I, sleeping, by a brother's hand
Of life, of crown, of queen, at once dispatch'd:
Cut off even in the blossoms of my sin,
Unhousel'd, disappointed, unanel'd,
No reckoning made, but sent to my account
With all my imperfections on my head:
O, horrible! O, horrible! most horrible!
If thou hast nature in thee, bear it not;
Let not the royal bed of Denmark be
A couch for luxury and damned incest.
But, howsoever thou pursuest this act,
Taint not thy mind, nor let thy soul contrive
Against thy mother aught: leave her to heaven
And to those thorns that in her bosom lodge,
To prick and sting her. Fare thee well at once!
The glow-worm shows the matin to be near,
And 'gins to pale his uneffectual fire:
Adieu, adieu! Hamlet, remember me.

MAKE YOUR OWN QUILL PEN

———— ◆ ————

THE MAIN INGREDIENT in a quill pen is, of course, the quill. As not all of us live in close proximity to ravens, crows or geese, it may be necessary to ask your local poultry farmer for a spare feather. You can always try an art supply shop or a calligraphy studio if you get stuck. Wherever you find your feather, it's best to get more than one, just in case. The other tools you'll need are a sharp knife or razor, a cutting board and a pencil.

MAKING THE QUILL

Hold the tip of the quill in boiling water for a minute or two to soften it up so that it can be cut without splitting or breaking off. (It should become soft and somewhat pliable, like your finger-nails after a hot bath.) You may also strip some of the feathers off to make room for your hand to hold the quill.

For this you will need adult supervision. Use the knife to slice horizontally across the end of the quill. This angled cut should begin about an inch from the end of the shaft on the underside of the quill.

Make a second cut at a steeper angle, about a half-inch from the end, to shape the nib (the 'point' of the pen). Clean out the hollow part, scraping out any fluff or fuzz from inside the quill.

Use the knife to make a slit in the middle of the nib.

Use your pencil to open the slit slightly by pressing up gently from underneath. Lay the nib on a cutting board and slice the tip off so that it is square. At this point you may refine the nib by further cutting down the angled sides or using fine sandpaper to gently smooth out rough edges.

USING YOUR QUILL PEN

It's a good idea to practise on newsprint or scrap paper before moving on to fancier papers. You may want to pencil in some lines or margins as guides before you begin, but this is not required. Dip your quill into the ink you've bought and then begin to write on your paper. Try not to drench your quill with the ink – the nib should be saturated just enough to write a few letters at a time. Otherwise you'll get blots, drips and splats. Writing with a quill pen is a leisurely task; the ink takes a while to dry and the nib will need re-dipping every word or so. Depending on the angle of your nib and the way you hold your pen, your quill will make thin lines as well as thick lines, so feel free to experiment. Practise by writing your favourite sentence – a famous quote or favourite saying – over and over until you can write it without any blots or errors.

HIKING

What is the difference between hiking and plain old walking? Well, we always think of hiking as being walking in the wilderness, out in the countryside where you can really appreciate the beauty of nature.

A few tips before you set out:

* Make sure you take a detailed map and that you know how to read it.
* Always go with a friend and tell someone where you are going and what time you plan to get back.
* Take provisions such as a torch, some water, some snacks and a mobile phone in case you get into trouble.
* Plan your route and work out how long it should take to complete it so you can avoid walking at night.

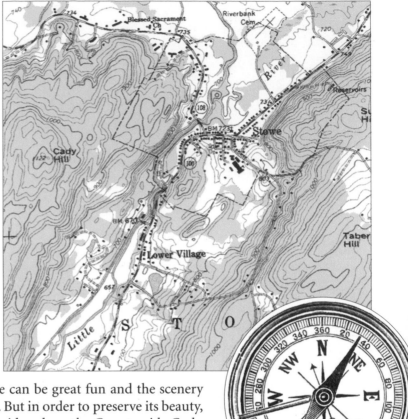

Hiking in the British countryside can be great fun and the scenery is worth getting out of breath for. But in order to preserve its beauty, remember to keep to the countryside rules – the Countryside Code. Always stick to the footpaths, close gates behind you, don't leave naked flames burning and make sure you take all your litter home with you.

Things to see along the way

The scenery around Britain changes with every county, but there are some things you should keep your eyes open for.

Trees
If you look closely at the trees you should be able to see how they are different from one another. With a good guide to identification you will be able to figure out the various trees by leaves, bark and fruit.

1. Crab apple
2. Juniper
3. Larch
4. Oak
5. Poplar

Animal prints

You may want to try to work out which animals have passed along the trail by identifying their tracks and droppings.

front *hind*

Badger

Cattle

front *hind*

Deer

front *hind*

Hedgehog

front *hind*

Rabbit

front *hind*

Squirrel

Nettles and dock leaves

When you walk anywhere in the countryside, you are almost certain to get stung by nettles. This can be pretty painful, but nature provides its own cure in the form of dock leaves. Nettles and dock leaves often grow next to each other so you have the cure handy whenever you are stung. Just rub a dock leaf over your sting, squeezing a little of the juice onto your skin.

How to make a walking stick

A walking stick should only be fashioned from a fallen branch, not pulled from a tree, and should reach from the ground to your shoulder. First, use your Swiss Army knife to remove the bark and whittle away extra branches and spurs. Then sand it down until the stick is smooth to touch, and finally just shine it with a little linseed oil.

Great walks

FOLLOW IN THE FOOTSTEPS OF CELIA FIENNES

Celia Fiennes was quite a novelty for her time. Born in 1662, she was one of the first women to travel around England purely for the pleasure of the journey. At the time, travel was seen as dangerous and uncomfortable, but Celia was determined to explore the country and to try to improve her health, which had always been poor since she was a child. She travelled by horseback and was the first woman to visit every county in England. Along the way she kept a journal which, although it was only ever meant to be read by her family and friends, was published as *Through Britain on a Side Saddle*.

She travelled throughout England, but here is just one suggestion from her Newcastle to Cornwall route starting at Buxton in Derbyshire:

Buxton we saw 2 or 3 tymes and then lost ye sight of it as often, and at last did not see it till just you came upon it – that 9 mile we were above 6 hours going it … Another wonder [to see in Buxton] is that of Pooles hole, that's just at ye town's end, a large cavity underground of a great length. Just at the entrance you must creep, but presently you stand upright, its roofe being very lofty all arched in the rocks and sound with a great ecchoe. Ye Rocks are continually dropping water all about, you pass over loose stones and craggy rocks. The dripping of the water wears impression on ye stones that forms them into severall shapes, there is one looks like a lyon with a crown on his head … The [next] wonder is that off Elden hole about 2 mile from Buxton; it's on ye side of a hill about 30 yards if not better in length at ye brimm, and half so broad, and just in sight is full of craggy stones like a rock for about 2 or 3 yards down, which contracts the mouth of ye hole to about 4 yards long and 2 broad or thereabouts; which hole is suppos'd to run down directly a vast length and has been try'd with a line and plummet severall fathom and the bottom not sounded … The [next] wonder is Mamtour which is a high hill that looks exactly round, but on the side next Castleton which is a little town in the high peake on that side its all broken that it looks just in resemblance as a great Hay-Ricke yet cut down one halfe on one side – that describes it most naturall. This is all sand, and on that broken side the sand keeps trickling down allwayes especially when there is the least wind of which I believe this country scarce ever is without; many places of the hill looks hollow and loose which makes it very dangerous to ascend and none does attempt it, ye sand being loose slips ye foote back againe … The [final] wonder is at Casleton 4 mile from Elderhole; its a town lyes at ye foote of an exceeding steep hill which could not be descended by foote or horse, but in a compass and yet by ye roads returning to and agen on ye side of ye hill at least 4 tymes before we could gaine ye bottom or top of said hill. This is which they call the Devill's Arse a peake, the hill on one end jutting out in two parts and joyns in one at ye top, this part or cleft between you enter a great cave which is very large, and severall poor little houses in it built of stone and thatch'd like little styes, one seemed a little bigger in which a gentleman liv'd and his wife yet was worth above 100 a year which he left to his brother, chooseing rather like a hermite to live in this sorry cell … From Castleton to Buxton is 6 mile, but they are very long. You might go 10 of miles near London as soon as you are going halfe so many here.

From *Through Britain on a Side Saddle* by Celia Fiennes

You would be well advised to check a map before you leave, but keep your eyes peeled for the sights described by Celia.

Walk in *Lorna Doone* country

Lorna Doone is a story of forbidden love and jealous rivalry, set in Exmoor, Devon, in the seventeenth century. If you haven't read it, you must hurry along to your local library as it's a story that girls have loved for generations. Ask your mother, she'll almost certainly have read it.

The countryside in which the story is set is some of the most stunning in Britain. And it is possible to trace the story in the hills and valleys of Exmoor, visiting the places where famous scenes from the book are set.

Doone Valley is actually called Badgworthy Valley, and to start this walk you need to head to Malmsmead, the tiny village where the book is set. Here you'll find the Lorna Doone farm. Your walk starts by heading away from the village, up the hill to a public right of way where you'll find a sign to Doone Valley. Head across the fields, with the Badgworthy Water to your left until you reach Cloud Farm. Here you need to descend to the river, and a little way on you'll find a mem-orial stone laid in honour of the author of the book, R.

D. Blackmore. Continue by heading into Badgworthy Woods, crossing over the Lank Combe Water using a footpath. Keep going until you see a sign for Brendan Common, and then your walk will bring you out onto moorland that once held a settlement. Continue uphill until you reach Lank Combe Ford where you need to cross the stream and go on towards the ridge. You'll soon come across a sign for Malmsmead and you should follow this until it takes you down the hill and back into the village. You'll have walked about six miles so you'll be ready for a hot bath and a rest.

Discover the world of *Swallows and Amazons*

This is perhaps more of a wander than a walk but it is inspired by a book, and another book that every girl ought to read. *Swallows and Amazons* is perhaps one of the greatest adventure stories ever written for children. Written by Arthur Ransome, it follows the adventures of John, Susan, Titty and Roger – the Amazons – and Nancy and Peggy – the Swallows – both groups named after the boats they find and borrow. With the summer ahead of them and the freedom of the lakes and countryside around them, they create a fantastical world where grown-ups are not invited.

Arthur Ransome told his readers that the places in his book could all be found in the Lake

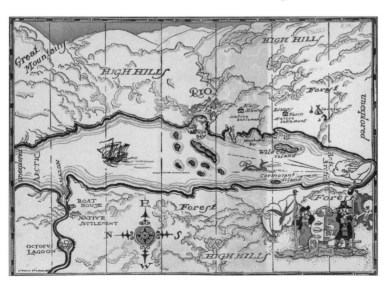

District. We can tell you that the lake in the book is based on Windermere and Wildcat Island in the book is most likely to be Peel Island in Coniston. But the fun of this walk is exploring the countryside around this area and discovering for yourself the landmarks which correspond with the book. We recommend taking the book, some friends and some ginger ale out on a boat and discovering this world for yourself.

GREEK AND LATIN ROOT WORDS

◆

M ANY ENGLISH WORDS have their origins in Latin and Greek. Knowing a word's roots, prefixes or suffixes can be your clue to its meaning – even if you don't understand it at first glance.

A word's 'root' is the part of the word that carries the main component of meaning. Adding a prefix to the beginning of the root word, or a suffix to the end of it, can add other layers of meaning, but the core concept of the word is in its root. Here is a chart of Greek and Latin root words, their meanings and some examples (the Greek terms are in *italic*).

Greek and Latin roots	Meaning	English examples
-anthrop-	human	anthropology
-arch-/-archi-	ancient	archetype
-astro-	star	astronomy, astral
-audi-	hear	audible
-bene-	good	benefit
-bio-	life	biography
-brev-	short	abbreviation
-chron-/-chrono-	time	anachronism, chronicle
-dem-	people	democracy, demagogue
-dict-	to say	dictate, predict
-duc-	to lead; to take	produce, reduce
-gen-	kind, type; birth	generation
-graph-	write	graphic

Greek and Latin roots	Meaning	English examples
-gress-	to walk	progress
-hydr-/hydro-	water	hydrate
-ject-	to throw	eject, project
-jur/just-	law	jury, justice
-logo/logue-	word, thought	dialogue, monologue
-luc-	light	lucid, luculent
-manu-	hand	manual
-meter/metr-	measure	thermometer
-morph-	form	amorphous
-olig-	few	oligarchy
-op/oper-	work	operation
-osteo-	bone	osteoporosis
-path-	feeling, suffering	empathic, sympathy
-pel-	to drive	compel, dispel,
-pend-	to hang	depend, pendulum
-philo-/-phil-	love	philanthropy, philosophy
-phon-	sound	polyphonic, phonetics
-port-	to carry	export, support
-proto-	first	prototype

Greek and Latin roots	Meaning	English examples
-pseudo-	false	pseudonym
-scrib-/-script-	to write	describe, transcribe
-sect-	cut	dissect
-sol-	alone	solitary, solo
-struct-	build	construct
-ter/terr-	earth	territory
-tract-	to pull, drag, draw	attract, contract, extract
-vac-	empty	vacant, vacuous
-ver-	truth	verify
-vert-	to turn	convert, revert
-vid/vis-	see	video, visualize

A prefix is a word part added to the beginning of a root word to change its meaning. Here are some Greek and Latin prefixes, their meanings, and examples.

Greek and Latin prefixes	Meaning	English examples
a-/an-	without; not	amoral, atypical
ad-	to	addict
amb-/ambi-	both	ambidextrous
anti-/ant-	opposite	antifreeze, antacid

Greek and Latin prefixes	Meaning	English examples
auto-	self	autobiography, autopilot
bi-	two	bipedal
bio-	life	biology
centi-	hundred	centimetre, century
circum-	around	circumvent, circumnavigate
co-	together	coauthor
con/- com-	with	concert
de-	off; from; down	depart, defrost
deci-	ten	decimetre, decade
di-	two	diameter
dis-	opposite; not	disable, discomfort
e-/ex-; ec-/ex-	out	exit, exegesis
hyper-	too much	hyperactive, hypersensitive
hypo-	too little	hypoactive
in-	not	invalid
intra-	within	intramurals
macro-	large	macrobiologist
micro-	small	microscope
milli-	thousand	millipede

Greek and Latin prefixes	Meaning	English examples
mis-	bad	misnomer
mon-/mono-	one; single	monochrome
nano-	billion	nanosecond
neo-	new; recent	neophyte, neonatal
omni-	all	omniscient
pan-	all	panorama
para-	alongside	paralegal
per-	throughout	pervade
peri-	all around	periscope
poly-	many	polygon
pre-	before	precede, prepare
pro-	forward	protest
re-	again; backward	rearrange, rewind
retro-	back	retrograde
super-	more than	supermarket
sym-/syn-	together	symbol, symbiotic
thermo-/therm-	heat	thermal, thermometer
trans-	across, beyond, through	transatlantic

A suffix is a word part added to the end of a root word to change its meaning. Here are some Greek and Latin suffixes, their meanings, and examples.

Greek and Latin suffixes	Meaning	English examples
-able/-ible	capable or worthy of	likable, flexible
-al	relating to	maternal
-algia	pain	myalgia, neuralgia
-arium	place of	aquarium, terrarium
-ation	action or process	civilization, strangulation
-fy/-ify	to make or cause to become	purify, humidify
-gram	something written or drawn	cardiogram, telegram
-graph	something written or drawn; an instrument for writing, drawing or recording	monograph, phonograph
-ic	relating to	poetic
-ile	quality; state	juvenile
-ism	the act, state or theory of	criticism, optimism
-ist	one who practises	biologist, cyclist
-ize	to cause to be or to become	legalize, modernize
-logy/-ology	the study of	biology, dermatology
-ment	action or process	entertainment, amazement

Greek and Latin suffixes	Meaning	English examples
-oid	like or resembling; shape or form	humanoid, trapezoid
-ous	quality; state	nebulous
-phile	loving	audiophile, Francophile
-phobe/-phobia	an intense fear of a specific thing; a person who fears that thing	agoraphobe, agoraphobia, xenophobe, xenophobia
-phone	sound; device that receives or emits sound; speaker of a language	telephone, Francophone
-ty/-ity	quality; state	certainty, frailty, similarity
-tion	quality; state	preservation
-ular	relating to	cellular

Now that you know roots, prefixes and suffixes, you can work out what new words mean – and you can mix and match word parts from the charts to make your own words, like hyper-logophobia!

FABLES AND STORIES

◆

EVERY CULTURE HAS its own fables and stories. They are usually tales with morals designed to teach children the virtues to which they ought to aspire. Here are just a few from around the world.

Indian fables

THE GEESE AND THE TORTOISE

Once upon a time there lived a tortoise and two geese. They went everywhere together and had become great friends. But the lake that they lived in was drying out and would soon run out of water. They could only survive by leaving their home and looking for another lake to live in. The only way of reaching another lake was by flying, but the tortoise could not fly and begged his friends not to leave him behind. They thought and thought about how to solve this problem and decided that the geese would hold a stick between them as the tortoise hung on to the stick with his mouth. They could then carry him to safety. But the tortoise was a talkative fellow, so the geese warned him not to to speak or he would fall from the stick and to his certain death. Reluctantly the tortoise agreed, seeing it was his only escape route. And so they set off. But as they flew through the air, people down on the ground started pointing and laughing. Unable to control himself, the tortoise spoke out: 'What are you all laughing at?' But, as he was warned, he lost his grip on the stick and fell to his death.

Moral: Sometimes it is wiser to keep quiet.

THE MOON LAKE

In the jungle lived a large herd of elephants, presided over by their leader, the King of the Elephants. When a drought hit the jungle, the king elephant knew that if he didn't find water for his herd they would surely die. He had to find water, and quickly.

And so it passed that he discovered a lake far away in another part of the jungle. He spread the good news among the herd, and they set off to their new home. Arriving at the lake, they were so overjoyed to find water that they did not notice the colony of rabbits living near the lake, and trampled on hundreds of them as they stampeded towards the water.

The King of the Rabbits, horrified by the massacre, called a meeting with his remaining rabbits. 'I will reward any one of you who can find a way to save our fellow rabbits.'

After much scratching of heads, one little rabbit stood up and said, 'Your Majesty, I think I have a solution to our problem. Please send me to talk to the King of the Elephants.'

The King of the Rabbits gave his blessing and the little rabbit hurried off. He approached the elephants carefully, fearful of being trampled, and scrambled atop a rock. 'King of the Elephants,' he shouted, 'please hear my words.'

The King of the Elephants turned to the little rabbit. 'Who are you?'

'I am a messenger from the mighty Moon and I have a message for you.'

The King of the Elephants was paying full attention to the little rabbit now.

'But you must not be angry with me, O King of the Elephants, for I am only the bringer of the message,' said the little rabbit.

'Very well,' agreed the king. 'I shall not be angry with you.'

'The Moon has this to say: "King of the Elephants, you have come to my sacred land and to my holy lake and made dirty its waters. You brought with you your herd of elephants and killed hundreds of the rabbits who are under my protection. I will warn you now: you must not harm any more rabbits or you will pay a very heavy price."'

The King of the Elephants was shocked. 'The Moon is right. We killed many of your fellow rabbits when we arrived at this lake. I must make my apologies to the Moon. Please tell me how I can speak to him.'

The little rabbit pointed down towards the lake. 'Come with me and I shall take you to the Moon.'

The elephant and the rabbit made their way to the lake and stopped to look into its waters. 'There, King of the Elephants, there is the Moon,' said the little rabbit.

'Let me worship the mighty Moon,' said the elephant, dipping his trunk into the water.

The waters of the lake were disturbed, making the Moon appear to move to and fro.

'You have angered him further,' warned the rabbit. 'You have touched the waters of his holy lake.'

The King of the Elephants was penitent. 'Please tell the Moon that I will take my herd and I will leave you and him in peace. I am sorry we came and destroyed your lands and rabbits.'

And so the elephants left in search of another lake. Soon the rains came and they could drink water again.

The rabbits lived in peace and safety once again. And never did the elephants realize that they had been tricked by a tiny rabbit.

Moral: Wit can win over might.

Roman mythology

A STORY OF POVERTY AND HOSPITALITY

In Ancient Rome there lived a married couple, Philemon and Baucis, who were known for their kindness and generosity despite their poverty. Jupiter, king of the gods, tired of humanity and its greed and degeneracy, was about to destroy the world but, on hearing of this one virtuous couple, decided to give it one last chance.

Disguising themselves as poor travellers, Jupiter and his grandson Mercury came among the neighbours of Philemon and Baucis. As they asked for shelter from each of their neighbours, they were turned away again and again. But at Philemon and Baucis's house they were welcomed with open arms, fed and watered with what little the couple had.

As the evening wore on, the married couple began to notice that their jug of wine was not getting any emptier. Realizing that their guests might be immortal gods, they decided to kill their only goose in their honour. But just before the goose could be killed, the gods revealed themselves, and as a gesture to thank the couple for restoring their faith in humanity they offered to grant a divine favour. The couple said they wished to become priests and then die together. And after their death they became trees intertwined with each other for eternity.

Moral: Treat everyone well, as you never know when a god is present.

Buddhist fables

You may well recognize this fable. It's one that has passed into English folklore.

CHICKEN LITTLE

There once was a chicken called Chicken Little. One day Chicken Little was minding her own business, eating her lunch, when she felt something land on her head. 'Oh!' she thought. 'The sky must be falling, for a little bit of it has fallen on my head!' Little did she realize that it was just an acorn, fallen from the oak tree above her head. 'The king will know what to do,' she decided, because something had to be done. Putting her headscarf on and saying goodbye to her chicks, she set off to the palace, which was far, far away.

Along the way she met Henney Penney, who stopped her, 'Chicken Little, why are you hurrying so?'

'I am on my way to see the king, for the sky is falling and I must warn him.'

'How do you know that the sky is falling, Chicken Little?' asked Henney Penney, quite reasonably.

'I felt a bit of it land on my head,' replied Chicken Little.

'Oh! In that case, can I come with you?' said Henney Penney, now worried.

And so the two set off together to see the king far, far away.

Further along the way they met Cocky Locky, who stopped them and said, 'Why are you two hurrying so?'

'The sky is falling and we are going to tell the king,' they replied.

'And how do you know?' asked Cocky Locky, quite reasonably.

'Because Chicken Little told me so,' said Henney Penney.

'Because a bit of it landed on my head,' said Chicken Little.

'In that case, can I come with you?' said Cocky Locky, now worried.

And so the three set off together to see the king far, far away.

Further along the way they met Goosey Loosey, who stopped them and said, 'Why are you three hurrying so?'

'The sky is falling and we are going to tell the king,' they replied.

'And how do you know?' asked Goosey Loosey, quite reasonably.

'Because Henney Penney told me so,' said Cocky Locky.

'Because Chicken Little told me so,' said Henney Penney.

'Because a bit of it landed on my head,' said Chicken Little.

'In that case, can I come with you?' said Goosey Loosey, now worried.

And so the four set off together to see the king far, far away.

Even further along the way the four met Foxy Loxy, who stopped them and said, 'Why are you four hurrying so?'

'The sky is falling and we are going to tell the king,' they replied.

'And how do you know?' asked Foxy Loxy, quite reasonably.

'Because Cocky Locky told me so,' said Goosey Loosey.

'Because Henney Penney told me so,' said Cocky Locky.

'Because Chicken Little told me so,' said Henney Penney.

'Because a bit of it landed on my head,' said Chicken Little.

'But you are going the wrong way to the king's house,' said Foxy Loxy, a greedy glint in his eye. 'Follow me, I know a short cut.'

And so they all followed Foxy Loxy into a dark and scary wood.

First went Goosey Loosey, and SNAP! off came her head, eaten by Foxy Loxy.

Next went Cocky Locky, and SNAP! off came her head, eaten by Foxy Loxy.

Then went Henney Penney, and SNAP! off came her head, eaten by Foxy Loxy.

And last came Chicken Little, and SNAP! off came her head, eaten by Foxy Loxy.

Moral: Don't believe everything you are told.

PAPER FLOWERS AND CAPILLARY ACTION

---◆---

You will need

* A piece of paper (notebook paper is fine)
* A pencil
* Scissors
* A large bowl or dish of water

To MAKE YOUR PAPER FLOWER, draw a large circle on your piece of paper and then draw triangle-shaped petals all around it. Cut out the shape and close the triangle parts down on top of the paper. Place your closed paper flower on the surface of the water in your dish or bowl and watch what happens: your flower will blossom, thanks to something called capillary action. Capillary action, or capillary motion, is the ability of one thing to pull another thing inside it – think of sponges or paper towels and how they soak up spills. When your paper flower is placed in water, the paper begins drawing the water in through capillary action. As the paper fibres swell with water, the folded petals unfurl.

Capillary action isn't a phenomenon restricted just to science experiments or wiping counters – it happens every day in our bodies, with the circulation of our blood and even the draining of constantly produced tears from our eyes. And some modern fabrics use capillary action to draw sweat away from skin. You can try this experiment with other kinds of paper to see how capillary action works with different materials, from construction paper and watercolour paper to tracing paper and tissue paper.

> **FUN FACT**
>
> Albert Einstein's first paper published in the 1901 Annalen der Physik, titled *Folgerungen aus den Capillaritätserscheinungen* ('Conclusions from the capillarity phenomena'), was on capillary action.

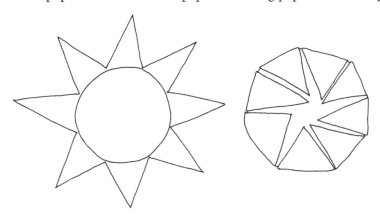

JACKS

JACKS, ALONG WITH MARBLES, is one of the oldest games in the world. Shop-bought jacks are six-pointed star-shaped objects, with a ball to bounce as we scoop them up, but in its early form the game was played with whatever was at hand – stones, small animal bones, or even crumpled-up paper.

Players decide who goes first by 'flipping' or using any rhyming game to determine the first player. Flipping means tossing jacks in the air and trying to catch as many as you can on the back of your hand. The player who catches the most gets to go first.

To begin play, toss the ten jacks onto the playing surface. Then bounce the ball in the air, pick up one jack using your throwing hand and catch the ball in the hand holding the jack before the ball bounces. (Place the jack you've collected in your other hand or off to the side before you try to pick up another one.) Do this again, picking up one jack at a time without the ball bouncing twice, until you've picked up all ten jacks. This is 'onesies'. Once you've done that successfully, move on to 'twosies': scatter the ten jacks again and this time pick

up two jacks at a time. Do this until you've picked up all ten jacks. Continue to 'threesies', where you pick up the jacks three at a time, 'foursies', four at a time, and on all the way to 'tensies'.

(When there are 'leftovers' – one jack in 'threesies', two jacks in 'foursies' – you pick them up individually. If you pick them up before you've picked up the groups, that is known as 'putting the cart before the horse', and you must call 'cart' as you pick up the individual 'leftover' jacks. 'Threesies' has three groups of three and one jack in the 'cart'; 'foursies' has two groups of four and two jacks in the 'cart', etc.)

Your turn is over when you don't pick up the correct number of jacks, you miss the ball or the ball bounces. When it's your turn again, start up where you left off – if you lost your turn on 'twosies', start at twosies. The winner is the player who is able to successfully pick up the largest number of jacks.

TIPS AND VARIATIONS

Usually, only one hand may be used to throw the ball and pick up the jacks, but play can be simplified to allow two hands. You can also make it more difficult by only allowing players to use their 'bad' hands (right hand for left-handed players, left hand for right-handed players).

Kissies
When two jacks are touching. They can be separated by calling 'Kissies!' while a player moves them apart.

Fancies
Complicated ways of picking up the jacks, like not being allowed to touch the jacks you don't pick up.

Around the World
Toss the ball, circle the ball with your hand and then pick up jacks before the ball bounces.

Cats in the Well
Make a loose fist with the thumb and first finger of your non-throwing hand. The jacks you pick up ('cats') are dropped through the opening (the 'well').

Eggs in the Basket, or Picking Cherries
Toss the ball, pick up the jacks and transfer the jacks to your other hand before catching the ball.

Pigs in the Pen
Make an arch with the thumb and first finger of your non-throwing hand. Then toss the ball, flick a jack through the arch and then catch the ball.

Pigs over the Fence
Make a 'fence' with your non-throwing hand by putting your hand on its side, thumb facing up. Toss the ball, transfer the jacks to the other side of your 'fence' and catch the ball.

PICKING WHO'S IT

Rhymes to determine who goes first can be used for any game, from jacks to tag to board games to truth or dare. Here are some fun schoolyard ways of figuring out who gets to be first.

Eeny, Meeny, Miny, Moe
(Point at each player for each word said; whoever the rhyme ends on is out and you start again until there is only one person left who is 'it'. That person gets to go first.)

Eeny, meeny, miny, moe
Catch a tiger by the toe
If he squeals let him go,
Eeny, meeny, miny, moe.
O. U. T. spells out
And out you must go.

One Potato
(Players put their fists in a circle. The 'potato peeler' puts her fist on the players' fists as she says the words. Whoever lands on 'more' removes her fist. The last player left goes first.)

One potato, two potato
One potato, two potato, three potato, four.
Five potato, six potato, seven potato, more.

QUEENS OF THE ANCIENT WORLD V

◆

Zenobia, Queen of the East

IN THE THIRD CENTURY AD, Zenobia of Palmyra was the famed Queen of the East. According to the author of *Historia Augusta*, she had long black hair and warm brown skin, piercing dark eyes and a lyrical, strong voice. Known for her boldness, determination and fairness as a leader, she was just in her twenties when she built and ruled an empire that covered most of what is now the Middle East.

Zenobia was born around 240 AD at Palmyra, a sparkling, palm-tree-filled paradise deep in the desert of Syria (now the ruins of Tadmor, about 150 miles northeast of Damascus). Her father was a tribal ruler who had enticed her mother from Egypt to this prosperous and cosmopolitan trading outpost.

Zenobia's full given name was Iulia Aurelia Zenobia. 'Iulia' was a popular girl's name in Rome, which, even though it was far away,

ruled the Syrian desert. 'Aurelia' meant that her family were Roman citizens, an important honour. 'Zenobia' came from her family's Aramaic tribe. Historians know that by the age of eighteen, she had already married the governor of Palmyra, a man named Odainat (known in Latin as Septimius Odaenathus). Then she changed her name to Septimia Zenobia, to match his.

As wife to the land's governor, Zenobia was well educated and her court was filled with philosophers and poets. Many an evening was spent lingering over sumptuous meals, talking about Homer and Plato, making speeches and laughing at riddles and wit. The peace was disturbed in 260 AD, however, when the Persian king, Shapur, tried to take Syria from the Romans. As allies of Rome, the Palmyrans guarded the frontier where the Roman Empire met the Persian, so Odainat and Zenobia prepared for combat.

The emperor of Rome, Valerian, faced rebellion everywhere – to the west, north and now to the east. His troops were dispirited, but nonetheless he marched them to battle. The Persians had superior strength and fighting skills, so they easily routed the weary Roman soldiers. Valerian and Shapur agreed to meet at the city of Edessa and negotiate terms. When Valerian showed up, the Persians ambushed him and took him into captivity.

That's when two Roman messengers urged their horses across the desert sand to Palmyra, bringing the terrible news of Valerian's capture. Odainat and Zenobia were ready. Side by side, the couple donned armour, saddled their horses and led the army of Palmyra against the Persians, in search of Valerian.

While Odainat was a courageous and daring warrior, ancient writers tell us Zenobia was even more so, and praised her battle skills, including her exceptional way with the troops.

She rallied them, kept them inspired and at times even got off her horse to march for miles with the foot soldiers. Unfortunately, the Persians killed Valerian before Odainat and Zenobia could save him, but the couple's brave leadership earned them the complete respect of the Palmyran army and people.

Was it odd for these troops to see a woman in front, her long black hair streaming out from beneath her helmet? The ancient cultures of Greece and Rome often portrayed the deity of war as a woman, and female Victory statues graced nearly every city. In fact, the Palmyran soldiers followed Zenobia to battle again and again in the following years.

In 267 AD, seven years after their first battle together, Zenobia's husband Odainat was assassinated. The royal line fell to Zenobia's toddler son, Vaballathus, who was clearly too young to rule. Zenobia, then twenty-seven years old, became queen in his stead. She dreamed of an empire of Palmyra and prepared the troops for a battle of independence.

The Romans were busy in Europe defending themselves from the Goths, Zenobia knew, so she attacked the Roman province of Egypt. The Egyptians, too, were distracted, off battling pirates in the Mediterranean Sea. She conquered them and then went to conquer cities in Arabia, Palestine and Syria. By 269 AD, she declared her empire's independence from Rome and minted new coins with her image and the word 'REGINA' – Queen.

Historians tell us that Zenobia ruled tolerantly as Queen of the East, drawing on the Palmyran traditions of hospitality and openness to treat all people with fairness, including the pagans, Jews and Christians of her empire. She opened new trade routes and met Christian bishops and other leaders of the cities she conquered.

As Zenobia expanded her Palmyran empire, armies threatened the larger Roman Empire on all sides. The new Roman emperor, Aurelian, was battling the Goth and Visigoth tribes in northern Europe. When his messengers arrived with news of Queen Zenobia's expanding kingdom, Aurelian set off for Egypt, determined to win the territory back, and then to Turkey (which in ancient times was called Asia Minor). After these small victories, he prepared to attack Antioch, a city in northern Syria that Zenobia now ruled.

Zenobia had never faced the vast legions of the mighty Roman army. She could have given up and returned to the Roman fold, but decided instead to take a last stand and save the heart of her hard-earned empire. She assembled the troops along one side of the north-flowing Orontes River. Her soldiers fought all day, Zenobia along with them. Then, as the sun dipped towards the western horizon, the tired soldiers, bleary and water-starved after a long day, fell into a trap, in which the Romans massacred them from all sides.

Zenobia managed to escape with seventy thousand soldiers and retreated to the city of Emesa. They found a hill and, under cover of night, climbed to the top and lay in wait, ready to rain down arrows on the Roman soldiers.

The Romans, though, pulled out their colourful shields, held high overhead, each shield meeting the next to cover the men and protect them from the Palmyrans' arrows and darts. In this formation, the Romans pushed forward up the hill. When they reached the Palmyran marksmen, they moved their shields forward and down and attacked.

Thousands of troops died on the battlefield. Zenobia herself barely escaped and even her trusted horse fell in the battle. She commandeered a camel and turned the slow beast towards the sandy hinterlands of the Syrian desert, with hopes that the plodding animal could take her one hundred miles east to Persia, where she would be safe from Rome.

'I promise you life if you surrender,' Aurelian wrote to her. Zenobia had other plans, but it was Aurelian's turn for victory. He lay siege to her beloved Palmyra and sent his best soldiers on horseback to capture the fallen paradise's fugitive queen. As she neared the Euphrates River, so close to freedom, the emperor's horsemen reached Zenobia and captured her.

The remainder of Zenobia's life is shrouded in myth. Where one ancient historian reports that she died in captivity, another writes that Aurelian took her to Rome. It is said that in 274 AD, Zenobia was wrapped in chains of gold and made to walk down Rome's main boulevard as Aurelian celebrated his triumph over the many tribes he had battled. Still another tale suggests that some time later, Zenobia was released. In her absence, Palmyra had rebelled against Rome once more and had been crushed. Some tales hold that, with no home to return to, Zenobia lived the rest of her life not far from Rome, in Tivoli.

CYCLING

———— ◆ ————

CYCLING IS A GREAT WAY to get out and about, and it's good for you and the environment too. Before you set off, make sure your bicycle is in good working order, your tyres are pumped up and puncture-free, your chain oiled, and your brakes nice and tight. A few more things to remember:

* Always wear a helmet. It will protect your head should you come off your bike.
* Always follow the Highway Code when cycling on the roads. This means stopping at all traffic lights and not cycling on the pavement.
* Always make sure you have lights on you in case it becomes dark while you are out, and make sure they have working batteries too. Reflective strips are also a good idea.

If you follow these simple rules, you'll have fun and will keep safe too.

GREAT DAYS OUT BY BIKE

These are just a few ideas. If you are inspired and would like to find out more, visit www.sustrans.org.uk which has routes for cyclists of all abilities in all areas of the country.

The Great North Way

This is a route of 32 miles that takes you out of North London into Hertfordshire along cycle-friendly roads. The route is clearly marked along the way – just follow the 'Route 12' signs.

Start by taking the train to Hadley Wood train station. The first location you are heading towards is Welham Green, so take a left out of Hadley Wood towards Ganwick Corner. Then follow the road to Dancers Hill and you'll already feel as though you are in the countryside, even though you are close to the M25 and A1. Here you'll even go under the M25, and then you need to follow Mymmshall Brook towards Water End. Then a little way on you'll get to Welham Green. Time to stop for a well-deserved ice-cream.

Next stop on the route is Codicote. Follow Traveller's Lane towards Stream Woods and Howe Dell where you'll go through the secluded woods on the outskirts of Old Hatfield. Continue up Mill Green Lane towards Welwyn Garden City and then take a left onto Turnmill Dale, leading to Ayot Green and Ayot St Peter. After stopping to see the church of Ayot St Peter, take the St Albans Road towards Codicote, mentioned in the Domesday Book. It's probably time for a swift break for sandwiches around here too.

Don't stop too long; you still have a way to go yet. Take Slip Lane towards Old Knebworth, passing Knebworth House and then heading on to Stevenage. Take the Gunnelswood Road and then the Hitchin Road and you'll emerge to the north-east of Stevenage. Ahead is Willian with its famous arboretum, and then Letchworth. This is a lovely market town; you can stop here or, if you are feeling energetic, continue on to Baldock, one of the oldest towns in the county of Hertfordshire. It's up to you now: either catch a train back or cycle back to Hadley Wood.

Pottering around the Cotswolds

This is a shorter route that runs through pretty Cotswolds villages.

Start by taking the train to Moreton-in-Marsh. From here you need to turn left onto the A429 towards Stretton-on-Foss. You'll only need to stay on this road a few miles, so keep an eye out for the turning to Aston Magna on the left. Once on this road you'll be deep in the countryside, surrounded by fields. At Aston Magna take the first right towards Paxton. This is a rough track and one with a couple of hills but it is worth the effort once you arrive in the pretty village of Paxford. Here is a good place to stop for some lunch. After lunch, keep going along a road called The Cam and you'll get to Chipping Campden.

Chipping Campden is a lovely place to stop for an ice-cream. From here, take the road to Broad Campden, then Draycott, and then on to Batsford. From here you'll have a long, easy, downhill ride all the way back to where you started, just in time to get the train back home.

A stately cycle ride in Yorkshire

This ride is easy and fun, all along flat roads and paths. It takes you from York to Beningborough Hall following cycle route 65.

Start in York by the River Ouse at Lendall Bridge. The first part of the route follows the river and is on traffic-free cycle paths. Then follow the signs to Overton and then Shipton where you'll go through the pretty villages on a quiet country lane. From Shipton follow the signs to Beningborough Hall. The hall is a stately home that is well worth a visit in itself. A grand Georgian house, it is filled with impressive paintings and surrounded by a magnificent walled garden. To get back to York from Beningborough, simply retrace your route the way you came.

Canal life in Scotland

This is an easy and picturesque ride along one of Scotland's greatest canals.

Start at the canal centre in Linlithgow, dropping in at the museum to find out more about the canal you'll be cycling along. Take the cycle path west (following signs for cycle route 76). And that's it! The route is entirely straight along the canal so you'll be able to concentrate on seeing Scotland's longest waterway tunnel, the Avon Aqueduct, marvelling at the length of this canal which is uninterrupted by locks – a first at the time it was built. The route ends at Falkirk where you can see the Falkirk wheel, the only rotating boat lift in the world.

TAKING CARE OF YOUR BIKE

A daring girl should be able to take care of her own bicycle, so here are a few tips on what to do if your bike goes wrong.

How to mend a puncture

However lucky you are and however good your tyres are, you'll get a puncture at least once in your cycling life. Hopefully it will be somewhere close to home, but you should be prepared and able to fix the puncture at the side of the road if necessary.

* First let all the air out of your inner tube so you can take the tyre off the wheel. Tyre levers can help you here.
* Then take the inner tube off the wheel. You'll need to find the hole, and the best way to do this is to pump the inner tube up and then hold it underwater and look for the bubbles which indicate where air is escaping. If you are on the road this is trickier and you may have to just listen for the sounds of air escaping.
* Having found the hole, mark it with a piece of chalk so you don't lose it again.

* Your puncture repair kit should have a slightly abrasive section on the outside of the case; use this to gently rough up the area around the hole – it will help the patch stick.
* Cover the area around the hole with glue and leave for a few minutes to go tacky.
* Then cover with a patch and hold down for a couple of minutes to make sure it sticks.
* Then you need to put the inner tube back into the tyre (inflating it slightly before you put it in the tyre will make sure you don't trap it or kink it under the tyre). Then place the tyre and inner tube back onto the wheel. You'll notice an arrow on the tyre – make sure that this is pointing in the direction that the wheel rotates.
* Finally, using the tyre levers again, attach the tyre to the wheel rim and pump up the inner tube once more.

It's a bit of a messy job but one that is very satisfying to be able to do yourself, and it gets easier with practice.

Tightening your brakes

Good brakes are vital to your safety as a cyclist, so it important that you keep them in working order. You don't want to regret not knowing how to do this.

* Loosen the cable clamp bolt. You'll find this next to your brake levers on your handlebars – the brake cable comes out of it.
* Pull the brake cable through very slightly to tighten the brakes.
* Screw the cable clamp bolt up again.
* Check that your brakes are tighter and more responsive, and always take care the first few times you use your brakes after tightening them – they'll react faster so you may skid if you are not careful.

While you are tightening your brakes, check that your brake blocks are not worn down. You'll need to replace them every six months or so (depending on how often you cycle) so keep an eye on them and go to a bicycle repair shop when they need replacing.

Lights

Before you go out, especially in winter, make sure your lights are working properly. You need a white front light and a red rear light at the very least. You want to be seen by the traffic at all times. Rechargeable batteries are good, but remember to charge them up regularly.

GAMES FOR A RAINY DAY

———— ◆ ————

THERE ALWAYS SEEM TO BE too many of those days when the weather is too bad to go outside and you are doomed to spend the day watching raindrops race each other down the outside of the window. Staying inside is never going to be as fun as being outside with the wind in your hair and the world at your fingertips, but here are a few ideas to pass the time more quickly until the sun comes out.

Board games

Normally kept stacked inside a cupboard waiting for Christmas, board games are a great way of passing a rainy day. Old favourites such as Monopoly, Cluedo, and Snakes and Ladders can last for hours and are good fun, too. But even better is making your own board game.

HOW TO MAKE A BOARD GAME

* Start off with some stiff cardboard, with white paper glued onto it to create a board.
* Using your imagination, create a scene for your board. We suggest using the format of an existing board game – take Snakes and Ladders for example – and adapting it. Mark off squares in a sequence, decorating along the way.
* Now you need to create scenarios for each player to do as they land on a square. These can be fun and physical: 'You've landed a job testing space hoppers. Jump thirty times on your space hopper to show you can do the job,' or more quiz-based: 'You have landed on a Brain Square. Name the capital of Canada.' Have fun coming up with challenges and questions to fox your friends.

* Make sure you decide on the rules before you play – you don't want to give your brother a chance to cheat!

Card games

See the chapter on playing cards for some ideas. If you've played those and it's still raining, how about a game of Patience?

RULES OF THE GAME

Patience is a game for one person.

Start by setting out the cards in preparation: from the left, place one card facing up in front of you and then a row of six cards facing down. Then place another card facing up on top of the first concealed card, and then five cards facing down on top of the cards already laid out. Continue until you have seven cards facing up, each with a growing pile of cards facing down underneath them. You'll have a few leftover cards which you will deal from.

The aim of the game is to create four straight suits from King down to Ace, in alternating colours. You can move whole runs from one column to another. If you have a space left by moving one card from one column to another, this can be filled with a King.

Aces can be kept to one side and used as a piling station for other cards of the same suit –

but only in numerical order, so only a Two of Clubs can go on top of an Ace of Clubs, followed by a Three of Clubs and so on.

Use the cards in your hand to help you move, turning them over three at a time and moving them into columns as and when you can. You should aim to release the cards from under the piles by moving the cards on top of them; as soon as a face-down card is revealed, you can turn it over and start a new column with it.

Good luck – and have patience.

Putting on a play

Putting on a play for your friends and family can be really good fun. It gives you a chance to be really creative and to show what a great actor you are.

You can choose a play that already exists and use it to work from. Even better, though, is to come up with your own story or to act out one of your favourite books. Decide who will play which part (you might want to bagsy the most exciting, attractive or interesting character for yourself, of course!) and improvise from there. Think about their personalities, their likes, their dislikes, their relationships with the other characters.

Designing the set can also be a lot of fun. If you are holding it in your living room or even in your garden, you can devise a backdrop to show any setting you like. Make use of any props you find around the house. Raid dressing-up boxes, kitchen cupboards and airing cupboards for props – the more flamboyant, the better!

When it comes to the moment of revealing the play, your family sitting waiting expectantly, remember to take a deep breath, forget those nerves and break a leg!

Charades

Charades is a good old-fashioned parlour game that is still fun to play today. One person is the actor and has to think up something – a book title, a person, a thing, anything – that they will act out, and no words are allowed. It is up to everyone else to guess what they are acting out.

Here are a few tips to get you started:

Show what type of thing it is by starting off with one of the following:

* Film – imitate an old cine camera by circling your hand near the side of your head.
* Book – open your palms out, like a book.
* TV show – draw a rectangle, TV shape, in the air.
* Person – stand with your hands on your hips.
* Quotation – make quotation marks in the air with your fingers.

Everyone else should shout out until they have the right answer. Show them they are right by nodding or point at your nose to indicate that they are 'spot on'.

Show the number of words by raising the appropriate number of fingers in the air.

Show which word you are acting out by raising the appropriate finger, i.e. your first finger if it is the first word.

If the words have more than one syllable, show this by placing the appropriate number of fingers together on your left arm with your right hand.

Show you are acting out something that sounds like your word by cupping your ear with your hand.

After that, use your imagination!

MAKE YOUR OWN PAPER

◆

ANCIENT EGYPTIANS wrote on paper made from papyrus plants and parchment, which was made from stretched and dried skins of calves, goats and sheep. In China, early paper was made with silk, bark from mulberry trees and other plant fibres. Today, paper is mostly made from wood fibres, though speciality paper is made from linen, cotton and even synthetic materials like latex. But the most basic technique for making paper is essentially the same today as it was in ancient times and you can try it out in your own home.

To make your own paper, you'll need:

* Recycled paper (such as newspaper, magazines, toilet paper, paper bags, notebook paper, construction paper, tissue paper, napkins)
* A sponge
* Wire mesh screen (an old door or window screen)
* A wood frame (you can use an old picture frame, or you can build a frame yourself using four pieces of wood and some nails)
* Plastic basin or tub (should be large enough to fit your frame)
* A food mixer
* Felt, blotting paper, flannel, or other absorbent fabric (newsprint will work at a pinch)
* Stapler
* Liquid starch
* Rolling pin
* Iron

Tear your paper into small pieces and fill the food mixer halfway full with it. Add warm water until the mixer is full. Blend the paper and water for about thirty seconds, starting at low speed and then gradually increasing. Blend until you get a smooth, well-blended pulp with no chunks or bits of paper.

Use your screen and wood frame to make what's called a mould. Stretch the screen over the frame as tightly as possible and use a stapler to affix it. Trim off any excess. Now is also a good time to lay out the felt or blotting paper that you will use later. Place it next to your basin so that it will be ready when you need it.

Half fill the basin or tub with water. Add the pulp from the mixer. Make two more mixers of pulp and add these to the basin. Stir the water and pulp in the basin – feel free to use your hands – and then stir in two teaspoons of liquid starch. Mix well, then submerge your mould (the screen and wood frame) in the basin, with the screen side on the bottom. Move the mould from side to side until the pulp settles on top of it evenly.

Carefully raise the mould out of the water and hold it above the basin while the water drains. The pulp mixture should be in a uniform layer across the screen. (If there are holes, or if the pulp is not lying evenly, submerge the mould again and give it another try.) Press down on it gently to squeeze out the moisture and use a sponge to soak up excess water from the bottom of the screen.

After the mould stops dripping, flip the screen paper side down onto your felt, flannel, or other blotting material. Press out any moisture with the sponge and then carefully lift the mould, leaving the wet sheet of paper on the fabric. Use your hands to press out bubbles or other slight imperfections.

Place another piece of blotting material on top of the paper and use a rolling pin to squeeze out the moisture. Now your handmade sheet of paper needs to dry. Find a good spot and let it sit for a few hours. You can also use an iron (on a medium setting) to encourage the drying process; just make sure to iron the paper through the blotting material, not directly on the paper itself. When the paper is fully dry, carefully remove the top cloth and then peel off the paper. Now you are all set to begin using your handmade paper for whatever you desire.

LETTERS HOME FROM
A GREAT ADVENTURER

◆

ISABELLA BIRD was not an obvious candidate to become a great explorer. She was born in 1831 in Yorkshire, the daughter of a clergyman, and her early days were marked by ill health. This poor health would follow her throughout her life but she felt strongly that travel was a way of improving oneself, both in body and in mind, so she persuaded her father to allow her to travel. She first went to visit relatives in America, and then continued her journeys on to Australia, Hawaii, the Rocky Mountains, Japan, China, Persia, Tibet and Kurdistan. She was intrepid and certainly not scared of a bit of hardship, discomfort or even danger. And throughout her travels she wrote home regularly to her sister, relaying her adventures. Her letters show her spirit and her courage and are an inspiration to girls over 100 years after Isabella's death. Here are just a few extracts; you can read all her letters in *A Lady's Life in the Rocky Mountains* and *Unbeaten Tracks in Japan*. She also wrote several travelogues, including *The Englishwoman in America* and *Amongst the Tibetans*.

Cheyenne, Wyoming, USA,
September 7, 1873

" As night came on the cold intensified, and the stove in the parlour attracted everyone. A San Francisco lady, much 'got up' in paint, emerald green velvet, Brussels lace, and diamonds, rattled continuously for the amusement of the company, giving descriptions of persons and scenes in a racy Western twang, without the slightest scruple as to what she said. In a few years Tahoe will be inundated in summer with similar vulgarity, owing to its easiness of access. I sustained the reputation which our country-women bear in America by looking a 'perfect guy'; and feeling that I was a salient point for the speaker's next sally, I was relieved when the landlady, a lady-like Englishwoman, asked me to join herself and her family in the bar-room, where we had much talk about the neighbourhood and its wild beasts, especially bears. The forest is full of them, but they seem never to attack people unless when wounded, or much aggravated by dogs, or a shebear thinks you are going to molest her young.

Nameless region, Rocky Mountains, USA, September, 1873

This is indeed far removed. It seems farther away from you than any place I have been to yet, except the frozen top of the volcano of Mauna Loa. It is so little profaned by man that if one were compelled to live here in solitude one might truly say of the bears, deer and elk which abound, 'Their tameness is shocking to me.' It is the world of 'big game'. Just now a heavy-headed elk, with much-branched horns fully three feet long, stood and looked at me, and then quietly trotted away. He was so near that I heard the grass, crisp with hoar frost, crackle under his feet. Bears stripped the cherry bushes within a few yards of us last night. Now two lovely blue birds, with crests on their heads, are picking about within a stone's-throw. This is 'The Great Lone Land', until lately the hunting ground of the Indians, and not yet settled or traversed, or likely to be so, owing to the want of water. A solitary hunter has built a log cabin up here, which he occupies for a few weeks for the purpose of elk-hunting, but all the region is unsurveyed, and mostly unexplored.

Kasukabe, Japan, June 10, 1878

From the date you will see that I have started on my long journey, though not upon the 'unbeaten tracks' which I hope to take after leaving Nikko, and my first evening alone in the midst of this crowded Asian life is strange, almost fearful. I have suffered from nervousness all day – the fear of being frightened, of being rudely mobbed, as threatened by Mr Campbell of Islay, of giving offence by transgressing the rules of Japanese politeness – of, I know not what! Ito is my sole reliance, and he may prove a 'broken reed'. I often wished to give up my project, but was ashamed of my cowardice when, on the best authority, I received assurances of its safety.

Kanaya's, Nikko, Japan, June 10, 1878

I don't know what to write about my house. It is a Japanese idyll; there is nothing within or without which does not please the eye, and, after the din of yadoyas, its silence, musical with the dash of waters and the twitter of birds, is truly refreshing. It is a simple but irregular two-storeyed pavilion, standing on a stone-faced terrace approached by a flight of stone steps. The garden is well laid out, and, as peonies, irises and azaleas are now in blossom, it is very bright. The mountain, with its lower part covered with red azaleas, rises just behind, and a stream which tumbles down it supplies the house with water, both cold and pure, and another, after forming a miniature cascade, passes under the house and through a fish-pond with rocky islets into the river below. The grey village of Irimichi lies on the other side of the road, shut in with the rushing Daiya, and beyond it are high, broken hills, richly wooded, and slashed with ravines and waterfalls.

Shingoji, Japan, July 21, 1878

Travelling along a very narrow road, I as usual first, we met a man leading a prisoner by a rope, followed by a policeman. As soon as my runner saw the latter he fell down on his face so suddenly in the shafts as nearly to throw me out, at the same time trying to wriggle into a garment which he had carried on the crossbar, while the young men who were drawing the two kurumas behind, crouching behind my vehicle, tried to scuttle into their clothes. I never saw such a picture of abjectness as my man presented. He trembled from head to foot, and illustrated that queer phrase often heard in Scotch Presbyterian prayers, 'Lay our hands on our mouths and our mouths in the dust.' He literally grovelled in the dust, and with every sentence that the policeman spoke raised his head a little, to bow it yet more deeply than before. It was all because he had no clothes on. I interceded for him as the day was very hot, and the policeman said he would not arrest him, as he should otherwise have done, because of the inconvenience that it would cause to a foreigner. He was quite an elderly man, and never recovered his spirits, but, as soon as a turn of the road took us out of the policeman's sight, the two younger men threw their clothes into the air and gambolled in the shafts, shrieking with laughter!

Yashimaya, Yumoto, Nikkozan Mountains, Japan, June 22, 1878

Today I have made an experimental journey on horseback, have done fifteen miles in eight hours of continuous travelling, and have encountered for the first time the Japanese pack-horse – an animal of which many unpleasing stories are told, and which has hitherto been as mythical to me as the kirin, or dragon. I have neither been kicked, bitten nor pitched off, however, for mares are used exclusively in this district, gentle creatures about fourteen hands high, with weak hind-quarters, and heads nearly concealed by shaggy manes and forelocks. They are led by a rope round the nose, and go barefoot, except on stony ground, when the mago, or man who leads them, ties straw sandals on their feet. The pack-saddle is composed of two packs of straw eight inches thick, faced with red, and connected before and behind by strong oak arches gaily painted or lacquered. There is for a girth a rope loosely tied under the body, and the security of the load depends on a crupper, usually a piece of bamboo attached to the saddle by ropes strung with wooden counters, and another rope round the neck, into which you put your foot as you scramble over the high front upon the top of the erection. The load must be carefully balanced or it comes to grief, and the mago handles it all over first, and, if an accurate division of weight is impossible, adds a stone to one side or the other. Here, women who wear enormous rain hats and gird their kimonos over tight blue trousers, both load the horses and lead them. I dropped upon my loaded horse from the top of a wall, the ridges, bars, tags and knotted rigging of the saddle being smoothed over by a folded futon, or wadded cotton quilt, and I was then fourteen inches above the animal's back, with my feet hanging over his neck. You must balance yourself carefully, or you bring the whole erection over; but balancing soon becomes a matter of habit. If the horse does not stumble, the pack-saddle is tolerable on level ground, but most severe on the spine in going up hill, and so intolerable in going down that I was relieved when I found that I had slid over the horse's head into a mud-hole; and you are quite helpless, as he does not understand a bridle, if you have one, and blindly follows his leader, who trudges on six feet in front of him.

If you find yourself lucky enough to explore the world, we hope you take inspiration from Isabella Bird and keep notes of your thoughts and experiences along the way. You could even add pictures and trinkets and make it a scrapbook of your time.

MAKING AND FLYING A KITE

◆

AS MARY POPPINS SO RIGHTLY SAYS, flying a kite is one of life's pleasures. And flying a kite you have made yourself is the best way to do it. Here's how:

Take two sticks of wood – the sort of bamboo used to prop up plants works well – one longer than the other. Form a cross with the two sticks and tie securely at the middle so that they are at right angles to each other with the shorter stick being horizontal.

Cut a notch into both ends of the sticks and wind some string around them to form a rectangular frame of string secured in the notches of the sticks. This is your frame.

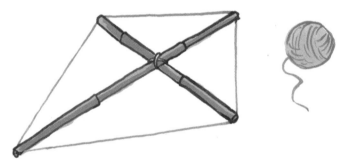

Cut your paper sail so it is the same shape as the frame but about 10 centimetres larger on all sides. Use thick, strong paper for this. Lay the sail on a table, with the frame on top of it, centred so there is the same amount of paper on each of the sides. Fold the paper over the string and tape down securely.

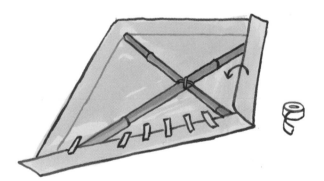

Tie a piece of string to the bottom of the upright stick, and one to the top. These two strings should be long – as long as you can make them – as they will be the string with which you fly the kite.

The final touch is to make a tail for your kite. Tie a long piece of string to the bottom of the upright stick and tie ribbons around that string at regular intervals as decoration.

Now wait for the next windy day so you can show off your kite!

Let's Go Fly a Kite

With tuppence for paper and strings
You can have your own set of wings
With your feet on the ground
You're a bird in flight
With your fist holding tight
To the string of your kite

Oh, oh, oh!
Let's go fly a kite
Up to the highest height!
Let's go fly a kite and send it soaring
Up through the atmosphere
Up where the air is clear
Oh, let's go fly a kite!

When you send it flying up there
All at once you're lighter than air
You can dance on the breeze
Over houses and trees
With your fist holding tight
To the string of your kite

Oh, oh, oh!
Let's go fly a kite
Up to the highest height!
Let's go fly a kite and send it soaring
Up through the atmosphere
Up where the air is clear
Let's go fly a kite!

TEN POINTS OF FASCINATION

——— ◆ ———

AS WE REACH THE END, there are some additional things one really should know and here they are, in no particular order.

1 **Skipping Stones.** Find a rock as close to smooth, flat and round as you can. Hold it flattest side down, index finger curled around one edge, and throw it sidearm, low and parallel to the water, snapping the wrist at the last possible moment before you let go to give it some spin. The stone should hit the water at a low, 20-degree angle or so. Keep practising till the stone bounces off the water a few times.

2 **Steering a Sledge.** We'll tell you here in case you do not know: it's opposite to how you steer a bicycle or a car and akin to a kayak or canoe. Lean left to go right. Lean right to go left.

3 **Water Balloons.** To fill, attach the mouth of the balloon to the tap and – this is key – keep the tap on low so the water pressure doesn't send the balloon into outer space. Once the water balloon smashes to the ground, clean up the colourful scraps, since when the fun's over, the balloon remnants turn into rubbish.

4 **Ping-Pong.** Forget nudging your parents for a horse; ask for a ping-pong table instead. Have a good supply of those air-filled white balls ready for when they lodge in the crevices between storage boxes that have been stacked high against the cellar walls to make space for the ping-pong table. If you're alone you can fold one of the table sides to vertical and push it against a wall to practise.

5 **Harmonica.** Invaluable for nights by the campfire when the embers are low, the camp songs are over and nearly everyone has fallen asleep. Hold with your thumb and first finger. Blow breath into it and draw it back through the holes. Experiment with sound. Flapping the other fingers up and down while you blow or draw will create a wavery vibrato.

6 **Temperature Conversions.** To convert Celsius to Fahrenheit, multiply by 9, divide by 5 and add 32. To convert temperatures the other way, from Fahrenheit to Celsius, subtract 32, divide by 9 and multiply by 5.

7 **Bicycle Wheelies.** Whether yours is a tough mountain bike or a ladylike pastel blue number with tassels on the handlebars and a basket, you'll want to know how to pop a wheelie.

Once you're at speed, lean forward, hands grabbing the handlebars and then shift your body weight slightly up and backwards. That should be enough to lift the front wheel off the ground, whether you're doing show-offs on the street in front of your house, or trying to get your bike over tree stumps on a rugged trail.

8 **Take Things Apart.** Old televisions and fax machines, a mobile phone that no longer works or a computer that's ten years out of date and living its final years in the garden shed: no discarded machine should go undismantled. Teensy-tiny drivers and hex

keys can unlock the smallest screws, so grab a hammer and whatever does the trick and see what's inside. That's how the world's best engineers learned what they know.

9 **Time Capsules.** This girlhood of yours is filled with days to remember. Make a scrapbook if you like, but really, any old box will do – an antique tin, a shoebox or a box hammered together from plywood and nails. Keep your mementos, letters, ticket stubs, the list of dreams scribbled on a napkin, a picture of your best friends and the poem or phrase you thought up last night before bed. Stow this box of inspiration somewhere safe, keep adding to it, and don't look at it for twenty years.

10 **Words to Live By.** Be brave and walk with confidence. And remember, in the words of Amelia Earhart: 'Adventure is worthwhile in itself.'

BOOKS THAT WILL CHANGE YOUR LIFE

◆

WE PRESENT THESE TITLES for your reading pleasure, knowing there are endless books beyond this list to discover and love, too. We know you will read them in your own fashion and at your own pace.

A Vindication of the Rights of Woman by Mary Wollstonecraft
Alice's Adventures in Wonderland and *Through the Looking Glass* by Lewis Carroll
Amazing Grace by Mary Hoffman
Anne of Green Gables (and *Emily of New Moon*) by L. M. Montgomery
Beauty: A Retelling of the Story of Beauty and the Beast by Robin McKinley
Black Beauty by Anna Sewell
Carrie's War by Nina Bawden
Charlotte's Web by E. B. White
Dandelion Wine and *Fahrenheit 451* by Ray Bradbury
Foundation and *Robot* series by Isaac Asimov
Frankenstein by Mary Shelley
Great Expectations by Charles Dickens
Harry Potter by J. K. Rowling. All seven, in time and as you grow.
His Dark Materials by Philip Pullman
I Am David by Anne Holm
Jane Eyre by Charlotte Brontë
Keep Climbing, Girls by Beah H. Richards
Little House on the Prairie by Laura Ingalls Wilder – the entire series
Little Women and *Jo's Boys* by Louisa May Alcott

Mary Poppins by P. L. Travers

Matilda (and *The BFG*) by Roald Dahl. Actually, make that anything by Roald Dahl.

Nancy Drew by Carolyn Keene. Starting with *The Secret of the Old Clock,* all the mysteries in River Heights end in Nancy's lap, and with her girlfriends George and Bess at her side, she always finds the secret passageways to solve them. The series began in the 1920s, and was revised twice, in the 1950s and the 2000s, each time becoming slightly less intrepid.

One Thousand and One Arabian Nights

Peter Pan by J. M. Barrie

Pride and Prejudice by Jane Austen

Private Peaceful by Michael Morpurgo

Robinson Crusoe by Daniel Defoe

The Adventures of Robin Hood

The Borrowers by Mary Norton

The Chronicles of Narnia by C. S. Lewis. Seven classic novels from the 1950s, including the most famous, *The Lion, the Witch and the Wardrobe*

The Complete Grimm's Fairy Tales by Brothers Grimm

The Complete Hans Christian Andersen Fairy Tales by Hans Christian Andersen

The Diary of Anne Frank by Anne Frank

The Famous Five, a series by Enid Blyton, with Dick, Ann, Julian, George (a girl!) and her dog Timothy

The Hobbit and *The Lord of the Rings* by J. R. R. Tolkien

The Jungle Book and *Just So Stories* by Rudyard Kipling

The Little Prince by Antoine de Saint-Exupéry

The Little Princess (and *The Secret Garden*) by Frances Hodgson Burnett

The Odyssey by Homer

The Once and Future King by T. H. White, about King Arthur's Court

The Owl Who Was Afraid of the Dark by Jill Tomlinson

The Railway Children by E. Nesbit

The Silver Sword by Ian Serraillier

The Wonderful Wizard of Oz by Frank Baum

Tom's Midnight Garden by Philippa Pearce

Treasure Island by Robert Louis Stevenson

What Katy Did by Susan Coolidge

Wind in the Willows by Kenneth Grahame

Winnie the Pooh by A. A. Milne. The original books and the poems.

Wuthering Heights by Emily Brontë

When we were young and bored, our parents told us, 'Go and read the dictionary!' We did and look where it got us. One should never underestimate the pleasure to be found flipping through a dictionary, an encyclopaedia or an old science book.

FIRST AID

———— ◆ ————

FIRST AID IS BASIC CARE in the event of illness, accident or injury that can be performed by anyone until professional medical treatment is given. It was a concept first put into practice by the Knights Hospitallers, who came up with the term 'first aid' and founded the Order of St. John in the eleventh century to train knights in the treatment of common battlefield injuries. In a life of adventure, accidents are bound to happen and a daring girl needs to know about first aid – even if she never plans to be injured in battle.

The information below is not intended to be a substitute for professional medical advice or treatment. Taking a first-aid class will provide even more in-depth instruction. But there are definitely actions you can take to help in the event of injury and below are some tips and techniques to keep in mind.

Remember your ABCs

When accidents happen, sometimes the first casualty is plain old common sense. It's easy to panic and forget about what's important, but these mnemonics can help you remember what to do. Mnemonic devices are formulas, usually in the form of rhymes, phrases or acronyms, to help you remember things. Some of the most familiar mnemonics in first aid are: the three Ps and the three Bs; the ABCs and CPR; and RICE.

The Three Ps
(Preserve life; Prevent further injury; Promote recovery)
Remembering the Three Ps helps you keep in mind what your goal is in responding to an accident or injury: making sure the person stays alive, ensuring that nothing is done to further injure the person and taking action to help the person get better.

The Three Bs
(Breathing; Bleeding; Bones)
The Three Bs remind a first-aid responder of what is most important to check when a person is injured and the order of importance in treating: Is the person breathing? Is the person bleeding? Are there any broken bones?

The ABCs
The ABCs stand for Airway, Breathing and Circulation and remembering this helps remind you to check that an injured person has a clear airway passage (isn't choking), is able to breathe and has a pulse. Open the airway by lifting the person's chin with your fingers, gently tilting their head

back. Listen for breathing sounds, look for a rise and fall of the chest, and feel for breathing movement. Check for a pulse by placing two fingers on the person's neck between the voice box and the muscle on the side of the neck. If a person is not breathing and does not have a pulse, call 999 and begin CPR.

CPR

CPR stands for cardiopulmonary resuscitation, a procedure performed on people whose heart or breathing has stopped. Once you have checked the ABCs, if a person is unresponsive, call 999. Begin CPR on an adult by pinching the person's nose as you give two breaths into their mouth. Using two fingers, check the person's pulse at the carotid artery (the neck, just under the jaw, between the voice box and the muscle on the side of the neck) for five to ten seconds. If there is no pulse, make sure the person is on their back, then place your hands one on top of the other on the lower half of the chest. Press down to give fifteen compressions, about one every second. Give two more breaths, pinching the nose and breathing directly into the person's mouth. Continue fifteen compressions with two breaths for four cycles. After one minute, recheck pulse and breathing. If the person has regained a pulse, discontinue compressions. If the person is still not breathing, continue giving a breath every five seconds until help arrives.

When performing CPR on an infant, use two fingers instead of your whole hand, and compress on the breastbone, just below the nipple line. For children, use two hands for chest compression. For infants and children, alternate five compressions and one slow breath, for a total of twelve cycles.

RICE

Use RICE (Rest, Ice, Compression and Elevation) for acute injuries like a sprained ankle or injuries due to overuse, like muscle strain.

R: REST
Rest the injured area until pain and swelling go away (usually one to three days).

I: ICE
Within fifteen minutes of an injury, apply ice by placing a damp towel over the injured area and putting a cold pack, bag of ice or a bag of frozen vegetables on top of that. Leave the ice on for ten to thirty minutes, then take it off for thirty to forty-five minutes. Repeat this ice on/ice off alternation as often as possible for the next one to three days.

C: COMPRESSION
Use a bandage to apply gentle but firm pressure until the swelling goes down. Beginning a few inches below the injured area, wrap the bandage in an upward spiral; if using compression in addition to ice, wrap the bandage over the ice pack.

E: ELEVATION
Try to keep the injured area above heart level to drain excess fluid for at least one to three days.

For burns, cuts and scrapes

Burns are classified by degree. First-degree burns are a reddening of the skin, as in a mild sunburn. Second-degree burns are when the skin blisters. Third-degree burns are when the skin is charred. Treatment for first- and second-degree burns is to immerse in cold water for fifteen minutes, then apply sterile dressing. For a third-degree burn, cover the burn with a sterile dressing and treat for shock (calm and reassure the injured person, help her maintain a comfortable body temperature with a blanket or remove her from wind or sun, or have her lie down and elevate her legs twenty to twenty-five centimetres). NEVER apply ice, butter, oil or any other substance to a burn.

For cuts and scrapes, rinse the area with cool water. Apply firm but gentle pressure, using gauze, to stop any bleeding. If blood soaks through, add more gauze, keeping the first layer in place. Continue to apply pressure.

For choking

The universal choking symbol is made by putting your hands around your throat. If you are choking and cannot talk, make this symbol to alert the people around you. If someone who is choking can still talk or is coughing, encourage her to cough more to expel the object. If she cannot talk, or if the cough is weak or ineffective, perform the Heimlich manoeuvre.

Heimlich Manoeuvre

Stand slightly behind the choking person and place your arms around her waist, below her ribcage. Make a fist with one hand, placing your thumb just above her belly button and grab that fist with your other hand. Give five strong upward-thrusting squeezes to try to lift the diaphragm, forcing air from the lungs and provoking a cough. The cough should move and expel whatever is blocking the airway. If it doesn't, perform the manoeuvre again to dislodge the object. If choking persists, call 999.

Emergencies

Any practised explorer can tell you that in an emergency what helps most is being prepared. Make a list of important phone numbers and put them on the wall next to your kitchen phone, or on a notepad stuck to the fridge. That way, in the event of an accident, you'll easily find the numbers to call your family doctor, the fire engine or the police.

The most important emergency number to know, of course, is 999. Calling 999 is free from any phone, even a pay phone. It can be scary to call 999, especially if you're not sure whether or not what you're dealing with is a real emergency, but it's the right thing to do when someone is dangerously hurt, not breathing or unresponsive. A good rule to remember is: when in doubt, make the call.

What to do when you call 999

* Try to speak as calmly as you can.
* Give the address you are calling from.
* State the nature of the emergency (fire, accident, injury, etc.).
* Listen to the 999 operator and follow any instructions you are given.
* Do not hang up until the 999 operator tells you it's okay to hang up.

First Aid Kit

It's always a good idea to keep a First Aid kit at home and making one for your family can be a fun project. For the kit itself, you can use a tote bag, backpack or other container that is clean, roomy, easy to carry and easy to open. A good First Aid kit should contain the following:

* Plasters of assorted sizes
* Bandages
* Safety pins
* Gauze and adhesive tape
* Sharp scissors with rounded tips
* Antiseptic wipes
* Savlon
* Tweezers
* Prescription medication
* Medicines including aspirin, ibuprofen, antihistamine, decongestants
* A page listing the contents of your kit for easy reference, your list of emergency phone numbers and a list of family members' allergies and medications.

First Aid on the go: You can make a mini-kit (with plasters, Savlon, tweezers and bandages) to take with you on a hike, or when you babysit.

ILLUSTRATION CREDITS

ILLUSTRATION CREDITS

ACKNOWLEDGEMENTS

---◆---

With thanks to our agents, Laura Gross and Sam Stoloff; Phil Friedman, Matthew Benjamin, Stephanie Meyers and everyone at HarperCollins and The Stonesong Press. And to Molly Ashodian and her friends, Barbara Card Atkinson, Rob Baird, Samira Baird, Dana Barron, Gil Binenbaum, Steve and Nurit Binenbaum, Rona Binenbaum, the Bromley-Zimmerman family, Sarah Brown, Bill Buchanan, Elin Buchanan, Jessie Buchanan, Shannon Buchanan, Betsy Busch, Stacy DeBroff, Katie Dolgenos, Asha Dornfest, Ann Douglas, Eileen Flanagan, Marcus Geduld, the Goldman-Hersh family, Kay Gormley, Sarah Heady, the Larrabee-O'Donovan family, Jack's Marine, Jane Butler Kahle, Megan Pincus Kajitani, Les Kenny, Killian's Hardware, Andy Lamas, Jen Lawrence, Sara Lorimer, Rachel Marcus, Molly Masyr, Metafilter (especially the women of Ask Metafilter), Jim Miller, Tracy Miller, Marjorie Osterhout, Myra and Dan Peskowitz, Deborah Rickards, Rittenhouse Lumber, Carol Sime, Lisa Suggitt of rollergirl.ca, Alexis Seabrook, Kate Scantlebury, Tom Sugrue, Carrie Szalay and Felicia Sullivan. Appreciation to everyone who offered advice and inspiration and to daring girls everywhere.